The Accidental Free Society

A Historical and Modern Worldview of Dictators, Democracies, Terrors, and Utopias

By MIKE SCHOBER

LIBERTY HILL
PUBLISHING

The Accidental Free Society
A Historical and Modern Worldview of Dictators, Democracies, Terrors, and Utopias
by Mike Schober

Printed in the United States of America.

Edited by Liberty Publishing.

ISBN 9781498458627

www.libertyhillpublishing.com

To my Dad and my grandson, Dylan,
enjoying each other's company
in Heaven

Contents

Introduction

The vicious dictatorships of the 20th century remained for a long time an enigma for me. How could the fantastic progress of the Scientific and Industrial Revolutions produce such a tragedy? What was it that made the three great dictators of that century, Hitler, Stalin, and Mao, possible? Because Totalitarianism had taken over in many different places and times, because different nations and cultures were susceptible to this contagion, I could not attribute it to a lone aberration.

I, like so many, was taught humankind's most fundamental desire is the desire for freedom. If true it would make these vicious dictatorships an impossibility. The key to this enigma is the thesis of this book. Totalitarianism is not something entirely new, but a modern version of an ancient human tendency. It is thus not, unfortunately, an aberration but a constant threat from which we can never escape.

Dictatorship has been the primary form of government since the dawn of civilization. When the society is pre-industrial, the Hereditary Dictatorship predominates, and in these societies the most common manifestation of the Hereditary Dictatorship is monarchy. Totalitarianism, which I simply call the Modern Dictatorship, is the incarnation of the Hereditary Dictatorship in the industrial age. Despite vast differences in technology and wealth, the characteristics of these two types of dictatorships are surprisingly similar. Fortunately, free societies appeared on occasion and this is also covered as part of the thesis. Thus, the study of dictatorship also becomes the study of freedom.

As the human population grew it became impossible to organize the large numbers of people, as had been done before, in the tribe. It was from this necessity man invented government. Like fire, another highly useful invention, it can be dangerous if not kept closely contained. Sadly, no matter where one looks, government's worst aspect, dictatorship, was on display. From the civilizations forming first in the four fertile valley regions of the world to Persia, Cambodia, Japan, and elsewhere across the globe, one finds only dictatorship. Forming in total isolation, as they did in the Americas, the story is the same. If one accepts the basic notion that monarchy is a form of dictatorship then the conclusion, although dramatic, is nonetheless entirely correct: the fundamental form of human government is dictatorship. For most of the last 5,000 years there was virtually no other type of government. The term, Hereditary Dictatorship, emphasizes this point—all monarchy is a dictatorship.

The essential reason governments tend toward dictatorship is all governments create a monopoly of violence. The control of violence from the courts to the army is the essence of this monopoly and a key feature of any government. In the enlightened industrial democracies of today, people are imprisoned against their will for crimes, property is confiscated in the form of taxes, and servitude extracted in time of war via a draft. The most minor rules or regulations are always backed up with the implied threat of force. How the monopoly is controlled determines the form of the government in each kingdom. Since there is an innate symbiotic relationship between the dictator and his army, the monopoly of violence tends toward dictatorship. From this primary monopoly the dictator creates secondary monopolies over the economic, religious, and intellectual life of each kingdom. This is in stark contrast to other worldviews arguing an economic or religious monopoly leads to dictatorship.

Because dictatorship is historically ever-present there are few counterexamples. The two most important of these counterexamples are the democracy of ancient Athens and the Roman Republic. These two highlight many of the themes essential for the free society. The development of a merchant community as a counterweight to dictatorship is particularly important. The control of the army with the use of citizen soldiers is another key ingredient.

The division of government power with checks and balances to keep each part under control was evident in these early democratic experiments.

Since freedom is the lesser theme in human government, it could only grow into a major theme by fortuitous circumstances and the courage of individuals to fight for freedom. While every other major center of civilization was dominated at one point by a single large empire, interrupted by occasional civil war (called a warring states period), Europe was stuck in a permanent civil war condition. The fractured political landscape allowed for a limited type of freedom, created by the power vacuum.

In European history, different movements—the Renaissance, the Reformation, the Enlightenment, and Capitalism—attacked the secondary monopolies and made them weak. The competition between European dictators pushed the Scientific and Industrial Revolutions. By a lucky accident of timing and geography, the free society and Industrial Revolution were most advanced in England, a nation isolated on an island, protected by a strong navy, and supported by a vibrant merchant community.

The free society came to fore as the Industrial Revolution was making the basis of the Hereditary Dictatorship obsolete. This was fortunate because Napoleon was demonstrating for the first time how Europe could be unified into a single empire. The first dictator to actually accomplish this task would thereby end Europe's permanent chaos and make it like every other major civilization.

To survive, the free society needed a champion, and she found it in the American Republic. Its formation and survival were, as was freedom in Europe, only made possible by a special set of circumstances and the willingness of people to fight. America was fortunate because it was free to develop without the many vestiges of monarchy and the other trappings of the pre-industrial society. It was free except for one curse: slavery. The exorcism of this evil nearly killed the experiment entirely. With the official abolition of slavery in 1865, America became the first major power in history to be free of both king and slave.

America also represented one particular strain of the Enlightenment disposed to limited government. This was important because the contrasting French Revolution, representing the opposite strain, tended toward utopian uses of large government. These two distinct approaches to government would echo down through history. Luckily, the American experiment created the most powerful nation on earth, something important in freedom's future survival.

With the Hereditary Dictatorships being swept away by the Industrial Revolution it might be tempting to think freedom had won. Though the Hereditary Dictatorship could not survive the industrial era, from its ashes the Modern Dictatorship was born. Our story has now come full circle; the natural tendency toward dictatorship has reemerged. The West, being the first to industrialize, faces this struggle first. The most massive wars in human history were fought over the issue of freedom. If the free societies had not had the powerful American Republic as a member of their crusade, it is doubtful freedom would have survived.

Two major forms of the Modern Dictatorship appeared in the 20th century. Fascism grew in numerous western countries and Japan while Communism flourished in Russia and China. The ideological differences between the two systems are irrelevant as they are both realizations of the same phenomenon. The other major lesson concerns the Cold War. It is part of my thesis the Cold War is a harbinger of things to come as new Modern Dictatorships appear. The industrial age will thus be marked by the constant struggle of democracies and dictators.

While the Scientific and Industrial revolutions promise greater well-being for the human race, the Modern Dictatorship promises a greater capacity for evil. The basis of this dictatorship remains the monopoly of violence and it uses this monopoly to dominate society. However, the Modern Dictatorship brings two new innovations not found in the past. The first innovation I term the Terror—a massive expansion of the monopoly of violence to every aspect of society. It creates a new kind of army, the secret police, to wage war upon the fabric of each nation. Everything has now become the business of government. The second innovation I term the Utopian Vision.[1] It replaces the role religion played in the Hereditary Dictatorships of the past. It seeks to

---

[1] I selected this term to mirror the term Beatific Vision where the direct experience of God in heaven produces ultimate bliss. For the fanatic on earth the Utopian Vision is the secular substitute.

tap into the emotion of hate in an atmosphere of hysteria to motivate people in the service of the dictator.

My enigma, Totalitarianism, is the ancient human tendency toward dictatorship updated with the Scientific and Industrial Revolutions. The progress of these revolutions is apparently a two-edged sword. Man has become more powerful but not fundamentally better. My worldview of government also makes it crystal clear how unusual this current period in history is. Freedom as a worldwide phenomenon only began in 1945 under the watchful eye of American military power. The natural tendency toward dictatorship haunts humanity and remains a threat from which we are never free. Athens and Rome are the real aberrations. The solution to my enigma has now become a warning. Care and courage are needed, or this period in history will become an aberration too.

Section I

The Fundamental Form of Human Government is Dictatorship

"I am the State"
Louis XIV of France

Man's Flaw

Chapter One

From the earliest records of human history, in each 'cradle' of civilization, the predominant form of government was dictatorship. The first civilizations formed in large fertile valleys along major rivers: the Nile, the Euphrates and Tigris, the Indus and Ganges, and the Yellow River in China. When new civilizations, kingdoms, or empires formed later, each was again ruled by a dictator. Persia is an excellent example of an empire created when different peoples were unified under one dictator. The kingdoms of Cambodia and Japan were examples from Asia, which developed later as the human population grew. The less developed areas of Africa and the Pacific Islands also spawned tyrannies. From Latin America, the kingdoms were interesting because they were totally isolated from any outside influences, and yet they too developed independently as dictatorships. Working across the globe, from the start of civilization around 3,000 BC to the modern era, dictatorship was the only form of government with few isolated exceptions.[2]

It is widely speculated the human race evolved into its current form during the last glaciation. The massive ice sheets lasted from over 100,000 years ago until about 10,000 when the earth began to warm. Once the earth began to warm, the human population began to grow and eventually cities formed in the most fertile areas created by great rivers. These rivers created

---

[2] The more traditional designation BC is used as indicated. When a date is in the modern era AD is omitted unless needed to avoid confusion.

a 'Garden of Eden' compared to the harsh conditions the human race had endured for tens of thousands of years, and in virtually every example the government chosen independently by peoples of widely differing cultures was dictatorship.

One could imagine an alternative story: a story in which the clan leaders of a village would meet and collectively decide the fate of the village. As the population grew into cities, each city had a council of elders chosen from the clans to administer to the needs of the city. As an empire, representatives from the major cities could be sent to form a 'pseudo-parliament.' Only in one area for a brief period of time did anything remotely like this happen. For most of the human race, none of this happened—ever.

2.1

The following historical survey (sub-sections 2.1 – 2.8) shows a universal devotion to dictatorship in different areas of the world. The sub-sections also demonstrate the cycle of dynasty and warring states.

In this sub-section, a brief history of Egypt is presented from 3100 BC to 30 BC.

One of the earliest recorded dictators was Narmer the first Pharaoh of Egypt. Narmer, the Scorpion King, unified a northern and southern kingdom along the Nile in approximately 3100 BC. Archeological evidence shows the unifier of Egypt wearing a white crown (southern kingdom) victorious over soldiers of the red crown (northern kingdom). Henceforth, every Pharaoh was the Lord of Two Lands depicted with a double crown, one white and the other red, representing the two original lands. The Egyptian dictatorship continued for over 3,000 years. This long period of time was divided into periods of unified rule by a single dynasty one after another and shorter periods of civil war between competing dynastic families. The Old Kingdom extended from 2707 BC to 2170 BC and included six dynasties. The Middle Kingdom extended from 2119 BC to 1793 BC with two different dynasties, and a New Kingdom extended from 1550 BC to 1069 BC with three dynasties in all. After the Persians conquered Egypt in 525 BC, the rule was maintained by foreign imposed dictatorships.

With the arrival of Pharaoh Nebka, the Third Dynasty and the Old Kingdom began. The Old Kingdom was most famous for building the pyramids and Djoser of the Third Dynasty built the first. The construction of this type, the step pyramid, was a marvel of engineering for its time. By the Fourth Dynasty, many design improvements had been made, most notably the outside was now smooth, and the pyramid now took on its classic shape. The largest of these, the Great Pyramid, was built to house the mummified remains of the dictator Khufu. The other trappings of state power were further consolidated in the Old Kingdom.

The Fourth Dynasty of the Old Kingdom put the army under the command of royal princes. The state religion was expanded with separate temple complexes in the provincial capitals and other lesser shrines in the countryside. The Old Kingdom eventually came to an end in 2170 BC when it broke apart beginning a warring states period. The cycle beginning with rule by a single dynasty (or series of dynasties) followed by a period of division until a single new dynasty eventually gained power was a common cycle in many civilizations. The period of division is called the warring states period. Egyptian historians use the term intermediate period for its warring states periods. The First Intermediate Period began with the end of the Old Kingdom.

The Middle Kingdom ended the First Intermediate Period in 2119 BC and began Egypt's first attempt to expand both in trade and territory. It highlights another common theme in all dictatorships: the constant need to expand territorially. The Middle Kingdom gradually annexed portions of Nubia to the south working its way up the Nile.

The Middle Kingdom saw a pronounced increase in trade sending representatives to numerous Near East city-states as a way of increasing the mutual exchange of goods. The trade reached as far as the island of Crete. It mined turquoise in the Sinai and in the eastern desert amethyst, greywacke, and galena. Gradually an influx of Semitic people from Syria and surrounding regions, called the Hykos, came to Egypt. When a Hykos petty dictator, Nehesi, was able to create a small realm in the Nile delta, the Middle Kingdom ended. The Second Intermediate Period had begun in 1793 BC.

After many years of struggle and the eventual expulsion of the Hykos rulers in 1550 BC, Egypt was reunited and the New Kingdom began. The New Kingdom was Egypt's time for empire as the territorial expansion began immediately and within one hundred years had expanded south into Nubia and east all the way to the Euphrates. A particularly energetic dictator of this period, Ahmose, instituted several reforms; the most important being a large standing army with professional soldiers. These rulers also took steps to increase the cult of the pharaoh and strengthen the Egyptian religion. A major innovation was to create a cult of the god Amun with the selection of a princess from the royal family as the "Oracle of Amun." Originally a local god at Thebes, Amun was elevated to the status of a main Egyptian god and eventually became Egypt's most important god.

The New Kingdom period saw an unprecedented increase in wealth for Egypt. The tribute, conquests, and trade of the time poured into the imperial coffers, and the new wealth made the temples and buildings of this period superior in grandeur to the Old Kingdom.

Like previous Intermediate Periods, the New Kingdom fell and split into competing factions after the administration of inept dictators. The Third Intermediate Period was characterized by two major power centers— the first in Tanis in the northern delta region and the second at Thebes. The center at Thebes used the Oracle of Amun as a source of power, and it was not uncommon for the dictator in the south to also be the high priest of Amun. After the Assyrians sacked Thebes in 644 BC, there was a short period of Saite pharaohs who ruled Egypt for around 150 years. In 525 BC Egypt fell to the Persians and was never independent again. However, the fiction of a divine pharaoh lived on as a method to maintain control over the populace and only ended with the suicide of Cleopatra in 30 BC.[3]

The Egyptian dictators reveal many of the characteristics common to all dictators. Dictators are aggressive and they are always looking for opportunities to expand their realm. They are full of self-aggrandizement, building huge monuments to themselves. They tend to promote orthodoxy and crush

---

[3] It is remarkable how little technological progress was made in over 3,000 years of Egyptian history. Putting it alongside the West would mean the discovery of the Earth's orbit about the Sun took place in 1490 BC and Egyptians walked on the Moon in 1131 BC.

dissent. One interesting characteristic of these early dictatorships was the divinity of the dictator. All secular and spiritual authority was concentrated in one man.

2.2

The first civilizations around the Euphrates and Tigris are chronicled in this next sub-section (2400 BC – 539 BC). The dictators in this fertile valley tended to rule over culturally different groups simultaneously. The term empire is usually used to indicate such a situation.

The Sumerian civilization, nestled between the two rivers Euphrates and Tigris, was likewise ruled by dictators. The area of Mesopotamia was divided initially into city-states each ruled by their own dictator. Sometime in the 24th century BC, a ruler from the city of Kish was able to conquer Mesopotamia and the surrounding area. Mixing culturally different peoples under one rule made Sargon I the first true emperor in recorded history.

The Akkadian Empire, taking the name from the new capital city Akkad, was the first to create a permanent standing army. In the capital city 5,400 soldiers ate their meals with King Sargon. His empire also had reforms seen in later empires. He standardized weights and measures, put into place a standardized tax system run by officials in the employ of the empire and also paid tribute to local deities by building temples to local gods. Propaganda from his reign has Sargon worshiping Enlil, the god of Elam in the east, and the Semitic god Dagon when Sargon went to the north.

Sargon's sons ruled a combination of twenty-four years after their father's death, re-establishing his kingdom of subject city-states like Ur and countries like Elam. When Naram-Sin, grandson of Sargon, took the reigns of power he brought this first kingdom in Mesopotamia to its apex. His Empire stretched from the Mediterranean north to present day Armenia. His Empire fell faster than it rose when nomadic tribes called the Gutains came from the mountains in the east. For the next 100 years the Gutains held sway over the fertile valley.

When more stability returned, the city of Ur became dominant. The subjugation of the region by one city followed by periods of inter-city conflict was a different version of the cycle of dynasty and warring states. During the city's third dynasty (2113 BC – 2029 BC) it grew into an empire. The Ur III Dynasty maintained monopolies as part of their power, particularly in textiles, and included a silver rod as the main unit of exchange. The first two dictators, Ur-Nammu and his son Shulgi ruled for eighteen and forty-seven years respectively, and created a bureaucracy for the collection of taxes and a system of scribes. Regional capitals were created with appointed governors. It was a period of prosperity and peace. Typical of the god-king rule of the era, Shulgi was said to be the husband of the goddess Inanna.

With the fall of Ur, a new city, Babylon, would become the major city-state in the valley in 1838 BC. The most famous of its early dictators was Hammurabi (1792 BC – 1750 BC) who recorded their laws. It was originally believed to be the first such formal codification of law, but it is now known to be a compilation of earlier Sumerian codes. Bodily injury was compensated monetarily based upon one's station in life. Sixty shekels was the going rate for a lost eye. A free man of lesser degree was worth only half of a gentleman. Regulation of slavery was also part of this law. As the practice of slavery is a nearly universal human depravity, it is found in the earliest recorded laws.

When the Hittite King, Murshili I, came from the north to sack Babylon, the history of the valley between the two rivers, Euphrates and Tigris, would no longer be a battle of city-states. The Hittites built an empire in what is now present day eastern Turkey. The Kassite Dynasty (1600 BC – 1155 BC) followed and ruled Mesopotamia from the city of Dur-Kurigalzu. Babylon, however, would re-emerge under Nebuchadrezzar I (1126 BC – 1105 BC). Later, the Babylonians would again fall victim to an invasion from the north—the Assyrians in the 9th century BC. The Assyrian Empire (745 BC – 612 BC) eventually encompassed all of Mesopotamia and Egypt. The next Babylonian kingdom, the Neo-Babylonian period, began in 626 BC. It lasted until conquered by Persia in 539 BC.

2.3

Indian civilization was likewise dominated by large empires. This sub-section covers the period of 2300 BC to 1785 AD.

The Harappan, situated along the Indus, was one of the earliest civilizations, existing from 2300 BC until around 1700 BC. Their cities were characterized by numerous single story homes arranged on wide streets with a sophisticated drainage system for the elimination of sewage. The Harappan civilization abruptly ended around 1700 BC, leaving only their brick homes and low-level stone buildings. Their form of government remains unknown.

Along the other major tributary in India, the Ganges, the eventual governments were dictatorial in nature. The basis of these civilizations was the Aryan tribal invasions in the second millennium BC. Tribes were led by a warrior class governed by either a group of warriors or a hereditary king. The evidence strongly suggests the eventual caste system in India began as a form of control imposed by the conquering Aryans. The four traditional castes of Brahman (priest), Kshatriya (warrior), Vaishya (merchant), and Shudra (cultivator) mirror a clear division of labor between conqueror and conquered. Sixteen "great realms," called Mahajanapadas as recorded in early Buddhist scriptures, formed between 560 BC and 500 BC mostly around the Ganges valley. During this period the Aryan tribes coalesced into these separate political entities.

Indian civilization was forever dominated by invasions from Afghanistan and Alexander the Great is perhaps the most famous example. This dictator of Macedonia and Greece began his string of conquest with Anatolia (modern day Turkey) in 333 BC. This was followed by the conquest of Phoenicia and Egypt. When he sacked the home city of the Persians, Persepolis, in 330 BC, the Persian Empire ended. Proceeding east Alexander mastered present day Afghanistan and surrounding areas. In 327 BC he was ready with 50,000 men to invade India.

Alexander was a brutal conqueror and an example of the close bond between dictatorship and military power. Frustrated the siege of the Phoenician city Tyre had taken too long, he slaughtered 7,000 male inhabitants, and sold 30,000 women and children into slavery when the city finally capitulated. However, he shared a sense of loyalty with his men. After taking several cities in the Indus valley in western India, Alexander had further ambitions to move deeper into eastern India, but his men would not have it. Under pressure from his troops, he sailed down the Indus and back to conquered Persia.

Leaving a weakened Magadhan Empire in the aftermath of the Macedonians' invasion, a rebel by the name of Chandragupta Maurya was able to start a civil war. By 320 BC he had become dictator of the Magadhan Empire. Historians designate this new dynasty as the Mauryan Empire. The third dictator of this new empire, Ashoka, ruled over almost all of India. This empire was the first to dominate India and lasted to around 200 BC.

The Gupta Empire (320 – 550) ruled over the Classic Age in Indian history and was a rigid enforcer of the caste system. The second ruler, Sumadra Gupta, conquered much of northern India and Bengal. Chanadragupta II, his son, conquered parts of western India. The Empire fell apart under pressure from the Hunas from Afghanistan. From the fall of the Gupta Empire, India entered a warring states period and Medieval India's regionalism was the dominant factor. It ended when India was split between a Muslim north and a Hindu south.

Two major empires during this period, the Delhi Sultans to the north, and the Vijayanagara Empire to the south, are worth mentioning. The earliest Muslim invasion from Afghanistan was by the Turk, Mahmud of Ghazhi, about the year 1000. Other invasions would follow, including a large one in 1186. The first Delhi Sultan, Iltutmish, ruled from 1211 to 1236. The Delhi Sultanate rule depended upon Turkish and Afghan nobles who were constantly at odds with each other. Eventually their power would extend from Punjab to Bengal. When in their ascendency, the Sultans and their cavalry were unchallenged plundering Hindu kingdoms to the south.

The Vijayanagara Empire consisted of three different Dynasties: the Sangamas (1336 – 1505), the Tuluvas (1505 – 1550), and the Aravidis (1550 – late 1600s). The Empire's first conquest to the east was the Tamil Kingdom with its rich farmland. These dictators liked to portray themselves as the protectors of Hinduism against the Muslim north.

The sub-continent of India was unified under the Mughal Empire (1526 – 1862), founded by Babur, a Turkish ruler, with another invasion from Afghanistan. His grandson Akbar (ruled 1556 – 1605) consolidated the dictatorship and it was characterized by brutality. The cities of Kari and Kataria were sacked and many villages were looted and destroyed. After this consolidation, Akbar set up a novel arrangement helping the Muslim rulers maintain power over the Hindu population for the next 150 years. In addition to areas ruled by Turkish commanders, Akbar allowed certain Hindu Rajput rulers to retain their lands as vassal states. Aurangzeb (r. 1658 – 1707) conquered in effect the entire sub-continent. Eventually, the Mughal Empire was forced to make various concessions to the British and in 1765 they allowed the British to collect the taxes in Bengal. By 1785, the British were the de facto ruler of Bengal and, in the end, all of India.

2.4

The Chinese civilization was dominated by rule under a single unified dictatorship versus by multiple dictators found during a warring states period than any other major civilization. This sub-section covers the period 2200 BC to 1644 AD.

The last of the major cradles of civilization, the Yellow River valley, produced the Xia Dynasty whose dictators ruled from 2200 BC to 1766 BC. The Xia dynasty was originally thought to be more myth than reality, however, archaeologists have been able to verify its existence with the discovery of a royal palace south of the southern bend in the Yellow River. For the actual names of the particular kings, one must rely upon traditional histories such as the one produced by Sima Qian.

The Shang Dynasty (1766 BC – 1122 BC) is on a much more firm archaeological footing than the Xia. Beginning in the late 19th century, commencing with discoveries of bones inscribed with Chinese characters, a huge number of artifacts from the Shang have been found. These human bones have a curious pattern in their inscriptions. The writing always asked a yes or no question. It is now understood these are oracle bones used to foretell the future or recommend a course of action. Once the question was carved into the bone, a hot poker would be used to burn a hole causing cracks to appear in the bones. The interpretation of these cracks, like the reading of tea leaves, would give the answer. The answer could be coming from an ancestor, or a deity, or in many cases the chief god named Di. Nothing comes for free, and the people of the Shang period had something valuable to offer in return—human sacrifice. Shang cemeteries provide strong evidence of a militaristic society and mass graves of the victims.

A western breakaway kingdom, Zhou, with King Wen at its helm started a civil war in the Yellow River valley in 1122 BC. Although he did not see the war to its conclusion, King Wu, his successor, did. The Zhou dictators officially proclaimed themselves the Sons of Heaven. Although the kingdom lasted until 221 BC it did not maintain control of all of China. 770 BC was the beginning of the Eastern Zhou period, when China became a region of competing dictators.

The Chinese narrative of the corrupt old kingdom being replaced with a new dynasty with a renewed Mandate from Heaven is a common theme in all civilizations. Ordinarily mankind loves security over freedom. Obedience is exchanged for security and stability. But the security people exchanged for their freedom has its limits. When the dictatorship's corruption, incompetence, or brutality becomes too severe, a new dictator, often a charismatic figure, comes forward to challenge the old. In many cases this person is a famous general. The Chinese would say the old regime had lost its Mandate from Heaven.[4] By habit people accept the current situation until a crisis forces them to re-evaluate, and only then can a new dynasty be established. This transition from the old to the new dictator can take time leaving the civilization in a warring states period.

The warring states period ended when the Kingdom of Qin imposed rule in 221 BC. Pronounced "cheen," it is from this Kingdom the word "China" is derived. Qin was located in the western region of China where natural geography provided a defensive advantage, and Qin was able to wage war in the territory of others while its land was secure.

---

[4] This term from Chinese history will be used to indicate humankind's innate point at which the dictator loses legitimacy.

The Qin dictator, Qin Shihuang unified China, and he was the archetype of a dictator. Using the same Chinese character found in the name of the god Di, he took the title, huangdi, meaning either magnificent ruler or magnificent god. He adopted a Chinese philosophy called Legalism, and outlawed the competing Taoist and Confucian beliefs. In 213 BC he had all non-Legalism books destroyed, and he buried alive four hundred intellectuals who would not recant. A megalomaniac, he created the now famous army of terra cotta soldiers on display in modern China's Shaanxi province.

The harsh methods of Qin created opposition and he lost his hold in a civil war. In 202 BC Liu Bang, a commoner who rose through the ranks of the imperial army, was able to unify China and founded the Han Dynasty (202 BC – 220 AD). He is an example of how a popular general replaces the dictator with himself.

The Han dynasty is considered one of the better ones in Chinese history due to its efficient administration. It reached its peak in 147 BC when Wudi, the military emperor as he called himself, became dictator. He followed a pattern of military conquest typical to many dictators. He initiated a war to the north against the Xiongnu and expanded China to the north, although it took a later emperor to complete the conquest of the Xiongnu. Wudi took many internal steps to solidify his power without the more harsh methods of Qin. To eliminate competition from wealthy merchants, he forbade them to purchase land. He created government monopolies of salt and iron. He made Confucianism the official state ideology.

The Chinese historian, Sima Qian, lived during this reign. An example of the dictator's absolute power involves the abuse of Sima Qian. When Wudi publically humiliated a general for a defeat at the hands of the Xiongnu, Sima Qian came to his defense. This so infuriated the dictator he gave Sima Qian two options: death or castration. Fortunately for future generations, he chose castration over death. Much of what is known about ancient China comes from him. Sima Qian has proved to be a reliable historian as many of his accounts have been verified with archaeological evidence.

After the end of the Han Dynasty in 220, China entered a second warring states period lasting until 589. Due to the lack of central control, Buddhism was able to spread throughout all of China, and by the 6th century almost all of China was Buddhist. The Chinese began to see Confucianism as pertaining to government and public morality while Buddhism and Taoism pertained to the private and personal life.

The period of warring states ended in 589 with the creation of the Sui Dynasty (589 – 617), and much like the Qin dictatorship, the Sui Dynasty employed harsh measures. The second dictator, Sui Yangdi, was another megalomaniac who required thousands of women to make silk flowers and paste them onto trees in the wintertime to alleviate his depression. He undertook several failed military adventures including three unsuccessful invasions of Korea. Eventually assassinated in 618, he was replaced by General Li Yuan who was the founder of the Tang Dynasty (618 – 907).

The Tang Dynasty rivals the Han in its historic reputation as a golden age in Chinese history. At the peak of its power, the capital city of Chang'an was the largest in the world. It sat at the beginning of the silk route across Asia and brought the Chinese into contact with many foreign influences. China's one and only female empress, Empress Wu, ruled during the Tang Dynasty, and it was during her reign Korea became a vassal state of China.

The efficiency of the Tang government rested upon a civil service system and a rigorous set of examinations. It was selective and few applicants made the grade. Technically, it was a system based upon merit, and anyone could take the test although they were primarily from elite families. The civil service system included a well defined set of levels with fixed salaries. To prevent these government officials from building any local power base, Tang dictators wisely rotated them every few years.

Monopoly over the land was an important component of both the Han and the Tang power. The Han Dynasty had already limited merchants from owning land and the Tang Dynasty extended this heavy-handed policy into agriculture by confiscating large land holdings. These holdings were then rented out to males between the ages of 16-60 physically able to farm. The Tang dictatorship made this policy universal throughout China. It also emphasizes another important theme; the distrust by the dictator of the merchant community.

The Tang Dynasty came to an end shortly after a rebellion in 879 led by Huang Chao when a large northern region was hit by a severe drought.

As part of this popular revolt, Jewish, Christian, and Muslim merchants by the thousands were killed in Canton. The rebellion was crushed, but the dynasty was never the same. A short warring states period followed until a general from one of these states, Zhao Kuangyin, consolidated the empire and began the Song Dynasty (960 – 1279).

Beginning with the Song Dynasty, China was continuously ruled by dictatorship until 1912.[5] The Yuan Dynasty (1279 – 1368) followed the Song and was established by Khubilai Khan, the grandson of Genghis Khan, with a Mongol invasion from the north. The Ming Dynasty (1368 – 1644) was known for its extreme centralization called the Ming Despotism. It was followed by the Qing (1644 – 1912), also known as the Manchu Dynasty, with a huge vassal state arrangement including Korea, Vietnam, Burma, Siam, Cambodia, and the Malay Peninsula.

The Ming despotism began with Zhu Yuanzhang in 1368 when he drove out the Mongols and began a period of restoration of all things Chinese. It was during this period the Chinese began to call their land "the fatherland." He called his dynasty Ming meaning "bright" in Chinese to represent the victory of culture over the barbarians. In his first year he set forth a new code of laws intended to dictate the new conduct of officials and commoners alike, excluding the Emperor. Whenever he found the penalties of the law were not to his liking, Zhu created the "law beyond the law" with harsh penalties only he was allowed to enforce. By the 1380s, these were compiled into the Grand Pronouncements and published. If any judge wished to enforce a provision of the Grand Pronouncements he could do so, but only with a lesser penalty.

By Zhu's official count, over 15,000 individuals were executed. When he became suspicious of his most important minister he initiated a purge. He had the minister executed by *lingchi*, the death by a thousand cuts or literally death by slow slicing. Other purges followed and upwards of 40,000 high and low officials met their demise. The death toll from these purges was the worst in Chinese history, excluding the 20th century.

---

[5] The Chinese have the unfortunate distinction of being the only modern people of a major power ruled continuously by a central dictatorship for nearly one thousand years. After a short warring states period, their suffering resumed in 1949.

Traditional Chinese governments of the past placed restraints on the dictator either through royal court procedures or Confucian traditions. Zhu was determined to eliminate those impediments to his reforms and centralized power. He eliminated the position of Central Secretariat and forced lower level bureaucrats to report directly to him. He also dismantled the Chief Military Commission and the office of Censorate. All power was concentrated in him. It was because of this unusual concentration of power the Ming Despotism gained its reputation. When an Emperor made a mistake it was always the fault of the minister. A minor punishment might have been a simple banishment or assignment to some remote frontier of the empire, while a significant blunder often meant death as well as the humiliation of the desecration of the corpse. The stifling impact of this policy would flow down the chain of command resulting in an extreme conservatism and reluctance to take risks.

The orthodoxy of the Ming Dynasty extended into religious matters as well. Tradition held the Three Teachings of Confucianism, Buddhism, and Taoism, in harmony, with each adding to its proper sphere of life. However, as more than one Ming official would state, the Four Books and Five Classics of Confucianism were all that was needed to run the empire. In 1391, the Hundred Day Edict gave all Buddhist monasteries 100 days to move into a single location in each county. Three years later, the Edict of Seclusion forced the monks to remain within their monasteries and to avoid contact with the public. In 1418, the monks were limited to twenty per monastery. The Taoists did not escape persecution—books displeasing to the Confucians were banned in 1417.

The Ming Dynasty made the population a priority, and it was for this reason they held on to power. They were not going to lose their Mandate from Heaven due to internal mismanagement. In each county, four Preparedness Granaries were established for the eventuality of a famine. Also, care was taken to keep a good system of roads and to maintain the Grand Canal, of 7th century origin, which connected northern and southern China and had a tremendous amount of traffic. The government alone had 11,775 grain barges, pulled and attended by 121,500 soldiers, to keep Beijing fed. At any given moment larger numbers of smaller barges could be found moving goods across China.

The previous system of coinage, based upon small copper coins, had a tiny hole in them, and the hole was used to string a large number of coins together. A string of 1,000 coins was called a guan. The increase in trade activity across the empire and the payment of taxes made these small denominations increasingly difficult. The Chief Grand Secretary Zhang Juzheng in the 1570s introduced a thirty-seven gram ingot of silver and this monetary reform is considered the most important reform in China prior to the Industrial Revolution as it moved the government and tax system away from barter. This new monetary system eventually required a large amount of imported silver from Japan and Peru. As a reflection of the improving prosperity, Zhang ordered a new survey of all cultivated land in 1580.

The Ming system would have appeared in the late 16th century to be one of considerable longevity. Unfortunately for the people of China, they were hit with a series of bad crop yields causing a famine, and in the early 1600s they were also hit by large scale epidemics killing upwards of 80% of the population in some provinces. The Ming Dynasty had lost their Mandate from Heaven and the answer was again to the north.

Nurhaci (1599 – 1626) was a warlord of the Jurchen tribes, lived in Manchuria, and united the tribes in attacks against China. By 1622 the Gate of the Mountains and Sea, the most eastern gate along the Great Wall, was closed. In 1636 the Jurchen formed a confederation with the Mongols to increase their pressure on the weakened regime. As Beijing fell to the invading army in 1644, the last Ming emperor hanged himself after killing his daughters.

2.5

Persia demonstrates how dictatorship forms in areas outside of the four major fertile valleys. This empire began in 559 BC and lasted until 330 BC.

Although the earliest civilizations formed around the four major fertile valleys of the four major river systems, others would soon appear as the population grew. However, these other examples were no different in their form of government and provided no counterexamples to dictatorship. The Persian Empire was one such example.

Beginning in 559 BC with the conquests by Cyrus the Great, who was from a minor kingdom, Media, in southwestern Persia, Persia became one of the largest empires in ancient history. The Persian Empire was one of the fastest examples of empire creation. Cyrus first conquered the Kingdom of Media where he was a vassal king. He defeated Astyages the Median dictator in battle, took him hostage, and looted the capital city of Ecbatana in 550 BC. Interestingly Cyrus did not claim to be a god. He only claimed to be a descendent of the legendary Persian hero Achaemenes. With the two kingdoms firmly in control, he consolidated his power in western Iran. His next move was to conquer the peoples of Parthia and Hyrcana in eastern Iran in 549 BC. From the secure base in Iran, he set out to the west in conquest. The first victim to fall was the King Croesus of Lydia. Croesus had overextended his own holdings after the collapse of Media. Cyrus captured the capital city Sardis around 547 BC. He next turned his eye towards Babylon. Upon his approach to the city, the peopled rebelled, and the King Nabonious fled. The entire Babylonian Empire was now in Cyrus's possession in 539 BC.

A particularly interesting policy carried out by Cyrus enabled him to maintain control over his many new conquests. He had a reputation for being magnanimous in victory toward his defeated enemies. Except for the sacking of their capital, the Medes were treated well. There are conflicting narratives about King Croesus, but one version has Cyrus sparing the defeated king's life. The Babylonian approach had been a severe repression of native religions. They had stolen subject people's sacred artifacts, and forced all to serve their god Marduk. Cyrus immediately returned these religious items to their rightful owners and allowed local peoples to serve their gods. He most famously ended the Jewish Babylonian captivity.

After the death of Cyrus, his son Cambyses conquered Egypt in 525 BC. Upon his premature death in 522 BC, the empire was in civil war. Seven royal families who banded together were victorious in the struggle, and one of their members, Darius I, became dictator. Darius's rule (522 BC – 486 BC) was one of consolidation and because of this, is often recognized as the real founder of the Persian Empire. He consolidated his power with a professional military made up with mostly ethnic Persians. His Empire of 50 million people stretched from the Mediterranean to the Indus in the east, and from Egypt to the Crimea.

Darius's administrative reforms were also impressive. He divided the Empire into twenty administrative districts, each with a governor called a satrap selected from a royal or prominent family. There was not a permanent capital city as the royal entourage moved between different conquered capitals and the home city of Persepolis. There was also the now familiar standardization of weights and measures, and a new system of coinage was issued. He also set up a system of well-policed royal roads and a postal system. However, he did not centralize religious observances in the Empire but continued the toleration policies of Cyrus. The empire ended when the last dictator, Darius III, was conquered by Alexander the Great in 330 BC.

2.6

Other areas of the world bolster the dictatorship thesis. This sub-section is devoted to an evaluation of Cambodia (253–1863) and Japan (c. 200–1543).

Other highly developed regions of the world, areas like Southeast Asia and Japan continued the same pattern as other civilizations, and Cambodia serves as a good example. Chinese sources show a small kingdom, Funan, existing between 253 and 519 providing irregular tribute. Archeological evidence does not support the existence of a major kingdom but stone inscriptions indicate some level of development, enough to construct buildings and temples. Certain social divisions were already evident including a separation between those who knew Sanskrit, the language of the sacred, and those who knew only Khmer, the common language of Cambodia. Sanskrit inscriptions recorded poetry, prayers or mighty deeds of kings while Khmer inscriptions documented administrative details like the number of slaves a king might own.

The Angkorian Period (802 –1431) centered on a state formed in the 9th century in northwest Cambodia. During this period it was the most

25

powerful kingdom in the region exacting tribute from places as far away as Burma and Malaysia. The kingdom's beginnings coincide with the coronation of Jayavarman II (770 – 850) as universal king. Inscriptions declare him the god-king and associate him with the Hindu god, Siva. Starting with King Indravarman, the rulers began to build step pyramids for their burial. Thirteen Cambodian dictators followed his example.

Eventually Buddhism became Cambodia's predominant religion due to the patronage of several kings. Suryavarman (r. 1003–1050), who organized rice production, required loyalty oaths although he allowed Hinduism to be practiced. Jayavarman VII (1125 – 1200) came to power in 1181 after a time of political turmoil and perhaps civil war. He was a strong devotee to Mahayana Buddhism using his position to foster its practice and he made efforts to de-Hinduize society. The fate of the Kingdom depended upon the King's and Kingdom's devotion to Buddhist principles. Historically he had one of the most consequential impacts of any ruler upon Cambodian history.

The Cambodian Kingdom did not end in 1431 but simply shifted their capital to Phnom Penn. The new capital was a center of trade and Theravada Buddhism became predominant thanks to influence by monks from Thailand. The kingdom sent several tribute missions to China between 1371 and 1419 as trade became more important than rice production. The Portuguese missionary Gaspar de Cruz visited the kingdom in 1556.

Cambodian history from this point forward would be characterized by its interaction with its neighbors much more than internal developments. As the power of Vietnam and Thailand grew, the king of Cambodia had to become adept at manipulating the two to keep his independence. When the French offered to help him end vassal status in 1863, it was a reasonable course of action. Eventually Cambodia would become a French colony as a result.

The islands of Japan appear to have been inhabited from pre-historic times. Four main islands dominate the archipelago starting with Hokkaido in the north, followed by Honshu the largest and then Shikoku and Kyushu in the south. The government formed near the Yamato River in the southern part of the Honshu Island. A capital would eventually be built in Nara in the same vicinity by the Empress Genmei. The first formation of a central government appears in the 3rd century under the woman dictator Himiku the Sun Princess. She was followed by her daughter Iyo.

One characteristic unusual about Japan was the high number of female dictators in the early part of the country's formation. Early Japanese society was matriarchal as men went to live with their wife's family and inheritance followed the female line. Perhaps the early power of women could be attributed to the worship of spirits called Kami. The most powerful Kami was the Sun Goddess Amaterasu. An early Chinese chronicle says the Queen Himiku ruled by magic, perhaps an indication she was a female shaman.

Buddhism arrived in Japan in 552 and over the years combined with the worship of the Kami to form Shinto, the official religion. Confucianism from China also had its influence when in 702 the Great Law of Taiho became an official document of governance.

The capital city of Nara had huge Buddhist temples and eventually the monks began influencing policy. When the dictator Kanmu moved the imperial residence to Heian (modern day Kyoto), to escape their influence, the Heian Era (794 – 1185) began. Kyoto would be the official residence of the Emperor for the next 1,000 years. This era is considered to be the high point of classical Japanese civilization.

Power was not always in the hands of the Emperor as powerful families often ruled from behind the throne. After a short warring states period, the first Shogunate was established. From this point forward, Japan entered a feudal period where power was found in nobles called daimyo supported by their samurai (a warrior caste). All this took place while the most powerful daimyo ruled as the Shogun—a military dictator ruling in the name of the Emperor. The samurai followed the bushido code or way of the warrior. They took the symbol of the sakura (a cherry blossom) because the blossom was both beautiful and short lived. Women were not initially excluded from being samurai, but the necessity of keeping the inheritance intact to maintain power gradually found women samurai disappearing. Japan was in a warring states period when the Portuguese arrived in 1543.

2.7

In Africa dictatorships existed as far back as 1000 BC. In the Pacific islands, Hawaii is used for an example as the islands are unified under a single king (1756 – 1810).

For those areas underdeveloped, such as Africa and the islands in the Pacific, the dictatorial pattern was the same. The oldest African civilizations would develop in the upper Nile. Stimulated by trade, Nubia grew into a large vassal state of Egypt. It was supported by a major trading post along the Nile between the first and second cataracts. By the year 1000 BC, Nubia gained its complete independence. The new kingdom, Kush, became powerful enough to conquer Thebes in 730 BC and rule Egypt for 60 years. Under pressure from the Assyrians, they moved their capital to Meroe (540 BC) at the junction of the blue and white Niles. Rule was similar to Egypt with a divine king. The kingdom survived to about 300 AD when it was conquered by the Aksum. From then to the 6th century, the Christian Kingdom of Aksum existed off of trade from the Red Sea. Persia would gain control of the trade after 600 causing a gradual decline in the Kush kingdom until about 800.

The kingdom of Ghana (1000–1235) in West Africa was the first to be built up both from trade and the agriculture from fertile soil around the Niger River. The dynasty consisted of warlike, semi-divine rulers. Both gold and salt were major exports. From about 1230 forward, Mali would become the dominant kingdom in the area. At first a breakaway province from Ghana, Mali came to control the three major cities of trans-Sahara trade: Jenne, Gao, and the most famous, Timbuktu. When the king, Mansa Musa, converted to Islam he took a pilgrimage to Mecca. When he returned he brought Islamic scholars and established an Islamic university at Timbuktu. When Mali fell into succession disputes, Sunni Ali would establish a new kingdom of Songhay in 1468. An attack by Morocco in 1591 provided the fatal blow to the kingdom and cities like Timbuktu were sacked.

The kingdom of Kuba in central Africa existed from the 17th century to the late 19th century until conquered by Europeans.[6] It was ruled by

---

[6] It was not out of any benign intentions the Europeans conquered Africa so late. It was African diseases preventing any earlier conquest.

the Matoon dynasty from its founding in approximately 1620. Having no writing, the dictators proclaimed themselves in statues or "royal doubles" across the kingdom. The king was a chieftain of the most powerful clan centrally located within the kingdom. Within the capital, royal slaves under the command of the king's son enforced the king's commands. When needed, a larger force of 2,000 men was on call for more serious operations.

The king was a direct descendent from the first king, Shyaam, who was selected as chief of chiefs by the nature spirits. Being of divine stock he was prohibited from eating in the presence of his wives or seating himself on the bare ground. Ncyeem was the supreme creator-spirit of the nature gods and the king was called Ncyeem Akwoonc translating as "god on earth." A system of civil servants, called the kolm, and a series of tribunals with the king at the head, insured the laws were kept and the taxes paid.

Hawaii is a good example of dictatorship in the Pacific islands. The dictator Kamehameha (1756 – 1819) was of high rank but was not in direct line to be king. The islands were divided into four different kingdoms at the time of his birth. The two most powerful kings were Kahekili of Maui and Kamehameha's uncle, Kalaniopuu. Kamehameha grew up as a warrior and fought with his uncle in battle against Kahekili on Maui in 1775. Eventually Kamehameha would be appointed guardian of the war god, while the King's son, Kiwalao, would be named heir to the throne. When Kiwalao became King in 1782 a succession struggle began. The two forces met at the Battle of Mokuohai where Kamehameha killed Kiwalao. For the next 10 years the big island of Hawaii was in civil war with occasional interference from Maui.

Warfare between the islands was a constant affair. While Kamehameha was making war on Maui and Oahu, Keoua the brother of Kiwalao, attacked the Hilo district and plundered it. When Keoua's army later passed by a volcano as it erupted and killed 1/3 of Keoua's men, it was said the gods favored Kamehameha. A holy man told Kamehameha to build a shrine to the war god if he wanted to become ruler of the big island. After the shrine was built, Keoua felt he should visit the shrine and upon his arrival, Kamehameha ambushed and killed him in 1791.

Meanwhile, Kahekili had managed to add Molokai, Oahu, and Kauai to his Maui kingdom. He had nearly been defeated by Kamehameha in the

Battle of Iao Valley in 1790 but now was a serious threat. Both sides began to acquire guns and ammo from fur traders who would stop at the islands for supplies.

When Kahekili died in 1794, two relatives fought over the kingdom. Kamehameha saw this as an opportunity and assembled the largest army and canoe fleet ever seen in the islands. He then set out and immediately captured Molokai. The army next landed at Waikiki beach on Oahu where at the Battle of Nuuanu Cliffs hundreds of vanquished warriors were driven over the cliffs to their death. After building a fleet of forty double-canoes with small sails, the holdouts at Kauai and Niihau joined his kingdom in 1810. Known as the Peleleu fleet, it was the most formidable naval force ever seen in Hawaii.

2.8

In the Americas, three different civilizations formed: the Inca, the Mayan, and the Aztec. These civilizations are salient examples since they developed without any influence from Asia.

The Incas had a small kingdom in the Andes Mountains when King Wiraqocha Inca came to power. He took a wife to cement a local alliance and added "Creator God" to his royal name. The Chankas attacked him in part for this insult to the gods but their three-pronged attack against Cuzco failed. As the legend goes, the Inca Prince Yupanki saw a vision of the Creator and he promised to send warriors. At a critical moment in the battle warriors appeared out of thin air to lead the Incas to victory. Many archaeologists speculate this battle, along with the divine support provided by the legend, put the Incas on their road of conquest. Wiraqocha was replaced by his son who added a new name to his title, Pachakuti, meaning "Son of the Sun."

Pachakuti began to expand south first subduing the Qolla in the Titicaca basin. It was the Inca practice, much like the Romans, to leave a garrison behind to keep control over their new possessions. Pachakuti continued south through parts of Bolivia before setting his sights to the north.

Expeditions were sent into present-day Ecuador and up the Peruvian coast with armies as large as 30,000.

The next Inca king, Thupa Inca Yupanki, build a settlement at Inkawasi, called the new Cuzco, used to conduct the northern military campaigns. When the Incas attempted to take a fort at Ungara, they used a faked withdrawal to lure the defenders away from the fort and left sacrifices of food on a nearby beach. The enemy warriors left the fort to celebrate their victory, falling into the Inca trap. The Incas massacred them on the beach and hung survivors on the wall of the fort. The Incas would call these people Guarco derived from the Inca word "to hang."

Consolidating the young empire, the next king Wayna Qhapaq, conducted up to eight campaigns in the north to subdue Ecuador. In one battle the enemy was trapped beside a lake, and there were so many dead the lake would be called Yaguarcocha or Lake of Blood. The Incas did not tolerate rebellion. When the rebel, Pinta, was captured his skin was used for a ceremonial drum in Cuzco. After the king's death, two half-brothers contested the throne. After a bitter civil war, Atawallpa, one of the two half-brothers, ascended to the throne in time to meet the Spanish in 1532.

The original picture of the Mayan civilization was of particular interest in comparing and contrasting early human civilizations and dictatorships. The view, held prior to the deciphering of the Mayan glyphs, was of a peaceful people ruled by astronomer kings. There was no obvious record of conquest, dictatorial propaganda, or empire.[7] However, this original view by the archaeological community changed completely when over a period of forty years the Mayan text was decoded. The picture to emerge from the Mayan ruins was startling. The Mayan civilization was one of warring city-states. Each city had an emblem glyph representing the city's "divine lord." A complex vassal state arrangement existed consistent with the observed disparity in city size among the many different Mayan cities. Thus the Mayans are like all the other early human civilizations, as they provide no counter-example to dictatorship.

---

[7] Projecting one's desires onto another civilization is a common fault of intellectuals particularly when little is actually known about the civilization.

The Aztec empire was one of the more brutal dictatorships, engaging in human sacrifice on a grand scale. The Aztecs who called themselves the Mexica began with a migration into the Valley of Mexico. The Valley of Mexico is a highland plateau in central Mexico and its fertile fields had been home to several different peoples prior to the migration of the Mexica to the area. The Aztecs were a fierce warlike people who were often hired as mercenaries by local chieftains. In one particular example a chieftain, Coxcox, hired the Aztecs as mercenaries. After the Aztec's victory, Coxcox sent a daughter to solidify their alliance. To his horror when he paid a visit to her village, she had already been sacrificed, and a priest was dancing about wearing her skin. Coxcox attacked the Aztecs forcing them to relocate to the mudflat regions of the valley. Exiled to the most undesirable part of the valley, the Aztecs built the city of Tenochtitlan.

After the 1431 conquest of the city-state Atzcapotzallo and its allies, the Aztecs set up a system of tribute for conquered peoples, preferring this to occupation. With each new victory, the Aztecs increased the sacrifices to their god Huitzilopochtli. To satisfy the ever-increasing demand of their god, the Aztecs embarked upon a series of Flower Wars. These were wars with only one aim—the capture of victims for human sacrifice. As the Aztecs became more powerful they looked outside of the Valley of Mexico for fresh victims, and after the 1450s, resistance to their collection efforts began to grow.

When the dictator Montezuma II came to power in 1502, the Aztec empire had anywhere from ten to twenty million people. The Aztec domination of the valley was so complete their native tongue, Nahuatl, was now the dominant language in the region. Their empire was one of grand buildings, and sophisticated aqueducts rivaling those in Europe.

3

Except as noted in chapter two, no historically significant counter-examples to dictatorship exist in the ancient world.[8]

In early India some tribes perhaps influenced by Jainist or Buddhist teachings formed governments based upon more democratic methods. Historians have coined the term gana-sangha, literally meaning clan-government for these realms. It is not clear how egalitarian they were, but clearly they were not absolutist monarchies. They represented the only reliable example of non-dictatorial governments in early human civilization. The term raja was used in these states to indicate an elder or clan representative.

A raja from a noble family was elected to hold executive power sometimes in consultation with a council. The accounts indicate an assembly of some type presided over all weighty state matters. Decision making, which could include voting, was more based on consensus viewing silence as consent. In the capital of the Licchaui Republic, Vaisali, their assembly of 7,707 rajas did not appear to have met on a regular basis while a council of nine elders met more often. How the power was split between the two currently is not known. With the caste system already in place at this time, it is doubtful members of these bodies were anything but members from the two upper castes. Given the most generous interpretation of these governments as fledgling democracies or evidence human government does display on occasion something other than dictatorship, their ultimate impact upon history was nil.

The experiment in non-dictatorial rule ended when Vaisali lost its independence in a protracted struggle with the Magadhan Empire. Vaisali was a leader of an alliance of lesser republics and using a professional army was the key to Magadhan's success. By the time of the Second Buddhist Council in the fourth century BC, Vaisali was part of the Magadhan Empire, and Magadhan eventually became a major power dominating the lower Ganges valley. Its territory extended from the Bay of Bengal to the Himalayas. When Mahapadma Nanda became dictator despite being from a lower caste, he

---

[8] To be historically significant one must be victorious on the battlefield and survive long enough to matter.

began to expand the empire. By 326 BC the Magadhan Empire contained the entire Ganges valley and neighboring territories. The fledgling democracy of the Licchaui Republic was by this time long gone.

There is also speculation among academics as to possible democratic institutions in Mesopotamia and surrounding areas prior to the dictatorships already described. Hard archaeological evidence to support this proposition is scarce and analysis relies upon favorable interpretations of inscriptions as an indication of democratic institutions and habits. For example, in the Hittite Old Kingdom, the kingship appears to have a term limit. The *pankus*, possibly an assembly of warriors, had some say over judicial matters and served as the king's advisory committee. The sense of equality seen among warriors who share common dangers and sacrifices in battle is a theme seen from time to time historically and, depending upon the circumstances, can support or retard democratic trends already present.

4

Government tends to concentrate all secular and spiritual authority in one individual. Examples from ancient Egypt to modern Japan are cited. So powerful is this centralization the myth of the god-king extended into the 20th century.

One prime feature of these early dictatorships is the close association between the dictator and the official state religion. The dictator is either seen as a god or directly descended from a god. It was the union of all secular and spiritual authority in one individual. The Pharaoh of Egypt provides a good example for he is shown on temple walls both as worshiping the gods and associating with them.

The Egyptian religion maintained the common people needed Pharaoh for eternal salvation. He alone had the key to the afterlife since the state religion of Egypt proclaimed the pharaoh a mighty god. On earth he was the son of Ra, the sun god and was also the god who acted as an intermediary between men and the other gods of the Egyptian religion. When he died, he became another god, Osiris, the god of the underworld. It was through his intercession ordinary Egyptians obtained eternal life.

The pyramids, built to hold the remains of these dictators, stands as mankind's greatest monument to dictatorship. The divinity was closely tied to the hereditary transmission from father to son and the purity of lineage and blood was therefore paramount. The practice of incest marriages between brothers and sisters was a way to ensure purity of blood.

At the end of the Third and beginning of the Fourth Dynasty, the cult of the dictator was notably expanded. Economic settlements were sponsored throughout Egypt. Fishing villages, farming communities, and towns of craftsmen were created to produce goods directly shipped to the capital and each of these communities had a small pyramid replica as part of the royal patronage.

So powerful was the pharaoh over religious matters he could make huge changes to worship without meaningful opposition. The Pharaoh Amunhotep IV invented a monotheistic religion around the god Aten. Aten was the visible disc of the sun. Amunhotep changed his name to Akenaten and created a new capital city in the desert. At the same time he sent royal representatives throughout the entire Kingdom of Egypt to suppress their polytheistic worship, but he neglected his political duties as pharaoh and lost large parts of the Empire. Historians call him the Heretic Pharaoh.

The emperor as god has many more examples in the ancient world. Atawallpa was dictator of the Incas at the time of the Spanish conquest and regarded by his subjects as a sun-god. The Incas obeyed his commands without question despite being held as a hostage by the Spaniards and this proved useful to the Spaniards as they accumulated a vast ransom prior to Atawallpa's execution. In another example, the grandson of Sargon, Naram-Sin, used the cuneiform sign of divinity before his name when he declared himself King of the Four Regions.

The Mayan kings were exalted as the great sun lord, holy lord, or lord of lords. No distinctly priest class appears to have existed with all major religious duties concentrated in the king. Many Mayan kings were associated with the jaguar sun-god. During different astronomical events of the year, Mayan kings would mount to the top of their step pyramids in their full regalia to perform bloodletting and human sacrifice. In this way they made contact with the spiritual realm.

Another example of particular interest is from the Chinese civilization. Their dynasty system lasted into the 20th century incorporating this key element from their first dictatorships. From its earliest beginnings the Chinese emperors used the term *huangdi* as their title. Literally translated it means "magnificent god" since Di was an early Chinese deity. As the dictatorship progressed, the emperor was considered a Son of Heaven and the Chinese court was called the Celestial Court. His residence, known to the westerners as the Forbidden City, was called the Great Within. When an official presented himself before the Dragon Throne, he was required to perform the *k'o-t'eu* known in English as the kowtow. This ceremony required groveling on all fours while banging one's forehead loudly on the floor nine times. During the "Holy Birthday of the Lord of a Myriad Years," almost the entire ceremony was conducted with the Son of Heaven absent and the participants prostrating themselves before the empty Dragon Throne. Western observers were amazed at the level of adoration paid to the emperor and put this on par with any devotional worship service they had seen in the west. It is truly remarkable how the myth of the divine king survived to sustain dictatorship in the 20th century, and this shows the power dictatorship has as a form of government.

Japan provides another example of emperor as god lasting into the 20th century. This dictatorship traced its roots to the time when the ancestral gods sent the grandson of the sun-goddess to earth to establish the kingdom. The imperial line was said to extend unbroken to the first emperor, Jimmu (660 BC).

The Japanese imperial succession ceremonies were full of divine references. The ceremonies could take up to two years to complete, as they did from December 25, 1926 to November 30, 1928. It began with the new emperor taking possession of the imperial regalia with its own divine origin. Proclamations were made before holy sites such as the sanctuary of imperial ancestors. In one such ceremony, the *daijo-sai* or great food festival, sacred dances were performed before the Sacred Regal Mirror, and the emperor worshiped at the shrine of the gods of Heaven and Earth.

5

Government is the struggle for power, to establish a monopoly of violence, and expand the kingdom via constant warfare, with all secular and spiritual authority concentrated in one individual, the dictator.

The previous historical survey shows how humankind loves the concentration of government power ideally in one man and the word "dictator" best describes that man. Human civilization had its earliest beginnings in four distinct regions of the world, and these regions were each characterized by large areas of rich and fertile soil. From the bountiful harvest grew an ever larger human population, eventually filling large cities. Later in other regions, the same general pattern repeated itself. A rich diversity of cultural practices, religions, and human languages could be found in these many different peoples. However, only one form of government could be found—dictatorship.

It might seem strange at first to categorize these governments as dictatorships. The English language contains so many words for the same thing— emperor, chieftain, king, pharaoh, sultan, maharaja, monarch, etc.—but their effect was the same. All government power was concentrated in a single individual. All secular and spiritual authority was concentrated at the top. It does not matter if a particular dictator is enlightened. He is still the dictator, whether for good or ill, because the manner of his rule is entirely at his own discretion.

The dictator passed the dictatorship on to future generations in the same family creating a dynasty. When each dynasty ended, a new one took its place either via a civil war between powerful families or by an external military force under the command of a foreign dictator. Men so love security over freedom only an extreme condition, in China termed losing the Mandate from Heaven, causes them to change dictators. When a rebellion of the people or civil war has unseated the current dictator, because his reign has been either too oppressive or too incompetent, and he has lost the Mandate from Heaven, another dictator is put in his place. In this manner a cycle is created between dynasties and warring states periods.

Several important conclusions can be drawn from the previous historical survey. First, there is a near universal presence of dictatorship in all early human civilizations. Since the survey includes all areas of the world, except Western civilization, and in many cases follows these areas up to the modern era, one is forced to conclude dictatorship is the natural form of human government. Human government is consequently the struggle for power. Second, the dictatorship maintains its power via a monopoly of violence.[9] The dictatorship is maintained in almost all cases by a professional standing army under the control of the dictator. The dictator uses his command of the instruments of state violence to bend others to his will. Third, these dictatorships display a strong aggressive tendency. Constant warfare characterizes their behavior. Fourth, these dictatorships tend to concentrate all secular and spiritual authority in the person of the dictator. In the extreme he is a god-king.

There is no human taboo not broken in service of the dictator. The wholesale slaughter of people did not stop Alexander. The theft of an entire empire's resources to build a grandiose monument to oneself, i.e. the Great Pyramid, did not stop Khufu. The abasement of a servant forced to kowtow before the Dragon Throne did not trouble the Son of Heaven. The total suppression of dissenting views did not bother Qin when he had four hundred intellectuals murdered. The practice of human sacrifice and the incest between siblings were all for the continuation of dictatorship—not to mention the nearly constant warfare all for the increased power of the dictator.

---

[9] Different than the similar term "monopoly on violence" first coined by the sociologist Max Weber.

The Nature of the Beast

Chapter Two

For most of the 5,000 years of human civilization, the only form of government was dictatorship—one that was hereditary with each dictator attempting to pass the dictatorship from father to son. If this was not possible then an attempt to keep it within a family or clan was made, resulting in a pattern of dynastic rule. The power sustaining the dictatorship was a monopoly of violence under the control of the dictator usually taking the form of a professional army. A priesthood provided the moral justification while the finance of the kingdom or empire was almost always a monopoly over agriculture and control over the surplus of food production. The dictator was constantly looking for opportunities to expand his realm via military campaigns. Thus this form of government, the Hereditary Dictatorship, is characterized by constant warfare.[10]

The Hereditary Dictatorship took place in a pre-industrial society and the control over the land was its key to domination. The pre-industrial society was stratified looking much like the pyramids many of these societies built. Many Hereditary Dictatorships were divided into an aristocracy who ruled over the land and a peasant class who worked the land. The aristocracy in these pre-industrial societies viewed themselves as their kingdom's guardians. Their society was seen as the pinnacle of human development and it was their job

---

[10] Not to be confused with the term "Family Dictatorship" found in political science.

to preserve it against the outside barbarians. This included a body of writings or sacred texts codifying this perceived superiority.

One should not make too much of the aristocrat versus peasant or oppressor versus oppressed paradigm. In a society with a pyramid structure the distinction is completely arbitrary as it is much like drawing an arbitrary line at a certain level of bricks in the pyramid. Those bricks above the line are the oppressors and those below the oppressed—the line could be drawn at any level. This paradigm obscures the most important feature of these societies: dictatorship.

2

The Hereditary Dictatorship's various forms are characterized by how the new dictator is selected and how power is distributed within the government.

The most dangerous time in any dynasty is the transition from the old dictator to the new. Numerous methods have been used to smooth this transition. In Europe, from the medieval period onward the son's inheritance of the dictatorship was derived from Salic law. The law's name comes from a criminal code dating back to the Franks making it illegal for women to inherit land, and so male children became the presumptive future king or baron. Nonetheless, Europe was more disposed to female rulers like Maria Theresa or Catherine the Great than most other areas of the world. The Christian religion's prohibition against harems and concubines limited the number of legitimate children a king might have, thereby reducing the probability of a boy.

A closely allied concept with Salic law is primogeniture. Primogeniture holds the first-born as king the moment the old king dies. The more absolute monarchists prefer this method because it does not require approval by any spiritual authority. Since only "God can make an heir," any approval of the clergy was unnecessary. The only complication occurs when the dictator is not an adult at the time of royal investiture. A regent is then appointed to act on the king's behalf until he comes of age.

In cases where the dictator had multiple wives the situation could get complicated. For the Ottoman Empire the situation became so bad the Law of Fratricide was used. Issued by Sultan Mehmed II of the Ottoman Empire in 1451, it allowed the Sultan to kill his brothers upon his production of a male heir. Wives and concubines were included in the royal carnage. Later it was changed to imprisonment for life, called "the Cage," but the goal was the same, avoidance of civil war and an orderly transition of government.

In a few limited cases an elective monarchy was used. However, this method never gained much favor. In Poland it will become apparent why. Poland had every reason to look to its future as a powerful nation in Europe. In the 17th century, it had a larger population than any other country in Europe save Russia. The king of Poland was however, limited by a set of obligations or contracts as part of his election as king. These *Pacta Conventa* became increasingly restrictive, and the king lost executive power becoming a figurehead. The ineptitude ended in 1772 when Poland was divided among its neighbors.

The use of adoption to pass power to the next dictator was used in rare cases with the most famous example being the five Good Emperors of the 2nd century Roman Empire. Making a virtue out of necessity, because these emperors had no male heirs, it was a short-lived attempt to avoid civil war and improve upon the qualities of the dictator and his governance. Nerva (r. 96 – 98) the first emperor elected by the Senate was old and adopted Trajan (r. 98–117) a popular general. Trajan adopted Hadrian (r. 117 – 138) who in time adopted Antoninus Pius (r. 138 – 161). The last in this line, Marcus Aurelius (r. 161 – 180) was a Stoic philosopher in addition to a competent ruler and is famous for his book *Meditations*. When the first male heir, Aurelius's son Commodus, appeared (r. 180 – 192) the seat of government went to him.

The other key characteristic of Hereditary Dictatorships is the relative power of the king versus his nobles or barons. This distinction has been noted by many observers of history, including Machiavelli in *The Prince*. When power is not solely concentrated in a king, a distributed monarchy is the result. In its most extreme form, called Oligarchy, no king is present at all, and power is shared between competing powerful individuals. When formally documenting the power arrangement between king, barons, and commoners it becomes a constitutional monarchy. England is the best example of this form of dictatorship. The Magna Carta was a document King John of England (1166 – 1216) was forced to sign by his barons in

1215. Fortunately his death in 1216 prevented civil war from resuming and made the document permanent. This was the first time in Europe a king explicitly limited his power.

Occasionally the king or emperor is a figurehead with the true dictator ruling from behind the throne with a complete separation of the sacred-king functions and the practical control of power. The Shogunate in Japan was a baron who wielded power from behind the Chrysanthemum throne and passed his power in a hereditary manner like a king. The Tokugawa Shogunate of Japan was a dynasty who ruled in the name of the emperor from around 1600 into the 19th century. The Praetorian Guard of the late Roman Empire and the "Mayors of the Palace" in medieval France are other examples.

A eunuch, who traditionally could be found guarding the harem, and by implication guaranteeing the paternity of any son born to a concubine, was used as a powerful minister in China, Assyria, and Persia. These men were used by the dictators because eunuchs could not establish dynasties. They played a particularly prominent role in the Byzantine Empire, as it was said, "no eunuch could attain the purple" i.e. could never be king. They often came from less important families who had their sons castrated as a way to improve their chances at high office. Prior to 1204, for roughly all of the Byzantine Empire, the chief minister was always a eunuch with one exception. They made excellent military commanders, and between the 6th and 12th centuries over forty were high level admirals and generals. The 6th century conqueror of Italy, General Narses, was a eunuch.

3

Political power is military power. The dictator uses this to establish a monopoly of violence. In the words of the dictator Mao Zedong (1893 – 1976) "Political power comes from the barrel of a gun."

Power's ultimate arbiter is the military because the military is used to establish the monopoly of violence for the dictator. It is from the dictator's monopoly of violence all other secondary monopolies are made possible. The military controls the internal security of the state as well as its external borders. It is used to dispense justice and keep the mob at bay. It is the principal means by which the Hereditary Dictator increases his power via campaigns of conquest.

Since government power rests upon this monopoly, as Mao indicated above, it is always present. The view seeing war and peace as two separate, opposite, things is an illusion. Violence by government is a continuum, and the perspective believing eliminating weapons and armies can eliminate war is no more realistic than the view that doing away with police and prisons can eliminate crime. Violence by government is ubiquitous and peace, as it is so called, is a low intensity conflict. Carl von Clausewitz, a Prussian Officer, wrote about this in his work *On War*. He wrote most famously how war was an extension of politics by other means. Clausewitz's dictum did not go far enough, from the dictator's point of view, all politics is a struggle for power and potentially violent.

Not only is the monopoly of violence ubiquitous, it is also unbounded. It is commonplace for commentators on war, such as Clausewitz, to say the object in war is to destroy the enemy's armed forces. Another commentator on war, Sun Tzu, a Chinese General who wrote around 490 BC, would argue it is the highest form of generalship to win without combat; however, nothing could be more false. The true object of government's violence is the human being and war as a consequence is tribal. Tribal warfare is genocidal because the destruction of the other tribe is the objective. The reason the destruction of the enemy's army compels them to do our will is the implied threat of annihilation. When Alexander the Great destroyed the city of Tyre, killing all adult males and selling all women and children into slavery, he was practicing tribal warfare.

The reason the monopoly of violence favors dictatorship and why dictatorship is so prevalent in history is because the principles of war favor a dictator. There is no universally recognized list of these principles, but found on almost all lists is the principle of a unified command. The military commander must have direct control of all forces in his area of responsibility. In the heat of battle there can be no confusion as to whose orders one is to follow. The dictator embodies this principle since he is always seen either directly or indirectly as commander of the armed forces. Clausewitz would see one single decisive battle as the ultimate abstraction of war and the complete concentration of power in the dictator is the ultimate abstraction of dictatorship. The more centralized the power—the more this ideal is approached.

Another principle commonly listed is the principle of the objective. In this principle the military coordinates all of its effort toward a common goal. Some key weakness of the enemy is often picked such as a gap in the enemy's formation. Again, the dictator is best in a position to implement this principle when he makes war an integral part of his foreign policy. War and peace become two sides of the same coin—the coin being the expansion of his realm.

When Sun Tzu said all war is deception, he was identifying another principle of war: the principle of surprise. This is much more than the simple psychological effect of being surprised. From the lowliest foot soldier who would have avoided the arrow if he had only known it was coming, to the dictator himself unaware of a soon to be sprung treachery, this principle permeates warfare. Clausewitz captured this when he described a "fog of war." It is in a state of imperfect and contradictory information where the struggle for power takes place.

Both because it permeates warfare and because it is so fundamental, this principle can be seen as a basis upon which other principles can be derived. Spying on one's enemy? This is about reducing the fog of war for one's self while the often listed principle of security is about increasing the enemy's fog of war. Other principles can be seen as means to achieve surprise like the principles of offensive action, maneuver, or concentration of force. Many wars begin with a surprise attack because of this principle. The dictator and a small inner circle around him are in the best position to implement surprise and its subordinate principles. This is particularly true if he already dominates his kingdom via restrictions upon personal movement, censorship of publications, or restrictions on trade at ports of entry.

On these lists are principles related to the efficient use of military force. Economy of force, use of internal lines of communication, and efficient administration are all about making the most of one's army. The old adage—armchair generals talk about strategy while real generals talk about logistics—is all about maximization of military power at minimum cost. Only a dictator can coordinate all aspects of the state to maximize military power. Only he can mobilize a nation in his service.

The dictator both loves and fears his military. He needs them more than any other group for without them he is nothing. From the beginning, the earliest dictators created professional armies. One of the first dictators in the ancient world, King Sargon, took his daily meals with his 5,400 soldiers. At the same time a powerful general or noble capable of gaining their loyalty is a huge threat to the dictator. He must always balance how much military command he reserves for himself and how much he allocates to his subordinates. The powerful, charismatic, general is frequently seen in history replacing the dictator with himself. If a particular general forms a special bond of shared sacrifice with his men, he is particularly dangerous. The general's successful military exploits can make him more famous and revered than the dictator.

Wars almost always last longer and cost more than initially anticipated. The dictator is limited in what he can spend on his army. This produces a conflict between what he wishes to spend and what he can confiscate in taxes. If the taxes are excessively high then he risks economic ruin or popular revolt but if they are too low then he risks military disaster. If anything there is a tendency for dictators to overspend on the military and get themselves into financial trouble.

Because military power is the key to the kingdom, changes in military technology will affect the structure of the dictatorship. The iron stirrup made the heavy cavalry dominant on the battlefield in Europe and helped usher in the age of Feudalism. The introduction of the longbow was used in a similar way to end Feudalism. Certainly the use of gunpowder had a profound impact upon the battlefield. The fall of Constantinople in 1453 was made possible by the use of cannons to breach the walled fortifications, which had withstood previous assaults for hundreds of years. Its use made the medieval European castle obsolete and shifted the balance-of-power from barons to kings. Along with certain naval technology improvements like the dry compass, gunpowder allowed the European dictators to create vast worldwide empires. Although military technology changes the way dictators maintain control, it never undermined the dominance of dictatorship.

4

The monopoly of violence is used to establish secondary monopolies. The dictator's monopoly over the economy is a secondary monopoly. It is important because it funds the army.

If each kingdom is idealized as a body, soul, and mind, then the monopoly of violence likewise dominates the economy, religion, and intellect of that kingdom. Economic domination is the most important of these three and in pre-industrial societies that means land. Food production into the 19th century required 80-90% of the population to be directly involved. The entire economy of this type of society is concentrated around a single enterprise. In each of the fertile valleys and then later in other population centers, a small surplus of food over the subsistence level was produced. Control of the land translates into control over this surplus and the society at large.

Since the monopoly of violence is unbounded, its secondary extensions are also unbounded. Each increase in government power extracts an additional amount of the surplus from the population, which then allows for an additional increase in government power. This is a form of positive feedback causing all governments to grow. The positive feedback continues until the cost of any additional effort equals the last amount extracted. This is the point implied by Machiavelli when he states in *The Prince* a prince needs to be feared but not hated. Confiscatory taxation is an example of overreach by the dictator where he risks being hated and losing his Mandate from Heaven.

With the land under the control of the dictator and the small group underneath him, the pre-industrial society becomes increasingly stratified as the government continues to grow. With most people forced to work the land for the benefit of the dictator, many pre-industrial societies split into two classes—a ruling class made up of an aristocracy and a much larger peasant class. Most peasants as tenants or serfs were unable to leave the land. Many could not leave for short periods of time without the landlord's permission, in some cases they could not marry without the landlord's consent, and for legal disputes the landlord was their only recourse. When the land was sold, they were sold with the land. A system with remarkable persistence, it survived into the 17th century in China, the 18th century in Western Europe, and 19th century in Eastern Europe.

Land was perceived as the prerequisite of one's status and closely tied to political power. In many societies the land of the aristocracy could not be sold. When lesser nobility or peasants owned land, there was no other economy to provide a living, and thus the land was kept as a family heritage. With the entire economy revolving around a single industry, it was impossible for the dictator to reward a subject without a grant of land. In its most extreme form, all land was owned by the dictator like the Incas and at certain times in China.

An additional advantage of the close connection between the land and the peasants was the ready access to forced labor. Forced labor as one's obligation to the landlord was common. Labor construction projects for roads, dikes—virtually anything—were forced upon the peasants. In Europe the forced labor was part of the tenant's rent and called *corvee*. In feudal societies it was not uncommon for peasants to be forced to serve as ground troops during war.

Because of the serf condition and as a practical answer of what to do with captured soldiers, the Hereditary Dictatorship had the ubiquitous use of slavery. The practice is found in essentially every pre-industrial civilization, and the slaves performed any task. They could be domestic servants or used in hazardous occupations such as mining. They appear quite frequently in agriculture working on Roman olive plantations in Sicily or on the sugar, tobacco, and cotton plantations in the New World. They were also used for their intellectual ability. Educated Greeks were used by the Romans as slaves. In the Islamic world slaves are found in prominent positions such as governors and generals. In addition, slavery was also a method to erase debts and a form of criminal punishment.

Many cultural practices reinforced the pyramid shape of the society and the separation of aristocracy from peasantry. One of these was the education of the nobility, scribes, and clergy. The education included study and memorization of sacred texts, as well as studying the writings of learned men in the past. Any literature studied was usually poetry. It was an education embodying the established truth, the wisdom of the ages, and it was the job of this upper crust of society to ensure these timeless truths continued.

This educational training took many years and was well beyond the means of the average citizen. It was a general education focusing on what made their civilization 'civilized' and separated them from the outside barbarians. It had the additional benefit of making these men, and a few women, appear superior to the people they ruled.

Dress and customs further separated the educated making them obvious from a distance. In many areas, these manners of dress and custom were enforced by laws called "sumptuary laws" and could be quite strict.

A consequence of using ancient texts was the ancient language itself became the language of the educated. The vernacular was for the peasants and not for the society's elite. The maintenance of revered ancient texts in a 'sacred' language was an important part of the Hereditary Dictatorship's power. This tended to make them conservative and resistant to change.

In the West, men of letters would be fluent in Latin, and sometimes Greek and Hebrew. In the Islamic world, classic Arabic was used. In India, Sanskrit was the key to the inner circles of power. Only in the ancient language was the true meaning of these sacred texts fully understandable. While this caused the official languages to become fixed, the vernacular languages continued to evolve. In many areas local dialects abounded. On the eve of Italian unification, Tuscan, which would become the official Italian language, was spoken by only 3% of the population. In France of 1863, a full 25% of the population did not speak French.

5

The dictator's monopoly over religion is another secondary monopoly providing meaning and values to the people in the dictatorship.

The close relationship between the Hereditary Dictatorship and the state religion was an important prop of the dictator. A monopoly of religion also flows from the monopoly of violence. Dictatorships provide meaning and values via this monopoly. The philosopher Plato (429 BC – 347 BC) recognized this and wrote about it in the *Republic*. In the first civilizations, the religious monopoly took the form of the god-king. This form of dictatorship had remarkable persistence and lasted into the 20th century in the Chinese and Japanese examples. For the most part, as the old empires expired, dictators were less god and more chief priest, so if calamity struck the misfortune was less the weakness of the gods than it was a lack of fidelity.

The type of religious monopoly depended upon the power of the dictator. When most powerful, the dictator was divine. A less powerful dictator would rule in the name of the gods, and the weakest would be in conflict with religious authorities or need their help.

The gradual development of a divine Roman Emperor was a good example of what a powerful dictator can do. Octavian, the future dictator of Rome, was at a military training camp in Epirus when he got the news his great-Uncle Julius Caesar had been murdered, and he was heir to two-thirds of his fortune. Although young and considered immature, his dictatorial impulses were not and he quickly set out on revenge, eventually killing the statesman Cicero. A secession civil war ensued, and Octavian proved victorious on 3 September 31 BC. He immediately began solidifying his rule by associating himself with the divine. He established a residence next to the temples of both Apollo and Venus. Preserving the fiction of the old Republic in the trappings of its old institutions he kept the Roman Senate. Proclaimed Augustus by the Senate, the title had strong religious overtones and literally meant, worshipful. He took on the title and priestly duties of *pontifex maximus*. Eventually the cult of the emperor became routine, and the Senate would declare the emperor divine upon his death. Within 200 years, the emperors would openly proclaim to be god and master from birth. The Christian refusal to worship the emperor as a god was the main reason for their persecution.

A new method of justification of dictatorship became necessary when the first Christian Emperor, Constantine, became dictator of the Roman Empire. Obviously, he could not claim he was divine. The new relationship was made clear by the historian Eusebius, Bishop of Caesarea. He saw a clear parallel between the founding of the Roman Empire and the birth of Christ. The *pax augusti* was proof the Romans had divine help when they quickly created an empire. The one kingdom on earth was a reflection of the one kingdom in heaven and the one king in heaven had his representative on earth in Constantine. It was only natural for Constantine to call a church council at Nicaea in 325 to establish religious orthodoxy within his realm. It was an integral part of his duties. Other examples of this justification of dictatorship include when, William the Conqueror was anointed and crowned king in Westminster Abby on Christmas Day 1066 by the Archbishop of York, and when Charlemagne was crowned King of the Romans on Christmas Day 800 by the Pope in Rome.

The divine right of kings is espoused in many places proving he derived his authority directly from God and not any Pope. The theologian Wycliffe (1328 – 1384) declared the king the vicar of God while lesser known is Dante's support in his *De Monarchia* (1310). Sir Robert Filmer writing in *Patriarchia* (1679) made the point since kingship was part of natural law, so too was the divine right of each particular king and the elders of Cambridge University in 1681 declared much the same thing. Kings too made this self-serving argument. James I of England informed his son he was like a little god and born to rule men.

When kings are weak, the spiritual authorities assert their will as was noted in the conflict between the Buddhist monks and the Japanese dictators. A famous example from Europe can be found in the conflict between the Pope and the German Princes. The Holy Roman Empire in later years was a combined throne of election by German Princes and approval of the Pope. During the Investiture Controversy between Henry IV and Pope Gregory VII in 1075 they came into direct conflict. Henry insisted upon appointing his bishops in his own territory as had been done in the past and declared himself to be following the example of Constantine, Justinian, and Theodosius. The Pope had recently instituted reforms and all bishops now needed a papal appointment. Henry refused to submit and was promptly excommunicated. The Pope not only removed him as Holy Roman Emperor but also removed him as King of the Germans. King Henry perhaps in a moment of true remorse or more likely buying time to marshal his forces went to the Pope's residence in Canossa to repent. The famous Walk to Canossa has the King walking barefoot in the snow as a penitent wearing a hair-shirt asking for forgiveness. Civil war broke out in Germany during his absence, but he was able to crush his opponent in 1081 and then proceeded to march on Rome to install his own Pope. However, the Pope fled making Henry's operation a failure and the conflict continued for many decades.

6

The dictator's monopoly over the intellect is the last of the three key secondary monopolies and includes a monopoly over the sacred texts.
Propaganda and the control of information were evident from the earliest civilizations. The control of information was another secondary monopoly to flow from the monopoly of violence. The close link between the priest and the scribe was part of this control.

The first forms of writing facilitated the monopoly of information because it was a complicated system of hieroglyphic symbols. Special training was needed to become proficient. It is speculated by some anthropologists this was an intentional form of control and made unnecessarily complicated for that purpose. So important was this early power when a Mayan king captured a scribe from an enemy king, his hands were mutilated so he could not write.

Caesar Augustus was a master of propaganda. While seizing control of the Roman Republic, he maintained the fiction it was intact. He did it gradually while always maintaining he was doing it for the common man. Augustus reinstated old religious practices fallen into disuse, increased the number and privileges of the Vestal Virgins, revived the augury of safety as well as the festivals of Lupercalia and Compitalia. In 17 BC he celebrated the secular games in a grand fashion after they had not been celebrated since 146 BC. He did much to show circumstances were getting back to normal after many years of civil war by closing the doors to the temple of Janus on 11 January 29 BC, symbolizing Rome was at peace.

Caesar Augustus was seen as a humble man. When he returned to Italy in 29 BC, he refused the *aureum coronarium*, a monetary reward to victorious generals. He dropped the title Triumvir in 32 BC, a title he used in the civil war period and he gave up the consulship in 23 BC. Also, he was generous with those loyal to him. It was the Roman custom to award captured war booty to the commanding general. Using the large treasure captured from

Egypt, he gave 250,000 individual citizens the amount of 400 sesterces. Any veterans willing to settle in the colonies received 1,000 sesterces each the equivalent of about one year's income. He was always sure to impress this money came from his personal funds.

One particular honor voted Caesar Augustus was the civic crown. This honor normally goes to a soldier displaying unusual bravery while saving a citizen's life. He got the honor for saving all citizens of Rome from the ravages of civil war. Thus he showed himself to be everything one could want in a leader. He was a devoutly religious man, humble, generous, and brave.

Propaganda also took the form of symbols of power such as royal purple for the Romans and royal yellow for the Chinese. Royal displays, like coronations, magnified the importance of the dictator. The coronation of Queen Elizabeth II in 1953 is an example of such a royal display. It took place in Westminster Abbey, a place used for twenty-eight coronations over nine hundred years. All kings and queens were seated upon the Coronation Chair while beneath it was the Stone of Destiny—a sacred stone used by Scottish kings and captured by the English King Edward I in 1296.[11] Elizabeth herself wore regalia dating back to Charles II in 1661. The king as warrior was symbolized during the coronation by the great swords as part of the procession. One sword, the "Curtana" or Sword of Mercy, with its tip cut off to make it impossible to use as a weapon, symbolized how the king can never kill someone unjustly. An anointing was the confirmation of the spiritual power of the monarch. It was performed by the Archbishop of Canterbury with a tiny spoon of oil given to him by the Dean of Westminster. Once the coronation was complete, the new monarch received an acclamation from the knights present in the hall, which in past years consisted of them banging their swords upon their shields. Then all nobility, dukes, earls, and barons knelt before the new monarch and pledged their loyalty. The monarch had been crowned in a sacred place, upon a magical stone, wearing sacred clothes and been declared the union of the warrior and the sacred head of the kingdom. All secular and spiritual authority symbolically rested in the king or queen.

---

[11] It was briefly stolen by Scottish undergraduate students in the early 1950s but was in place by the time of her coronation.

Censorship was one method the dictators used to directly control the intellectual life. It facilitates the domination of the sacred texts by banning alternatives. The most famous in the West was the *Index*. In 1554 local religious authorities were already making lists of prohibited books in places like Venice and Milan. By 1559, Pope Paul IV published the *Index Librorum Prohibitorum* or *Index of Prohibited Books*. Simply called the *Index,* it existed into the 20th century, although by then it had little force, and was officially abolished in 1966. The first *Index* was approved by the Council of Trent in 1564. It was sporadically updated over the next four centuries and included on its list was a number of important thinkers of the Enlightenment such as John Locke. It also included prohibitions against items one might expect, such as obscene works, works on magic, and astrology. It also prohibited histories of the Inquisition. Violation of the prohibition meant automatic excommunication unless given a dispensation from the Pope.

7

The distinction between despotism and monarchy is a false distinction. By making such a distinction it is easier for some to justify monarchy.

A curious distinction made in histories of these dictatorships is monarch versus despot. It is a distinction made by such notable historians of government as Montesquieu. It is a false distinction made by Hereditary Dictatorships to show those who have been particularly harsh are an entirely different type of government separate from monarchy. Thereby monarchy is made more acceptable since it is not "despotism." When a dictator is overthrown by popular rebellion or civil war because he is too harsh, then he is a despot. However, if he is able to retain power then history overlooks his indiscretions.

Louis the XIV (1643 – 1715) of France is the archetype of the absolute monarch, and despite his cruel policies toward the Huguenots, is not characterized as a despot. He came into full power when his prime minister, Cardinal Jules Mazarin, died in 1661. His immediate appointment of himself as prime minister would portend of things to come. He assumed direct control over the army and increased the efficiency of the State's tax collection. He bypassed previous representative bodies to create laws. Two traditional checks upon the central power of the dictator, the Estates General and the Assembly of Notables, never met during his reign. He extended the police powers of the central government in 1667 with the appointment of a police chief of Paris, called a Lieutenant-General of Police, who now reported directly to the King. By the year 1699 this practice had been extended to all major cities and parts of the countryside. Separate commissioners appointed by the King promulgated his edicts out to the provinces. The reform of tax collection was a boon to the dictatorship when the finance minister, Colbert, discovered how corruption had diverted 75% of the taxes collected. After Colbert's reforms 80% went directly into the national treasury.

Louis was an effective propagandist using a patronage system to project a favorable image of himself in his kingdom. He described himself as the Sun King meaning all in his kingdom orbited around him. A patron of the arts, he commissioned sculptures, plays and ballets, even performing in some of them. The Louvre was improved and grand streets built. He expanded the Academy creating separate academies for dance in 1661 and science in 1666. Excellence in the arts and sciences welcomed royal approbation so long as it did not challenge his authority. However, nothing symbolized the grandeur he wished to create more than his new royal residence, Versailles. The building of Versailles spared no expense, taking 5% of the general revenue for decades.

Orthodoxy became the standard. The Les Invalides, originally a retirement home for soldiers, became a dumping ground for state undesirables. It is estimated over 100,000 individuals from Protestants to the insane, from those accused of witchcraft to prostitutes, all found a residence inside its confines.

Since the Council of Trent (1543 – 1563), the Catholic Church had been on a rigorous campaign of reform and standardization called the Counter-Reformation. In Louis XIV, they found an ally. A campaign against Protestants included a ban on national synods and a destruction of churches, up to 700 by some counts. When the Edict of Nantes granting religious rights was issued in 1598, between one and two million Protestants lived in France filling 2,150 churches. In the Edict of Fontainebleau in 1685 Louis repealed the Protestant rights granted under the Edict of Nantes. After the

Edit of Fontainebleau, they poured out of the country in droves to places like England, Prussia, and Holland. As is typical of minorities in agricultural societies they specialized in crafts and trades, and their departure was a net loss for the kingdom. When they regained religious protections in 1788, the Huguenots as they were called, numbered only 600,000.

The success in Louis XIV's bid for absolute power made him the admiration of other royalty in Europe. His lavish patronage of the arts caused other nobles, particularly in Prussia, to adopt his new modes of expression. The French language became the universal language of nobility. His large professional army firmly under control of the king was a model for the rest of Europe and numbered 400,000 at its peak. Many historians call his reign the Age of Louis XIV because numerous other monarchs copied his example.

Although his internal power grab was impressive, his foreign adventures were much less so. Attacking the Spanish Netherlands in 1666 initially found success. The new army demonstrated its prowess against the Spanish, and the Treaty of Aix-la-Chapelle (1668) gave France part of the Netherlands. When Louis resumed the war in 1672 he at first made impressive gains only to be thwarted by William III, the Prince of Orange, from the complete conquest of the Netherlands. The Peace of Nijmegen in 1678 resulted in additional territorial concessions by Spain. In 1688, when James of England tried to impose absolute monarchy, Protestant leaders asked William III for help. James fled when William's invading forces arrived. The Glorious Revolution then cemented an alliance between the English and the Dutch. The resumed struggle ended in 1697 with Louis reluctantly recognizing William as the legitimate King of England.

Louis the XIV of France concentrated all power in himself and spent lavishly on his personal aggrandizement. He crushed internal opposition and oppressed a religious minority to the state's own disadvantage. His huge military expenditures brought little territorial gain. Culturally Louis was the Sun King of all of Europe, and while he was a despot in deed, he never earned the title from historians preferring the less pejorative "absolutism" to describe his regime.

8.1

There is much more to fear from men who love power than there is to fear from men who love profits. The merchant community has always represented an alternative to the pyramid shape of the pre-industrial society.[12]

Other sources of wealth outside of control of the land and food production were limited in the pre-industrial society. Trade either over land or water was one source, as was mining. Merchant wealth was a method to accumulate money outside of the aristocracy. Because they were beyond the control of the dictator's land monopoly, merchants were always considered a threat. This is why Liu Bang the founder of the Han Dynasty prohibited them from purchasing land. Culturally they were also considered beneath the ruling elites. Prior to the 13th century in China, merchants were not allowed to take the civil service examination. The samurai of early Japan were likewise forbidden from engaging in trade. The dictator could also impose other controls like regulating trade with grants of monopoly, or restricting it to specific ports of entry. When contact with the outside world became too dangerous the trade could be severely restricted, as it was in Japan from the 16th century until the Meiji Restoration. When a source of wealth was particularly attractive, like the mines of ancient Egypt, the dictator would monopolize them for himself.

Since travel by water was so much cheaper than land, a merchant could travel by sea far and wide. In 3rd century Rome, it was cheaper to ship goods over water a thousand miles to Egypt than to ship goods fifty miles over land. This had two important consequences. First, cheaper transportation by water meant a seaport would have a larger market, and as a result a larger, wealthier, merchant community. Just as there was a symbiotic connection between the dictator and his army, so too was there a similar relationship between the merchant community and the navy. Second, as a result of their

---

[12] The boogieman of the rich manipulating current events from behind the scenes is a common theme. It was used to great effect by dictators in the 20th century. In fact businessmen are easily intimidated. Fear of corporations is the most recent incarnation. The phrase "corporations are cowards" better describes their behavior.

wide travels, merchants were either used as spies or suspected of being spies. The Chola invasion of Ceylon (1017) was sparked by merchant reports from visits to Ceylon. The Mongols invaded Iran (1218) after learning over four hundred Mongol merchants were executed for being spies. Having a subversive reputation did not stop the merchants from being the king's banker. It was not uncommon for a noble to be deep in debt to a local merchant for lavish spending or gambling.

In general however the trade was limited. Only a small group of people could be sustained by trading in luxury goods meant mostly for the aristocracy. Typically not being proficient military men, their threat to the dictator was exaggerated. Nonetheless, merchants as a distinct community represented an alternative to the pyramid structure of the pre-industrial societies.

Three innovations helped slightly weaken the monopolies of the Hereditary Dictatorship in the first millennium BC near the fertile valleys of the Nile and Mesopotamia. The first was the transition from the Bronze Age to the Iron Age. Iron weapons were more effective and less costly. Without this innovation the citizen soldier would not be possible. Second, the monopoly of information was weakened with the invention of the alphabet by the Phoenicians. Since they were primarily a seafaring collection of city-states their innovation spread throughout the Mediterranean. Literacy had been made more accessible. Finally, the invention of coined money by Lydia (western Turkey) increased the power of the merchant community. Since these changes took place around the huge potential market of the Mediterranean Sea it is reasonable some challenge to the Hereditary Dictatorship would develop prior to the establishment of a Mediterranean empire. These challenges were Athens and Rome.[13]

---

[13] This will not be the only time rapid innovation favoring independence resulted in free societies. As discussed later a similar burst in innovation helped the free society develop in Europe and again the dictatorships eventually adapted. Many argue today the internet is a similar innovation. If true, dictatorships will eventually adapt to it as well.

8.2

The best counterexample to the universality of dictatorship is ancient Athens. Both the importance of the merchant community and its relationship with a powerful navy is strongly supported by this example. The citizen soldier had an important role in the new democracy, as did the government practices used to prevent a concentration of power.

Initially the city-state of Athens was unremarkable. In the 7th century BC the city was ruled by the aristocracy through a council of nine called *archons* and a larger advisory body the *Areopagus* or Council of Ares. Both bodies consisted of members by noble birth only. Land was increasingly in the hands of fewer and fewer people while those at the bottom were increasingly burdened by debt. The positive feedback concentrating government power was well underway, and this pre-industrial society appeared to be on a normal path of development. There was an Assembly of all male citizens, but it had little power. The Assembly was used more as a meeting to receive information about new laws or decisions by the aristocracy than to provide any input into these laws.

The lower strata of society was divided into clansmen who were increasingly tied to the land to pay one-sixth of the produce for debts, and guildsmen who were sold into foreign slavery. The debt laws were formalized by Draco in 621 BC. The code stipulated a death penalty for numerous offences and has enshrined this harshness in the word "draconian." In Draco's defense, he was most likely simply writing down what was already an oral tradition. Each *archon* only held office for one year, a reflection of the oligarchic stalemate existing in the government. By 600 BC the situation was reaching a breaking point.

To address the crisis, Solon was appointed in 594 BC as sole *archon*, a reconciler, with full legislative powers. Ordinarily one might expect him to become dictator. Order was desperately needed and this has been the universal solution. However, something different happened. Solon instituted a series of reforms later becoming the basis of a true democratic government in Athens. He first cancelled all debts, used public funds to purchase guildsmen who had been sold into slavery, and prohibited Athenian citizens from any further bondage. The laws would no longer differentiate between the high-born and low-born. He re-categorized the citizenry based upon their ability to pay taxes into four groups. From the highest group, the *archons* and military commanders were selected.

The *Areopagus* was kept, but a second Council of Four Hundred was also created. It and not the *Areopagus* had the power to propose new laws. These laws were then sent for a yes or no confirmation by the Assembly. The ordinary citizen now had some power.

Solon made economic reforms and encouraged the teaching of craftsmanship. He offered Athenian citizenship to immigrants if they were craftsmen so as to increase their numbers. He encouraged the export of olive oil, wine, and fine pottery. In the struggle between the merchant community and the nobility, it appeared the merchants had won, and Athens' path as a sea-faring city-state had begun.

The brief experiment ended after a return to dictatorship in 561 BC. Had Cleisthenes not staged a popular revolt in 507 BC and became chief *archon*, Athens would today be as unknown as Vaisali. Cleisthenes initiated reforms forming the basis of Athenian Democracy. He broke up the traditional four tribes and re-organized them into ten. Each tribe was further divided into individual *demes*. The total number of *demes* for all Attica (the area surrounding Athens) was 140. All Athenian male citizens at thirty years of age or older were members of the *deme*. This included clansmen, guildsmen, and immigrants. Once established, the membership was henceforth hereditary. They were in essence a municipal council and charged with maintenance of the local temple among other responsibilities.

To populate the new Council of 500, replacing the old Council of 400, each tribe supplied 50 members chosen by lot. The *demes* in each tribe would elect potential candidates to be included in the selection pool. The *Areopagus* was the only vestige left from the old system. *Archons* were now selected by lot from the Council of 500 and from this group elected by the Assembly. The Assembly now took on a powerful role in the life of the government.

In times of war, each tribe supplied one regiment—the bulk of which were citizen soldiers. Using the census classes from Solon, those wealthy enough to provide their own mounts would form the cavalry. The heavy infantry, the *hoplites*, represented the majority of the fielded army. They came from the ranks of the landed farmer and provided their own arms. The leadership was elected in many cases from the upper Solon classes. The lowest class provided the light infantry. It was the citizens who voted for war and the citizens who fought.

The Council of 500 had additional restrictions preventing any concentration of power. They could only serve for one year. During the year, each tribe rotated duty if the full council was not in session. While serving their one-tenth of the year to handle the day-to-day business of Athens and Attica, a secretary and the chairman were selected by lot freshly each day. If already chosen he was ineligible to be chairman again. Over time, additional restrictions upon the aristocracy were added. In 462 BC all remaining power of the *Areopagus* was given to the Council, the Assembly, or the courts.

Athens' rival, Lacedaemon with its capital Sparta, deserves some comment. In their two approaches to government they were polar opposites. While Athens' focus was as a naval power, Sparta had the best army in all of Greece. It was an army of occupation as Spartan citizens constituted only 2% of the total population of Lacedaemon. The society was highly stratified with *perioikoi* and *helots* below the Spartans. The *perioikoi* lived in local communities within the country primarily concentrating in the trades. As subordinate allies, they were expected to fight along side the Spartans if ordered to do so. The lowest class, the *helots*, were surfs bound to the land.

The government of Sparta was an oligarchy headed by two hereditary kings from different families. They ruled simultaneously and shared executive power with five *ephors*. The rest of the government consisted of a council and assembly. The council had twenty-eight members. It was the most highly regarded position to hold in the government and one was required to be sixty years of age to be a member. After selection by a panel of judges and acclaimed by the assembly, they sat for life. All men of Sparta, age thirty and older, had assembly membership.

It was the two kings who led troops in battle, in addition to some religious and judicial functions. The five *ephors* had the sole power to call up the army. They also supervised the education system, called up the council, and directed lesser officials. It was they who received foreign ambassadors. They each had a term of only one year. Sparta was a highly militaristic society and this paid off on the battlefield. They went for a 150 year stretch without a single defeat.

The Peloponnesian Wars were a struggle between Athens and Sparta. Athens, a democracy with a mighty navy, competed against Sparta, an oligarchy and the most powerful land force in all of Greece. Had Attica been an island the eventual outcome might have been different both for Athens and the rest of humanity. Fought in two phases, the First Peloponnesian War (460 BC – 445 BC) ended in a stalemate mostly because Athens wasted much of its military power in distractions. The Second Peloponnesian War (431 BC – 404 BC) ended in a decisive defeat for Athens when Spartan troops occupied the capital. Athens continued as a democracy well into the next century but was never the power it had once been. Eventually, Philip II of Macedonia, the father of Alexander the Great, conquered all of Greece.

8.3

A second counterexample to dictatorship is the Roman Republic where the role of the citizen soldier figured prominently as the foundation of the Republic. The Romans had elaborate procedures in place to prevent a concentration of power much like the Athenians.

Because the government structure tilted heavily in the aristocratic direction, the Roman Republic is not as good an example of pure democracy as was Athens. Nonetheless the Roman system of voting and the adherence to the rule of law was remarkable for its time. It was also the only example of a republic extending over a large territorial area, and because of this it was of interest to thinkers in the Enlightenment as an alternative to monarchy.

The Roman Republic began in 510 BC when the last Roman King was deposed. This ended the monarchy traditionally begun with Romulus in 753 BC. The government consisted of multiple deliberative bodies. The Senate was made up of the aristocracy called patricians, and they served for life. There were three lower assemblies and each of the lower assemblies used block voting. Voting took place in or near Rome, and the votes could be cast by any Roman citizen. Majority vote in a block determined how each block voted in the overall assembly. The *Comitia Centuriata* had 193 voting blocks and represented those who owned land. It was those individuals who were called into military service. A census was taken periodically to determine the wealth of each land owner who could serve in the army. The men ranged in age from eighteen to forty-six and had to be fit to carry arms. The census divided soldiers into four groups with the wealthiest group getting seventy to eighty block votes. During voting the blocks from the wealthiest groups voted first. An issue could easily be determined before the less aristocratic members had their chance to vote since the wealthiest two classifications from the census had a majority of block votes. Nonetheless, it was a body representing the citizen soldiers, and like Athens, they were expected to provide their own arms.

The next two assemblies had duplicate members. The larger, the *Comitia Tributa*, was composed of both patricians and the non-aristocrats called plebeians. It had twenty-one representatives. The third assembly called the *Concilium Plebis*, was composed of only the plebeians from the *Tributa*. The head of this third chamber was called a tribune. In 287 BC friction between patricians and plebeians increased the power of the *Plebis* and tribune. Henceforth, laws passed by the *Plebis* applied to all citizens, not only plebeians. These two lower councils also voted by blocks with each block originally representing geographic locations. The idea behind these assemblies allowed each tribe of Rome a voice. Eventually the number of tribes, and blocks were increased to thirty-five.

Since a majority vote was used to elect the members to these different assemblies, one might conclude the Romans had a democratic system much like the Greeks. However in practice this was an illusion as the power was all in the hands of the Senate. All high ranking officials were expected to obey the directives from the Senate. The *Comitia Centuriata*, mostly full of aristocrats, made the decisions about war and peace. The effect of the plebeian power in the government was only to protect them from abuses against them by the patricians.

The executive power of the Roman constitution rested in a number of high officials. The most important of these were the consuls, praetors, and censors. All three were elected by the *Centuriata*. The consuls were the most powerful, essentially acting as kings outside of the city limits. They were invested with the power of *imperium*, which included the command of the armed forces, the power to convene the assemblies including the Senate, as well as receiving foreign ambassadors since they acted as the head of state for Rome.

Two consuls were elected each year for one-year terms. As a protection against an abuse of power, any action by the one consul could be vetoed by the other. When both were on the field of battle at the same time, the army was either split or the command changed back and forth on a day-to-day basis. Severe discipline was part of the *imperium* as it included the power of life and death. The consul's decision was final and there was no appeal. Once their term was up they could be held legally accountable for their actions and they would not be eligible for re-election for ten years.

Six praetors were elected as inferior magistrates to the consuls, and their office also included the *imperium*. Their term of office was also one year. They could be found at the head of an army, but their specialty was the judiciary. Two had sole jurisdiction inside the city while the other four had jurisdiction exclusively outside of Rome. They too could veto the actions of another as it was a general principle of the Roman government allowing magistrates of the same level to veto the actions of each other. The two censors were elected for eighteen month terms once every five years. As the name implies they conducted the census which classified both one's status as a Roman citizen or slave but also one's level within the *Centuriata*. They drew up the list of new appointments to the Senate. This office was the one with the most prestige and was filled with ex-consuls. Other lesser officials included the *aediles* who attended to the maintenance of streets and buildings, and the *quaestors* who were the treasurers and tax collectors.

The most important magistrate elected by the Plebis was the tribune, which in the later days of the republic numbered up to ten. Their most important power was to come to the aid of a plebian fallen victim to the unjust actions of a magistrate. Any act could be suspended by his veto called an *intercessio*. Only another tribune could block his action. It was the tribune who convened the Plebis and set its agenda. Eventually they gained the right to attend Senate proceedings, propose resolutions for debate, and in 216 BC convene the Senate. The negative power of the tribune was a powerful check upon the arbitrary abuse of power.

A few additional comments are needed to give a complete picture of the Roman Republic. The office of dictator, from which the modern use of the term comes, was a sole individual with all authority vested in him though it was used only in the most extraordinary circumstances and only for a six month term. He had the power of *imperium* without any possibility of a veto. Next, the Senate had the sole power to extend the term of a magistrate. Beginning in 326 BC, it was used when the year long term of office was insufficient to accomplish a task. An official so constituted was called a proconsul or propraetor. In later years of the republic, this power was abused by the Senate to build its power base. Many governors of the provinces were appointed in this manner.

Finally, another check and balance in the constitution was called the *cursus honorum*. It was a restriction upon the qualifications for each office. It might be one needed to be of the highest propertied class, the *equites*, for ten years before one could run for office or it might be an age restriction. For consul the age restriction was forty-two years old. Since there were many lesser positions, the history of the republic is peppered with career politicians moving from one office to the next. As many as eighty offices were up for grabs each year with the lifetime appointment to the Senate the ultimate goal.

The Punic Wars were a set of three wars in which Rome was always victorious, the first from 265 BC to 241 BC and the second Punic war (218 BC – 202 BC), all caused by a rivalry with Carthage. The third Punic War (149 BC – 146 BC) was a war of revenge since by then Carthage was no longer a threat to Rome. The second Punic War is particularly important because of the way it changed the Republic.

The major key change in the Republic, needed to facilitate a dictator, was the transition from a citizen army to a professional one. A professional army was more likely to be loyal to the general they directly serve than the Republic. The bond formed in the shared sacrifice of combat can create tremendous loyalty among the troops particularly if the general often wins on the battlefield.

After his march down from the Alps in 218 BC, Hannibal was devastating Roman armies across all of Italy. Seeing how Hannibal was getting little supplies from Carthage and was forced to live off the land, the Roman general Fabius devised a new strategy. He followed Hannibal and harassed him, but only engaged in full combat if the conditions were extremely favorable. He did all he could to prevent Hannibal from providing for his troops and attacked his foraging parties. This indirect approach to warfare would come to be known as a Fabian strategy.

Hannibal did all he could to entice the Romans to fight by ravaging the countryside and putting villages and vineyards to the torch. This left many smaller landholders with nothing. The Romans were eventually victorious, and this victory provided a bumper crop of slaves from the captured prisoners of war. Land prices were on the rise due to the huge profits generals and territorial governors were making in the new conquered lands, and they were buying up the land as the citizen soldiers were leaving due to the devastation. The slaves provided cheap labor for the vast new landed estates.

The pressure of empire also created a need for a full-time army. In the beginning service in the citizen's militia was for one year. If service was required past the traditional summer campaign, a *stipendium* was paid to each soldier as compensation. Improved tactics, during the Second Punic War, were made possible with the additional training from longer enlistments. This was better afforded by professionals as the citizen soldiers needed to tend to their farms, and the many years away were becoming a burden. The demands of empire also could use full time soldiers for the construction of more roads and fortifications.

The wars to save the Republic had planted the seeds of the Republic's demise. The gradual lowering of property requirements illustrates this trend. They were first reduced in 213 BC and later in 126 BC. The consul Marius in 107 BC opened the army to those without property. He also eliminated the troop levy by tribe and allowed large numbers of plebeians to volunteer for service.

The crisis of Hannibal also increased the power of the Senate at the expense of the other more democratic institutions in the Republic. Technically its resolutions, *senatus consultum*, had no force of law, as this required a magistrate. The historian Livy shows how in their panic, the

Romans turned to the Senate to take the initiative in diplomacy and strategy, and after Hannibal's defeat it became more and more the norm.

Much of the Senators' power was indirect. The Senate did not assign a military commander to a foreign post, it was chosen by lot. However, these posts could be quite lucrative, and the Senate had the power to extend the term of the assignment beyond one year. By this and other means they wielded immense influence. They also began to control certain public finance like the expense accounts of the magistrates, and they could reward or punish magistrates depending upon their actions. Eventually the assemblies also became corrupt. The contemporary historian, Sallust, would record it was a city for sale. Individuals receiving public grain could be easily manipulated. Lavish games by an *aedile* would gain favor with the public. A struggle ensued between the *populares* in favor of more democratic institutions and the *optimates* who favored the Senate. As the struggle became increasingly violent one could find patricians on both sides.[14]

The first serious attempt to become dictator was made by Sulla. As one might expect, he was a competent commander having been in combat in several of Rome's campaigns and having become famous for his capture of King Jugurtha of Numidia. A determined social climber, he was elected consul in 88 BC, and intended to march east against King Mithridates who was in rebellion against Rome. Political maneuvering, including the use of mob violence, denied him the command despite being a consul of Rome, so he declared the law void and marched on Rome. The officers of his legions refused to take part in this unprecedented action. However, most of the legions were full of veterans loyal to him from past campaigns, so Sulla was able to restore order to Rome and then go on with his preparations for the march east.

When Cinna was elected consul the following year, he attempted to have Sulla put on trial for his actions, but Sulla simply ignored the court's request and left for war in the east. In 85 BC, Cinna and others had many of Sulla's supporters in Rome killed. Sulla's wife escaped to report the news directly to her husband.

---

[14] It is a misconception the powerful always support their "class interest." In our own time the super-rich are likely to be found anywhere on the political spectrum.

Quickly concluding the eastern campaign, Sulla returned to Italy in 83 BC where he marched again on Rome and took the city. He declared himself dictator, and this became official when the Senate made him dictator in 80 BC. This was the first Senate declaration of dictator in 120 years. Like many new dictators, he embarked upon a campaign of revenge. When a prominent citizen, Metellus, insisted Sulla should produce a list of people who were enemies of the state in an attempt to stop random and arbitrary assassinations, Sulla posted a list of 500 people. Many were on the list simply to seize their wealth and property. With his power secure, he gave up the title of dictator and became a consul, and eventually, in 79 BC, a private citizen. Sulla died of natural causes a few years later.

Sulla's march on Rome followed by his power grab was proof the army was now more loyal to their generals than the Republic. It was only a matter of time until a dictator in the true sense of the word would rule. Many, such as Cato the Younger and Cicero, feared the Republic was near an end. However, none of them were great generals. Of those who wished to become king, the one they most feared was Julius Caesar.

In 62 BC two former commanders under Sulla, Pompey and Crassus, along with Caesar, formed a private compact called the Triumvirate. As part of the agreement Caesar would become consul in 59 BC. Cato in particular put up many political roadblocks in Caesar's way, but to no avail. Crassus was killed in battle in 53 BC in the east, and open civil war between Caesar and Pompey was close at hand.

When Caesar made his famous crossing of the Rubicon River in 49 BC, he was in direct violation of the Senate's dictates, and civil war began. Nominally, Pompey was on the side of the Republic, but this was a fiction. A civil war between two potential dictators was the reality. Cato chose the lesser of two evils and sided with Pompey as the only possible way the Republic might be saved.

Because of the large force of seasoned veterans Caesar led into Italy, all those opposing him fled. Cato eventually fled to Africa with others. When Caesar defeated the force in Africa he attacked the city of Utica with Cato inside. Prior to his capture Cato committed suicide, and in many ways the Republic died with him. Caesar's assassination in 44 BC only delayed the inevitable, and a new Triumvirate followed his death. The Republic was completely gone when Octavian, now Caesar Augustus, became dictator. There was no one to challenge his power after he defeated Anthony and Cleopatra in 31 BC.

8.4

The merchant community in Europe was the dominant force in a number of small republics including some of the Swiss cantons, Genoa, Lucca, and Venice in Italy and the United Provinces, sometimes called the Dutch Republic. The longest lasting of these was the Republic of Venice with an intricate set of checks and balances to prevent a concentration of power.

Once free of Byzantine rule, Venice was dominated by the merchant community more so than any other city in northern Italy. Commerce at sea was their specialty and was their major source of wealth over other merchant pursuits such as manufacturing. Since the capital was situated in the sandbanks near the Rialto River, the city had natural defenses not afforded other city-states.

The Republic went through several stages of development until 1297 when the evolution ended in an arrangement lasting to the end of the Republic in 1797. Prior to 1032, a *doge* had exclusive executive authority for life with a citizen assembly called the *Arengo* needed to approve his major decisions. The *doges* were continually attempting to establish a Hereditary Dictatorship until the Orseoli family was driven into exile. A new *doge*, Flabiniaco, along with the *Arengo* established two advisors to assist the *doge*, and when the situation required he was to invite prominent citizens as advisors. This was the so-called Flabiniaco constitution of 1032.

As the city prospered and the population grew, the *Arengo* became increasingly unwieldy. When Doge Michiel was killed in mob violence in 1171, the Venetians decided more government reform was in order. In the new constitution of 1172, the *Arengo* lost its power to directly elect the *doge* instead electing an electoral college which nominated the *doge*. The *Arengo* only retained the power to approve the nominated individual and declare war. These reforms represented a trend toward the gradual restriction of the lower popular assemblies and the expansion of the upper branches of government. By 1297 a smaller body, the Great Council, originally elected by the *Arengo*, became a closed hereditary body. The *Arengo* was eventually abolished in 1423.

The Republic of Venice was now a complex set of checks and balances lasting for the next 500 years. The day-to-day operation was handled by the *doge* and a cabinet of twenty-six called the *Collegio*. This body answered to the Great Council, approximately 1,500 strong, made up of all the hereditary citizens of Venice. Checking the power of the *doge* and *Collegio* on a regular basis was the Council of Ten and the Senate. The Senate had about 260 members and both intermediate bodies were elected from the Great Council. While it was up to the *Collegio* to propose legislation, it was the Senate that approved it. When speed was required the *Collegio* sent the action to the Council of Ten. An additional Council of Forty was used for judicial review. The top three members of the Council of Forty were also members of the *Collegio*. Most of the elected positions had terms of one year or less, and as a result, the Great Council spent much of its time considering new appointments.

Of all the institutions in the Republic of Venice, the Council of Ten was the most peculiar. Made permanent in 1335, its role was the protection of the Republic from decay and subversion. Members were elected from the Senate for terms of one year. The Council of Ten elected three members to be president and rotated the presidency on a month-to-month basis. Political crimes and public morality were sent to it for review meaning cases of espionage, bribery, and outrageous political propaganda. Private meetings they deemed to be subversive were stopped.

The Ten acquired a reputation of secret arrests and murder. Although true in rare instances, ordinarily any secret trial before the Ten included the *doge* and six members of the *Collegio*. Conviction was by majority vote. Despite being a secret tribunal, the defendant could call witnesses. Though a gross violation of civil liberties by modern standards, the Ten stopped the conspiracy of Doge Marino Falier and the Spanish conspiracy of 1618 preserving the Republic.

Although active participation in government was limited by lineage, the governance of the Republic of Venice was superior to most other areas in Europe. The odd combination of merchant-aristocrat saw it as their duty to govern the Republic for the good of all, and this tradition was important in maintaining good rule. The average Venetian enjoyed free speech and an equality before the law. Public organizations like the Grain Commission helped the poor during times of famine. Procedures in criminal investigations were strictly followed. When evaluated by future historians, the police and court documents verify their reputation for fairness. During the 500 year rule, the city never saw a civil war and was never sacked.

9

The fundamental form of human government is dictatorship. If men loved democracy and freedom more than power and security, history would be full of democratic governments, but as it stands, they are short-lived, rare anomalies.

From human civilization's earliest beginnings dictatorships were the model. With their first appearance in four of the world's most fertile valleys to the many other places civilization began, time after time dictatorship flourished. The dictator in these earliest manifestations was of the god-king type and to challenge his rule was to risk natural disaster in this world and eternal punishment in the next. Gradually a pattern emerged— the Hereditary Dictatorship.

The Hereditary Dictatorship was one passed down from father to son or kept within the extended family. Different methods were employed to make the transition from old to new dictator as smooth as was possible. Since human government is a struggle for power, the transition from old to new was a vulnerable time for the dynasty. The most outrageous method seen was the Law of Fratricide in the Ottoman Empire when the new Sultan had his brothers strangled and the brother's concubines drowned—much like what is seen in a bee hive as a new queen bee emerges first from her cocoon and then proceeds to kill her rivals yet to hatch.

While all power tended to be concentrated as much as was possible in the dictator, the Hereditary Dictatorship had many variations upon this theme, depending in large measure on how powerful the dictator was in comparison to other competitors. When other competitors could control their own territory and establish separate dictatorships, the kingdom entered a warring states period. If the king was weak relative to the general aristocracy, his powers were limited by a treaty such as the Magna Carta. If a king was deposed but a stalemate ensued between barons, then an oligarchy or elective monarchy could result. Sometimes the dictator was weak relative to a general and became a figurehead. The Shogunate of Japan was a good example of this. The government in all cases was the result of dictators or those who wished to become dictators. It was the struggle to monopolize violence.

The monopoly of violence was maintained by the dictator's control over the military. The two had a symbiotic relationship with both depending on support from each other. Dictatorship was the natural result of this marriage, since a dictatorship was most in harmony with the principles of war. From this monopoly sprang three secondary monopolies over the economic, religious, and intellectual life of the kingdom. The most important of these was the economic, since it would provide the funds to pay and equip the army.

The agricultural based pre-industrial society was vulnerable to a positive feedback mechanism concentrating government power. The economy was one-dimensional and there was typically not a free market for land. Using the monopoly of violence to extract resources, people were forced to work the land for the benefit of the dictatorship. Slavery became the ultimate manifestation of the monopoly of violence.

Humankind's natural inclination toward religion, something predating any civilization, was harnessed to justify and promote the dictator. He was obviously not going to pay for anything else. The dictator, thereby, invented ideology and became a source of meaning and values. He proclaimed his magnificence across the kingdom in propaganda. He attempted to control what was written and established a corpus of sacred texts needing his protection. The society looked like a giant pyramid with the dictator at the top.

Only in the extreme, when the dictator lost his Mandate from Heaven, was he overthrown and replaced by a new dictator.

In all of early history, there were only a few counterexamples. The most famous of these counterexamples were Athens and Rome. Nevertheless the time spanned and areas controlled was small compared to those dominated by dictatorship over all of human history and across the globe. The experiment in Athens lasted less than 200 years. The Roman Republic was more oligarchy than democracy but did have strong democratic institutions and lasted about 400 years. Had the Greek phalanx or the Roman legion not been as effective on the battlefield these brief experiments, would have been much shorter.

A common thread of both Athens and Rome was the citizen soldier. Power was impossible for the dictator to maintain if he could not control the army. If the bulk of the ranks were filled by ordinary citizens, then he was in the odd position of asking people to oppress themselves. A second advantage for democracy of the citizen soldier was the shared sacrifice of combat. This produced a type of equality among citizens sometimes translating into democratic institutions. The third advantage was a citizen soldier could be more motivated to fight since he had a role in the decision to go to war. Lastly, the citizen soldier was an armed citizen. For both Athens and Rome, individual soldiers provided their own arms. Unfortunately, the Roman Republic was doomed when the citizen army was replaced by a professional one.

The republics in Europe reinforced the importance of the merchant community in creating democratic institutions. These republics tended to form in seaports because water transportation was much cheaper in pre-industrial societies. The cheaper cost made the seaport a larger market and produced a larger, wealthier, merchant community. The Republic of Venice was an example of this merchant-based republic and lasted for 500 years. Unfortunately, those republics were small when compared to the rest of Europe. This tended to support the idea a republican form of government was limited to small city-states and could never be adapted to a large nation.

These republics, along with the examples of Athens and Rome, also showed how peculiar traditions and elaborate checks and balances were needed to overcome the natural human tendency toward dictatorship.

Thinkers in the Enlightenment would take note, checks and balances were a method preserving liberty for extended periods of time. The methods employed included popular assemblies, a division of powers, and limitations on terms and qualifications for office, and they worked to counter the positive feedback propelling government growth.

One cannot escape the evidence. If democracy and freedom were things men loved more than power and security, then human history would have more examples of those types of governments. As it stands they appear to be aberrations—freaks of history. Had the Free Society not appeared later in the story of mankind, freaks of history they would have remained. The human race had made a clear choice—they much preferred the pyramid-shaped society to democracy. The fundamental form of human government is clearly dictatorship.

Section II

The Weak become Strong

"He who is Brave is Free"
Seneca

The Missing Dynasty

Chapter Three

All major civilizations alternated between periods of dynastic rule and periods of civil war in which powerful families vied for control. These periods of civilization-wide civil war are called "the warring states periods." The one exception to this was Europe, as Europe was in a permanent warring states condition for all of its history. So divided was Europe it was not until the 19th century when Germany and Italy were unified into nation states. Because Europe was never ruled by a single dynasty, alternatives to dictatorship could not be crushed. Liberty developed despite the best efforts of the European dictators.

Internal European factors made the conquest of Europe by a single power difficult. The stage was set by the barbarian invasions that destroyed the old Western Roman Empire. When weak kings began to assert their authority as Feudalism ended, they were met by forces disposed to freedom. The Renaissance was the beginning of this process in which two important themes emerged driving the eventual creation of the Free Society. The first was the importance of the merchant community as a counterbalance to the aristocracy. The disorganized and fractured political landscape in Europe served to amplify the influence of the merchant communities compared to other areas of the world. The second theme was the increasing importance of the individual via Humanism, a movement beginning in the Renaissance.

Europe was also un-conquerable because of religious disunity, balance-of-power wars, and an accident of geography. Western Europe had a pan-national religious authority producing a constant battle of power between Pope and King. When Christianity in Western Europe was further split into numerous factions by the Reformation, the unification of Europe under a single king became markedly more challenging. The Reformation further reinforced the earlier Humanistic trends emphasizing the role of the individual versus state authority. It was during the Reformation when Europe's balance-of-power wars began. When one power became dominant, another peripheral power entered to prevent final victory. Lastly, an accident of geography isolated a powerful merchant community in England on an island, and this was a major impediment to the formation of any European Empire.

Not only an accident of geography but in addition, an accident of timing was needed to make the Free Society a reality. The Industrial Revolution was destroying the economic basis of the Hereditary Dictatorships. This was driven by inventions created in the Scientific Revolution, most notably the invention of fossil fuel engines. However, the Industrial Revolution, though necessary, was an insufficient condition for the Free Society. Fortunately, the Industrial Revolution began first in the British Isles, the one nation in Europe furthest down the path toward freedom.

2

The Roman Catholic Church, a pan-national religious authority, was created by the barbarian invasions in the Latin West. This inverted the typical relationship between dictator and the secondary monopoly over religion.

Europe was overrun or nearly overrun several times by barbarian invasions. The most famous, the Germanic invasions toppling the western half of the Roman Empire, first began in the late 4th century. The Huns, perhaps motivated by dwindling food stocks, moved south into territory controlled by the Ostrogoths a Germanic people who lived outside the northern borders of the eastern half of the Empire. With the Huns on the move, large numbers of Ostrogoths congregated at the border across the Danube seeking refuge within the Empire. The eastern Emperor Valens allowed them in under certain conditions, but it was not long before both sides felt betrayed by the other, and the Goths were soon in full revolt. On 9 August 387 the Goths delivered a crushing military defeat to the Romans at Adrianople and killed the Emperor. The Empire was open to plunder by Goths and Huns.

In the west, the barbarian pressure was constant with Germanic tribes crossing the Rhine frontier. Within a few generations Franks had settled in France, Visigoths in Spain and Vandals in North Africa. Alaric, a Visigoth leader, sacked Rome in 410. When the young Emperor Romulus Augustulus was removed by barbarians in 476, the western part of the Roman Empire came to an end. Despite all the confusion in the east, the eastern half of the Empire, designated by historians the Byzantine Empire, survived.

These constant waves of invasions in Europe made secular authority weak. In the Greek east, people looked to Constantinople for guidance, while in the Latin West they looked to Rome. It was from this spiritual center, the Catholic Church at Rome grew in power. By the time central secular authorities began to develop in the West, the power vacuum had created a pan-national spiritual authority reversing what was typically found in most places of the world. Ordinarily a dictator tried to dominate the one or more religions he found within his kingdom, as the natural human tendency is to have all secular and spiritual authority concentrated in one individual. In this case, the Pope would try to dominate kings. Lacking his own army, in practice this would mean one king acting at the Pope's behest against another king.

This pan-national spiritual authority had an additional advantage— monotheism. In the sacred text of the Catholic Church, the *Vulgate Bible*, a Pope could point to the subordination of the king to both the moral laws of God and to spiritual authority as shown in the history of the Jewish people. This separation of secular and spiritual authority was a unique feature of the Jewish Kingdoms of Judah (1025 BC – 587 BC) and Israel-Samaria (930 BC – 722 BC). The struggle between Pope and King was a constant feature of the Middle Ages in Europe. Pope Gregory VII asserted these claims in *Dictatus Papae* in 1075 as part of the Investiture Controversy. In it he maintained the Pope's supremacy in all Church matters and, more importantly, his supremacy over all kings. Thus a Pope could remove the kings and release all their subjects from obedience to them.

3

The barbarian invasions also made the initial first kings of Europe weak. In their desperation they turned to representative assemblies to raise money for war as Feudalism ended.

A second major, unintended consequence of the barbarian invasions was the creation of popular and nobility assemblies in Europe—a universal phenomenon across all of Europe in the 13th and 14th centuries. Going by many different names—Parliament, Rigsdag, Estates-General—these assemblies formed in three different ways. The first occurred when barons or other nobility asserted their power relative to the king, and the second method occurred when other political entities copied their example. In the last method kings initiated an assembly on their own, and once an assembly was established in one jurisdiction, it tended to spread by imitation to others. This type of Hereditary Dictatorship—the distributed monarchy—found its manifestation in Europe through these assemblies. The driving force behind this change was the need by the dictators of Europe for funds to wage war as the feudal obligations were no longer enough. By assembling the leaders of each group or class, the king could use their agreement as a binding obligation on the entire group. These assemblies acted as primitive types of representative government. Since it was impractical to have everyone present to personally consent to any agreement, leaders from different areas, prominent individuals, or envoys from towns would act on behalf of all those who could not attend. Being from the same class, it was presumed they would understand and be loyal to their class interest as they negotiated with the king. Any agreement would thereby be seen as being as valid as if everyone was in attendance.

Generally these assemblies represented three different constituencies: the clergy, the aristocracy, and the commoners who were usually represented by major towns. Voting in these groups could be by majority rule sometimes using a secret ballot. In other cases, a small committee would be formed of interested parties to reach a compromise, which would be binding on the entire assembly. These methods were borrowed from examples in the guilds or religious orders.

The number of assemblies was not always the classic three. In the Iberian Peninsula, the non-landed gentlemen called *caballeros,* who were excluded from power by primogeniture, had their own assembly. Likewise in Sweden the more wealthy peasants had a separate assembly. In only one major nation, England, did the assemblies split into only two—the House of Lords and the House of Commons. This unique arrangement tended to magnify the influence of the commoners, and by 1377 the Commons would elect a Speaker.

The influence of these assemblies tended to wane with respect to the king as the kings of Europe became more powerful. Monarchs, such as the King of France, would convene these assemblies more and more infrequently. Kings Henry IV and Henry V convened Parliament on a regular basis. Although this was less frequent under the Tudors, all of Europe saw an increase in the dictators' power.

Only in England did the Parliament act in a manner one would characterize as anything approaching modern by today's standards. It could act as final judge in court cases, and it could hear petitions over grievances. The House of Lords discussed national policy issues, and made determinations in cases of impeachment. The Commons throughout the 14th and 15th centuries gradually accumulated more control over taxation and expenditures. By the end of the 15th century all taxes required approval by Parliament, funds could be allocated for specific purposes, and audits be conducted to ensure the money was only spent as intended. After 1351 only an ordinance by Parliament was considered permanent.

4

Because of the fractured political landscape of the Europeans, the Renaissance began to weaken the secondary monopolies of the dictators in Europe.

In the 13th century, with Europe in the High Middle Ages, northern Italy was a collection of prosperous city-states. Texts of the ancient Romans and

Greeks had been discovered in various contacts with the Muslim world, such as in Toledo, Spain. After Toledo fell to the Christians in 1085, it became clear a large intellectual deposit existed in the Arab writings. The Jewish scholar Abraham bar Hiyya and an Italian named Gerard of Cremona translated a large number of these works. Aristotle's *Physics*, Euclid's *Elements*, and Ptolemy's *Almagest* were rediscovered. The Scholastic philosopher Thomas Aquinas (1225 – 1274) and others worked to unify them with the existing Christian tradition. These texts revived interest in classical writings of all kinds and sparked a mini-Renaissance, called Scholasticism, in the 12th to the 13th centuries.

This desire to reconcile important texts of the civilization into a coherent corpus of knowledge was characteristic of the pre-industrial society. In this particular case, it also legitimized those ancients, like Cicero, who supported free institutions. The collection and analysis of these manuscripts was aided by the universities organized as corporations under legal traditions used by monasteries. Such organization gave them limited autonomy from secular and religious authorities. Venice had the famous University of Padua which it provided with lavish support and was a source of pride to the city. The interest in all things classical eventually became known as the Renaissance.

The Renaissance, meaning rebirth, was a cultural movement spanning several centuries characterized by a resurgence of learning based upon classical sources. Its influence was felt in many areas from the arts and literature to the sciences. As the Renaissance progressed, there was an increasing interest in Greek classics especially with the influx of Greek scholars who left the depravations of the Ottoman Empire. Chairs of Greek classics were established in many places, including the University of Florence.

The fractured political landscape of Europe kept the Renaissance alive in small city-states like Florence where no dictator was powerful enough to crush dissent and enforce orthodoxy. Florence was a republic run by representatives from a number of guilds organized around professions like medicine, or successful trades like wool and cloth, or humble occupations like carpenters or blacksmiths. Once an adult male between ages seventeen and twenty-one became qualified to practice in a guild, he became a full citizen of Florence, and the Ordinance of Justice, passed in 1293, made all citizens of Florence equal with no privilege of nobility. One overall weakness was Florence's lack of any well-trained army, which Leonardo Bruni argued for in 1422 in a short work entitled *Concerning a Citizen Army*. Being businessmen and artists, the Florentines would have none of it.

Where freedom reigns so does innovation. While working in Asia Minor, Leonardo Bonacci, a Tuscan, came into contact with a new method to compute arithmetic. Called the Arabic numeral system, it depended upon the digit's position to determine the number, and was far easier to do calculations. Europe was still using the old Roman system and an abacus, but the Florentines quickly adopted the new method. They also took measures to standardize currency, and in 1252 they minted a seventy-two grain coin of twenty-four carat gold. With their patron saint, John the Baptist, on the front and the city's symbol the lily on the back, the florin became a standard of exchange across Europe. With their other invention, the bill of exchange—a Renaissance traveler's check—they became bankers to kings and popes. A consequence of large amounts of credit being made available to a king was the money available to wage war was increased. Wars became larger in scale, longer in duration, and over time this would favor king over baron.

As Florence and other northern Italian cities grew in influence, the timing could not have been better as this was also a time when many pillars of power in the Middle Ages began to weaken. The French king had persuaded (some say coerced) the Papacy to move to Avion in 1308. The Avion Captivity, as it is also called, weakened the church's authority as did the Great Schism in 1378 when the church returned to Rome. During this time, until 1415, multiple individuals made claim to be Pope. The Golden Bull issued in 1356 by Charles IV, changed the election procedures in the Holy Roman Empire, and was another blow to Papal authority. The feudal system also came under increasing pressure with the Black Death (1348 – 1350) which killed upwards of 30% of the population and created a fierce competition for labor on the farms. Consequently, it made it impossible to keep peasants on the land.

Military technology improvements also made the enforcers of the feudal system, the knight, a thing of the past on the battlefield. At the battle of

Pointers (1356) during the Hundred Years War between the French and English dictators, the English longbow was able to decimate the flower of French nobility as it could be fired much more rapidly than the crossbow and penetrated the heavy armor as effectively at long range. The charge of the heavy cavalry of aristocrats was no longer decisive. In this power vacuum of the 14th century the Renaissance had begun.

The wealthy families had a strong incentive to become educated and foster themselves off as guardians of knowledge. In a pre-industrial society, the landed aristocracy normally fulfills this role. The merchant community was now asserting itself and this required putting themselves on par with educated nobles. The merchants were well aware they were part of the same process that had taken place in ancient Athens. They established private academies taking the term from ancient Greece and set up a curriculum called the *studia humanitatis* mirroring a classical education in Greece and Rome. It is from this word the term Humanism is derived, and it is because of this the Renaissance is said to be a Humanist movement.

The Humanism of the Renaissance was not the same as later humanist movements. Renaissance Humanism was not secular as many humanists were members of the clergy. It was a reaction to the narrow interpretation given by Scholasticism of these new discoveries. God's gifts were to be used in the active world and not only in the contemplative monastic life. The ancients had practical advice to give on living life in the here and now. The five areas of study, grammar, rhetoric, history, poetry, and moral philosophy, made for a more eloquent and thoughtful citizen who could participate actively in civic life and could be a successful civic leader. A citizen Cicero and other supporters of the Free Society in the ancient world would have approved.

The Humanism of the Renaissance also placed a significant emphasis on the value of the individual. Individualism was critical to the eventual development of the Free Society. Certainly the explosion of artistic expression in the Renaissance was one manifestation of Individualism. Based upon their own merit, anyone could become a person of letters or the arts. This belief meant the trajectory of one's life was due to one's actions alone. One's fate was not determined by any membership in a group, race, or any accident of birth. As Feudalism collapsed, it is easy to see how Individualism moved in to fill the void.

5

The Reformation significantly weakened the secondary monopoly over religion. The religious wars of the Reformation demonstrated how difficult it was to dominate all of Europe. This was the beginning of Europe's balance-of-power politics.

From the moment Martin Luther nailed his ninety-five theses to a church door in 1517, a unified Europe became more remote, as this made the secondary monopoly over spiritual matters more difficult. The movement would also reinforce the ideas of Individualism since Protestantism needed no Church as intermediary between the individual and God. The churches had already split into east and west in 1054 when the Patriarch in Constantinople and the Pope excommunicated each other. With the advent of the Protestant Reformation, Europe was now split into three distinct groups: Eastern Orthodoxy, pan-national Catholicism, and Protestantism in northern Europe. In addition to many other smaller groups, Protestantism was further divided with three major groups: Lutherans, Calvinism, and most importantly for the Free Society, the Church of England. While religious wars raged in central Europe, peripheral powers intervened to prevent any one power from becoming predominant. Balance-of-power politics, beginning in the Reformation, kept Europe in a permanent warring states condition.

Martin Luther (1483 – 1546) was an Augustine monk who held a doctorate in theology from the University of Wittenberg. He was a lecturer there on moral philosophy and his studies prompted his opposition to the Catholic Church's use of indulgences. Those at the University already knew of his disagreements with many Church doctrines but when he posted his ninety-five theses on a church door on All Saints Day in 1517, the wider world knew.

After several attempts at reconciliation, Luther was condemned on 15 June 1520 by Pope Leo X and given a few months to recant. He was formally excommunicated on 3 January 1521. Because many of the German Princes were sympathetic to him, upset with church corruption, and some desirous of Church land, they were willing to give him one more chance, so he was summoned before the Diet of Worms in 1521. While two of the electors abstained, Luther was officially condemned by the Holy Roman Empire under the Edict of Worms on 26 May 1521. Oddly, he was given safe passage away from the assembly as the condemnation did not take effect for one month. While making his way back to Wittenberg, he was kidnapped by one of the abstaining princes, Frederick the Wise of Saxony and taken to Wartburg Castle where he was safe. Luther used the time to translate the New Testament into the vernacular German. In June of 1525 he also answered the question of celibacy for ministers of the new religion by marrying a former nun, Katharina von Bora after she was able to escape from a convent. Luther died of natural causes in 1546—a luxury many heretics at the time did not enjoy.

Jean Calvin (1509 – 1564) was raised a Catholic near Paris. He began his university studies in philosophy but under pressure from his father switched to law. However, when his father died in 1531, he no longer felt obligated to finish and returned to more scholarly pursuits, publishing a commentary on Seneca's *On Clemency*. He was eventually forced to leave Paris with a friend, Nicholas Cop, for their heretical views landing in Basel where he wrote his *Institutes of the Christian Religion* which made him a major Protestant theologian. From Basel, he spent time in Geneva, then Strasbourg, and then back in Geneva. Calvin's particular branch of Protestantism began to adopt democratic methods in church government, and in many cases congregants voted for their own church officials.

Sadly, the new ideas of tolerance only went so far. When in Geneva, Calvin denounced Michael Servetus a Spaniard who was on his way to Italy and had stopped to hear Calvin speak. The first European to discover the pulmonary circulation of the blood, Servetus was traveling under a false identity because he too had heretical views, but they were extreme even for Calvin. After he was discovered, he was burned at the stake in October 1553. Luckily for both Luther and Calvin, they were protected by the political confusion of Europe. The German Princes protected Luther, and Calvin was safe thanks to the Swiss Cantons.

The third split in western Christian practice occurred when Henry VIII of England (1491 – 1547) separated from Rome in 1534 to divorce, remarry, and produce a male heir. He was forced to concede additional power to the English nobles and Parliament to secure the needed legislation for separation with many of them receiving church property at low prices to secure the deal.

After rule by the sickly Edward VI until 1553 and the Catholic Queen Mary until 1558, who had hundreds of Protestants burned at the stake, Elizabeth I (1533 – 1603) became queen. She stands out as one of the few rulers in Europe to navigate the hazardous religious waters of her time without too much bloodshed. With a predominantly Catholic House of Lords, thanks to Queen Mary, and a Protestant House of Commons, Elizabeth attempted to make a church with a Catholic external form and Protestant beliefs. The thirty-nine articles of faith were a mixture of Lutheran and Calvinist doctrines. There were no searches for heretics in this church, only fines for those who refused to attend public service. Over time, the Church of England became increasingly Protestant in its doctrine.

With Sir Francis Drake's (1540 – 1596) victory over the Spanish Armada in 1588, Elizabeth kept England independent. This battle high-lights another important theme—repeated again and again—the navy was the key to England's independence. Since England developed institutions of a Free Society, this accident of geography protected by its navy was key to freedom's survival.

The religious wars of the Reformation provide an example of how con-flicts between kings produced a balance-of-power and stalemate across Europe. This period of warfare can be divided into three general phases. The first (1529 – 1555) by and large took place in Switzerland and Germany. The second (1560 – 1609) was mostly concentrated in France and the Netherlands. The third took place across all of Europe. This last phase, called the Thirty Years War (1618 – 1648), was particularly devastating to Germany as a large segment of the populace died from the general destruc-tion it brought to the countryside. When Spain was on the verge of victory in Germany during the Thirty Years War, a great captain from the north,

Gustavus Adolphus was able to push back the forces and preserve Protestant Germany. It is an example of how peripheral powers worked to prevent the establishment of a unified European Dictatorship.

The seeds of the Thirty Years War were planted when the king of Bohemia, Ferdinand of Styria (1578 – 1637), in 1617 reversed religious tolerance granted to the Protestants in 1609. Protestant nobles responded by attempting to kill two of Ferdinand's advisors, and the crisis soon involved the entire Holy Roman Empire. The nobles gained the support of Frederick of Palatinate to be the new king of Bohemia, and this precipitated a war. The Catholic Prince Maximillian (1573 – 1651) sent troops, as did Philip of Spain, and in a quick campaign the rebels were crushed by 1622. Christian IV of Denmark entered Germany to protect the Protestants. Ferdinand defeated Christian and began to transform the Empire. By using mercenary troops under Albrecht von Wallenstein (1583 – 1634) Ferdinand was able to occupy Denmark and parts of the Baltic coast with 125,000 men, and he was powerful enough to issue the Edict of Restoration in 1629.

The 1629 edict made Calvinism illegal in the Holy Roman Empire and required Lutheran Princes to return to Ferdinand all Catholic Church land. Once again, Ferdinand used mercenary troops under Wallenstein to occupy Protestant cities and forcibly convert them to Catholicism when the Swedish King Gustavus Adolphus (1594 – 1632) came to the aid of Protestants in 1630. His army was mostly financed by the Catholic Cardinal Richelieu (1585 – 1642) the French King's Chief Minister as France was forever worried about the Habsburg Dynasty in Austria as part of the balance-of-power in Europe. Adolphus was an able general and defeated the Catholic army at Breitenfeld (1631) invading Catholic areas and sacking Bavaria. Wallenstein came out of retirement and the two met at Lutzen in Saxony in 1632. Adolphus was killed, but the Swedish were nonetheless victorious.

With the death of Adolphus, Richelieu sent more resources into Germany. The years 1635 to 1648 were particularly destructive with French and Swedish armies fighting against Habsburg armies. From all accounts the troops spent more time pillaging the countryside than fighting each other.

Overall, Germany lost upwards of one-third of its population—over half in some areas.

Peace negotiations began in 1644 and were finally completed in the Treaty of Westphalia (1648). The treaty in reality only re-confirmed the old Augsburg formula, existing before the war, where each German Prince could set the official religion in his realm with private liberty of conscience for Catholics and Lutherans. However, Anabaptists, Calvinists, and other Protestant sects remained illegal, and many of these groups left for the British colony of Pennsylvania in America. The horrors of this war kept the political boundaries fairly constant until the Napoleonic Era.

6

The Glorious Revolution was the first major victory for the Free Society.

The forces of the Reformation and the merchant community were able for the first time to challenge the Hereditary Dictatorship in England. Increasing attempts by Charles I of England to impose rule eventually broke out into civil war between him and Parliament in 1643. Parliament, using its own army called the New Model Army under the command of Thomas Fairfax and Oliver Cromwell, defeated the king in the battle of Naseby (1645). Among the diplomatic correspondence of the king captured in the battle, was the worst fear of Parliament—efforts by the king to enlist Catholic rulers to come to his aid. The king returned in 1648 in an alliance with Scotland, but he was soundly defeated and this time captured. On 30 January 1649 Charles I was beheaded.

On May 19th, 1649, Parliament declared the end to monarchy and England was declared a Commonwealth and a Free State. This was a historic declaration as no people of a major country had ever thrown off their monarchy. Not since the time of the Romans had the Mandate from Heaven been thrown off and a new dictator not installed. It was also the first time the merchant community assumed power in a major European country.

It was a confusing period of time, called the Interregnum, with a large Puritan influence in the New Model Army, along with radical preachers who desired godly discipline, the moral force behind this rebellion. However, after the control of the Church of England was removed, a large number of competing sects emerged. "Fifth Monarchists" thought the Monarchy of Christ was about to appear to begin his 1,000 year rule. "Ranters" were a group denying all Scriptural authority and instead followed the personal guidance of the spirit. "Quakers" were similar when they appeared in 1652 and followed what they felt were the promptings of the Holy Spirit. "Seekers" argued no true church existed and one must wait for God to send a prophet to establish the new church. This chaos caused many to look to Oliver Cromwell to provide more order. Cromwell was made Protector for life in 1654 and offered the English crown before he died in September 1658.

At the end of the Interregnum, the revolutionaries had made no provision for succession. Richard Cromwell ruled briefly in his father's stead, and then three army commanders took over. The nobility was anxious to return to normalcy as was much of the general population, and the monarchy looked better and better as everyone was tired of godly discipline and Puritan radicals. A restored Parliament opened in 25 April 1660, and by 29 May Charles II, son of the late Charles I, entered London.

Although no formal treaty had defined his powers, it was expected Charles II would rule with moderation. His Catholicism was tolerated since he had no heirs by his queen, and also because his brother James II was Protestant. However, when James II converted to Catholicism in 1669, every action of the two brothers came under suspicion. Charles II supported the French against the Dutch in the Dutch Crisis of 1672 and attempted in the same year to relax restrictions preventing English Catholics from holding office, including Parliament, and making Catholic education, publications, and public worship illegal. When England refused to participate in the League of Augsburg (1686–1689), a defensive pact against French aggression, opposition to the king began to grow. This was at the time of the revocation of the Edicts of Nantes, and large numbers of Protestant refugees were arriving in England.

When Charles II died in 1685, James II continued to rule in the same manner. Then in 1687, by royal edict, James II suspended all restrictions upon Catholics and appointed upwards of ninety Catholic officers to the army. The Declaration of Indulgence was to be read in all churches of the realm. Seven Anglican Bishops petitioned the king against being forced to read the declaration. When it became public his wife, the queen, was pregnant, the Protestant nobility had reached the last straw. They had pinned their hopes on Mary II, who was the daughter of James II and a Protestant. If James II had no children with his second wife, then Mary II or her heirs would be dictator. Holland's William III of Orange was Mary's husband, and he was asked to rescue England. He crossed over to England with his army, but before the battle James II fled. On 13 February 1689, the crown was jointly offered to both William and Mary with limitations on their rule known as the Declaration of Rights. This victory, called the Glorious Revolution, was the first time in history merchants had a permanent victory over kings.

The Declaration of Rights was passed by a Parliament dominated by the merchant community. The declaration was divided into thirteen articles. Parliament was declared supreme in matters of law and taxes. The king could be petitioned without fear of reprisal. The Declaration made it illegal to maintain a standing army in England without Parliament's permission. The citizen soldier was protected when Protestant men had the right to bear arms. Elections to Parliament were to be free, and Parliament was to meet on a regular basis. No Member of Parliament could be held to account for anything said in Parliament. Citizens were to be free from cruel and unusual punishments. The Free Society had finally won an important victory.

7

The European colonial empires were driven by a desire to end the stalemate in Europe. The Europeans conquered the world but no European power conquered Europe. The warring states condition of Europe continued with more balance-of-power wars.

The European exploration and conquest of other areas of the world was driven by competition between the different European dictators and was an important factor in making Europe a dominant actor on the world stage with many European nations creating vast empires. It did not, however, solve the basic problem of domination in Europe. While their empires grew, a stalemate continued, and Europe remained dominated by balance-of-power politics.

Maritime trade between northern and southern Europe was facilitated by several improvements in ship technology developed in northern Europe. A deep draught ship with square sails was developed to withstand the rough seas of the Atlantic. Called a cog, its deeper draught made it an ideal vehicle of trade, and in addition it had a rear axial rudder to add to its control. Also important was the invention of the dry compass for seafaring. Previously the compass needle would float upon a bowl of water pointing to north, but a dry compass mechanically suspended the magnetic needle and was much more satisfactory in rough seas. An additional navigation improvement was the use of the portolan chart containing a detailed map of the coastline making it easy to plot bearings to reach a particular destination. Combining the charts with dead reckoning, an experienced sailor could be surprisingly accurate. Royal patronage of better astronomical tables added to the improvements, and portolan charts were a state secret for Portugal and Spain when they first started exploration.

Particularly in European waters, maritime trade had been a fair weather event taking place between April and October, but with the advent of these new technologies, trade could be conducted longer and was dormant only two to three months out of the year. They also allowed for open-ocean sailing where in the past it was common practice to stay closer to shore. However, these improvements did not remove all of the danger of a sea voyage. In 1341, a group of Venetian merchants sent a voyage out to the Canary Islands. They were last seen heading out west into the Atlantic Ocean never to return.

A Portuguese royal, Prince Henry the Navigator (1394 – 1460) was the first to send out large European expeditions. These forays explored as far south as the Senegal River in Africa while others reached the vicinity of the Congo by 1474 and the Cape of Good Hope in 1488. Once the way to the east had been found, progress was rapid. In 1510 the Portuguese had established a base at Goa in India. Further trading bases were established in Malacca (1511) and at Ormuz (1515) in the Persian Gulf, and they dropped anchor in Canton China in 1513. For the next one hundred years, Portugal dominated the trade routes in the South China Sea and the Indian Ocean.

With the success of the Portuguese king, other kings in Europe attempted their own end run. Christopher Columbus (1415 – 1506) was a Genoese sailor who sailed west to reach the riches of the Orient. His historic sighting of land for Spain took place on 12 October 1492. Each European dictator followed with his own explorers. England sent a Venetian, John Cabot (1450 – 1499), who found Newfoundland in 1497. The French sent Jacques Cartier (1491 – 1557) who explored the St. Lawrence River between 1534 and 1541. The Dutch sent Willem Barents (1550 – 1597). The long sought after western route to China and India was eventually found by the Portuguese sailor, Ferdinand Magellan (1480 – 1521).

The small amount of gold the Spanish took from natives in the Caribbean islands told them there was a larger source someplace in the Americas. From their base in Cuba, Herman Cortez sailed with eleven ships and 500 men. In October 1519, they marched with only 200 men on the capital, Tenochtitlan, a city of 200,000. By April 1520 an important ally arrived at Vera Cruz—smallpox. Various estimates attempt to quantify the devastation wrought upon the natives of all North and South America who had never been exposed to the deadly disease. Although some range as high as 90%, and certainly are exaggerated, the devastation was severe and undoubtedly exceeded the Black Death of 1350 on a percentage basis.

An important part of the European strategy was to form local alliances. Cortez formed an alliance with the Tlaxcalan Indians who hated the Aztecs. By 1522 the Aztec Empire was destroyed, and the pattern was repeated with the Incas. Francisco Pizarro (1471 – 1541) with a band of 5,000 men invaded in 1530. Much as the Spanish did in Mexico, Pizarro was able to take advantage of Indian groups oppressed by the Incas and willing to fight against their former masters.

The territorial conquests of Mexico and Peru were a boon to Spanish power but did not allow Spain to dominate Europe. Spain could not pay its troops and defaulted on loans from Genoese bankers in 1575. Despite the addition of Portugal due to a royal inheritance, Spain could not win the religious wars in Europe nor could she crush the eighty year Dutch revolt begun in 1568.[15]

Gradually, military superiority shifted from Spain to Holland. By 1609 the Dutch were, on a per capita basis, the richest citizens in Europe. A twelve-year truce began with Spain in the same year, and the Dutch used the opportunity to expand trade creating a mostly unarmed ship called the *Fluyt* to maximize cargo-carrying capability. At the same time, the Dutch shipyards produced the higher quality ships at lower prices than the Spanish were able to build. Slowly the Dutch were able to replace the Portuguese as major agents of trade in the Indian Ocean.

The imperial struggle would now shift to be a gradual accumulation of British gains overseas and a European struggle to contain France. When William of Orange rescued Protestant England, an English-Dutch alliance against France was a certainty. Others in Europe became concerned with France, and in 1689 formed the Grand Alliance, with the explicit goal of forcing France back to its territory of 1659. The Nine Year War (1688 – 1697) was another balance-of-power war. At sea, a combined English-Dutch fleet defeated the French in the Battle of Logue in 1692 allowing a blockade of French ports, and eventually the French were pushed back.

Other balance-of-power wars produced substantial overseas results for Britain without changing the stalemate situation in Europe. The War of Spanish Succession (1701 – 1714) was a war to prevent Spain and France combining under one crown but proved costly to all sides in both men and material. Austrian General Eugene was able to force Spain out of Italy, and the English General Marlborough and Eugene were able to defeat the French at Blenheim (1704) in Bavaria. Later the French met Marlborough at Malplaquet (1709) and Marlborough crushed the French leaving 40,000 dead or wounded on the battlefield. The Treaty of Utrecht (1714) left a Bourbon King on the Spanish throne but kept the two crowns separate.

---

[15] A popular myth has developed around the European dictators' conquests of native peoples. Although many invasions by barbarians over more advanced civilizations is documented here, the myth claims when a more advanced civilization meets a more primitive it is always a disaster for the more primitive. It was disease and civil war that made the Spanish conquests possible.

Britain obtained Gibraltar, Nova Scotia, and Newfoundland. Spain was forced to relinquish her holdings in Italy and any claims to the Netherlands.

The other two major balance-of-power wars, the War of Austrian Succession (1740 – 1748) and the Seven Year War (1756 – 1763), produced no dominant victor in Europe. Prussia became a major land power in Europe during these wars while Britain became Europe's major naval power. The Seven Year War is sometimes called the first true world war in which major battles took place outside of Europe. The Treaty of Paris (1763) forced France to make major colonial concessions in North America and India. French rule in North America ended with their retention of two tiny islands at the end of the St. Lawrence and the two sugar plantation islands of Guadeloupe and Martinique. Spain was forced to give Florida over to the British while Canada was now solely in British hands.

8

The printing press and the Scientific Revolution significantly weakened the secondary monopoly over the intellect.

The disorder of Europe's political landscape allowed a type of negative free speech as ideas suppressed in one political jurisdiction could find a more favorable reception in another. The proliferation of new ideas was magnified with the invention of the printing press because it allowed for the cost of information to decidedly drop and had a wide impact in a variety of fields. Johann Gutenberg (c. 1390s – 1468) was a goldsmith in Mainz who had been experimenting with a new method of printing for about ten years. He attempted its use as a commercial enterprise in 1452 and soon began printing the *Vulgate Bible*–later known as *The Gutenberg Bible*.

The printing press made the secondary monopoly over the intellectual life of Europe nearly impossible. Particularly important was its impact on the Scientific Revolution. Once it was discovered the ancient texts were wrong, there was an explosion of discovery, with the printing press spreading the news.

The Scientific Revolution is typically dated to have begun in 1543 with the publication of *On the Revolutions of the Heavenly Bodies* by Nicolaus

Copernicus (1473 – 1543). First the artists of the Renaissance and then the natural philosophers, as scientists were called, discovered they could exceed the ancients. A huge number of original discoveries were made in a few short centuries. Andrea Vesalius (1514 – 1564) began to describe human anatomy accurately. Blood circulation caused by the action of the heart was discovered by Harvey (1578 – 1657). Microscopic life was seen for the first time in a microscope invented by Leeuwenhoek (1632 – 1723). Modern chemistry and the principles of chemical combustion were advanced by Lavoisier (1743 – 1794).

A Roman living in Alexandria, Egypt, Ptolemy (90 – 168) wrote *The Almagest* containing methods to calculate the positions of the sun, moon, planets, and stars. The book came to the Europeans via translations from Arabic in Sicily and Spain. As was typical in pre-industrial societies this text became part of the depository of the wisdom of the ancients. However, as the Europeans began to make their own measurements, the methods of Ptolemy appeared more and more contrived. Copernicus wrote about a heliocentric model since it appeared to be a more elegant solution, but it was not until Galileo Galilei (1564 – 1642) constructed a telescope from information he had learned about devices invented in Holland and pointed the new contraption at the sky that convincing data was found to confirm Copernicus. Galileo published his observations in *Sidereal Messenger* in 1610. Further advances were made when Johannes Kepler (1571 – 1630) proposed a heliocentric model for planetary orbits but his solution, the most accurate to date, used orbits in the shape of ellipses and not circles. Kepler's discoveries illustrated what would become known as the scientific method—a method to advance knowledge in a systematic way.

Each of these scientists' works were put on *The Index of Forbidden Books* and not removed until 1835. The Catholic Church's condemnation of the heliocentric discovery is a perfect example of how a dictatorship thwarts innovation. Had Europe been ruled by a single secular and spiritual power, the entire Scientific Revolution might have been nipped in the bud, but because of the intense competition between European dictators, the opposite came to pass.

Although the universities in Europe did not become centers of research until the mid 19th century, the kings of Europe became patrons of science long before then. In 1662, under a Royal charter, the Royal Society of London for Promoting Natural Knowledge was founded. As soon as 1665 the Royal Society kept track of its findings in its publication *Philosophical Transactions*. Other nations followed England's lead, with the most famous being the establishment of the French Academy of Sciences by the absolutist monarch Louis XIV in 1666.

This patronage by a dictator such as Louis XIV has some important lessons for the Free Society. Thus far the benefits of freedom can be seen through the artistic freedom of the Renaissance, the freedom of religion of the Reformation, and the freedom of inquiry in the Scientific Revolution. However, none of these challenge the basis of the pre-industrial society. To be sure, a dictator allowing these freedoms runs the risk people will challenge his rule as the secondary monopolies become more difficult to manage. The invention of the printing press had the potential to widely disseminate views contrary to the dictatorship. Nevertheless, dictators as autocratic as Louis XIV realized the potential of science to further their ends, and for many rulers this was worth the risk. Scientific progress can proceed in a dictatorship as rapidly as it can in a Free Society—if the dictator is so disposed.

9

The Enlightenment thinkers proposed alternatives to the Hereditary Dictatorship through two basic approaches to government. One of these inadvertently laid the foundation for future dictatorships, and this split in the approach to government would echo down through the ages.

The Enlightenment was a reaction to the excesses of the religious wars as well as an attempt to capitalize upon the individualism of the Renaissance and the obvious success of reason in the Scientific Revolution. Called the Age of Reason, the Enlightenment placed reason above all else. Nominally it dates from the Glorious Revolution of 1688 and ends with the French Revolution of 1789.

One of the first actions in England after 1688 was the Tolerance Act of 1689 allowing Protestant belief outside of the Church of England if the person remained loyal to the Crown. The Anglicans had adopted a policy of latitudinarianism, and it was under this policy the Anglican Church was prepared to christen, marry, and bury anyone—provided it was done without too many awkward questions. Conscience was the providence of God alone. Nonetheless, there were not major shifts in religious observances as individuals for the most part died in the same faith as their birth. Except for a few deists and the rare atheist, traditional religion carried on. The difference was tolerance. In England, Holland, and Frederick II's Berlin, one could profess a deist belief without fear of being exiled. Burning a heretic at the stake was becoming a thing of the past. In Lisbon *auto de fe* was last practiced in 1739.

The Hereditary Dictatorship was under pressure with each of its secondary monopolies being challenged. The Enlightenment provided an alternative to the idea of monarchy and its monopoly of violence. John Locke (1632 – 1704) was an early advocate of tolerance and liberty, and it was his belief faith and reason could find an accommodation acceptable to both. He wrote both a discussion on tolerance, from which the concept of the loyal opposition was derived, as well as two works on government. In his first work, he maintained the divine right of kings was inconsistent with civil society. In his second, he explained how civil societies were formed to protect life, liberty, and property, and created or implied a social compact based upon trust. It was when this trust was broken men take up arms against their government. Locke was theorizing how the Mandate from Heaven was broken and was specific in designating the legislature using majority rule as the will of the people. In his view, the legislature was the superior part of the government since it represented the people. The other half, the executive, he felt must be kept separate as a protection of life, liberty, and property.

The other notable philosopher whose ideas became important to the Free Society was Charles de Montesquieu (1689 – 1755). He was an aristocrat who made his life's passion the study of history and governments. Published a few years before his death, his masterpiece, *The Spirit of Laws*, was a comparative study of three different types of government. Each type had a spirit or organizing principle. Governments rose and fell based upon how well they adhered to their spirit. For a monarchy, the spirit was honor and for a republic, it was virtue. Despotism was organized around fear. It was his conviction a republic was limited in the amount of territory it could successfully administer. Only a monarchy, properly restrained, could avoid despotism and offer reasonable government to the majority of mankind.

The purpose of Montesquieu's life-long study was to determine which government type would maximize liberty to all men. England after the Glorious Revolution was the best government in attaining this goal. It could do so because it separated the different functions of government, and this prevented an absolute monarchy or a despotism. The executive would reside in the king, and if this monarchy had an aristocracy to further restrain the monarch, it was all for the better. A parliament should have the legislative function and write the laws. The judiciary should be separate from both and a check on both. Montesquieu's approach to government of checks and balances was an inspiration to those framing the American Constitution as both he and Locke were expounding upon the types of checks and balances, which historically worked to preserve liberty. They were attempting to make the study of the monopoly of violence and democracy scientific. Positive feedback caused governments to grow. Societies needed traditions and institutions producing negative feedback to keep governments in check.

There were others who represented a different aspect of the Enlightenment. While Locke and Montesquieu sought reform, these other men thought the entire old order needed to be extinguished. Reason demanded a fresh start, and they saw faith and reason as incompatible antagonists. The first view was populated with religious men including deists, the second were anti-Christian deists, agnostics and atheists. In this second camp we find Diderot (1713 – 1784) and Rousseau (1712 – 1778). Denis Diderot was a militant atheist and editor of *The Encyclodpedie,* an embodiment of the Enlightenment's love of reason as it was a compilation of subjects by leading experts in their field. It was Diderot's life work with publication beginning in 1751 and finishing in 1772. He was also a critic in his own right. One of his more controversial stands was his attack on the sexual repression of the Christian churches. Like many in the Enlightenment he used a foreign country, Tahiti, as a foil against the hypocrisies of his day.

No one can discuss the Enlightenment without a discussion of Rousseau. An orphan brought up by relatives, he briefly considered becoming a priest but would later advocate deism for the rest of his life. He made a name for himself when he won an essay contest in 1750 for which the Academy of Dijon had questioned if the modern arts and sciences had made a moral improvement of mankind. In Rousseau's view the present civilization had corrupted man. Mankind in their original state had a type of innocence— an innocence based upon instinct later replaced by a sense of justice with the advent of civilization. It was private property preventing man's sense of justice from being fulfilled. He never advocated a return to the savage condition as is popularly believed but wrote instead on how to remake society to implement this justice. Rousseau's work, *The Social Contract*, was his analysis of this improved society in which the citizen recognized the general will encompassing the general good of society. He opposed a parliamentary balance of competing interests and called this the will of all. The new society would be created through a special program of education written about in his book, *Emile*. It would create a civic creed much like a religion. Those who refused to submit to the creed would be exiled.

The two different trends in the Enlightenment portended the important distinctions in how governments would evolve as the old Hereditary Dictatorships declined in the wake of the Industrial Revolution. The first theme, represented by Locke, was the application of reason to questions of government and tended to be practical in its accommodation of religion. It sought to find methods to limit the power of government and maximize personal freedom via negative feedback to keep government small. The second trend, represented by Rousseau, was more idealistic and elitist. It saw government as a means to reorganize society. It was the application of reason to questions of the entire society and social justice. This second trend was hostile to religion and private property and was driven by an ideal of how society was to be organized.

10

The Industrial Revolution would destroy the secondary monopoly over the economy and thereby undermine the basis of the Hereditary Dictatorship. The timing and location were key to development of the Free Society.

The complexity of commerce resulting from the Industrial Revolution made the secondary monopoly over the economy more difficult. Since this was the most important monopoly of the Hereditary Dictatorship, after the monopoly of violence, many of these dictatorships ended. It was the practical discoveries of the Scientific Revolution that made the Industrial Revolution possible. Generally, without a practical application, science is mostly useless and needs to prove its value, or else it becomes an ivory tower intellectual exercise. In other words without the engineer, science is dead.

More than anything else the Free Society needed the Industrial Revolution. The pre-industrial society was pyramid in shape with agriculture as its base. When the power of human and animal muscle was the only source of energy employed in food production, the low efficiency necessitated most people working the land. The few who escaped to pursue other interests constituted the top of the pyramid. Since the entire economy was tied to one industry, agricultural production, the opportunity for monopoly and total control over the society was too great to resist. This changed with the Industrial Revolution.

The Industrial Revolution's key innovation was the use of machines to replace muscle, and the resultant exponential jump in productivity both on and off the farm destroyed the pyramid. The economic value of one's mind grew, and this would have profound implications later, especially for women.[16] Societies gradually transitioned from mostly rural to urban, and the mass production of an increasingly wide variety of products caused a large increase in the standard of living. With the pre-industrial society gone, the human race entered a second phase of human civilization.

---

[16] The Industrial and Scientific Revolutions were the real cause of "women's liberation." With the reduced need to produce large families and the capitalistic pressure for mental over physical work, individuals in free societies did the rest.

Machines powered by human or animal labor, by water or wind predated the steam engines. Spinning machines were an example of a human powered contraption used to make yarn. Early models broke threads or produced thread of uneven quality, but by the late 1700s, as the merchant trade grew more efficient, machines such as James Hargreaves' Spinning Jenny or Samuel Crompton's Spinning Mule improved the productivity of one person. Wind and water powered machines could produce a much larger output than those powered with human or animal labor, but were unreliable due to drought, freezing temperatures, or a calm day.

In 1712 an Englishman named Thomas Newcomen (1663 – 1729) invented a steam powered machine to pump water out of mines. By the 1730s it was in use in several European countries. In the 1760s dramatic improvements in the steam engine sparked the Industrial Revolution. James Watt (1736 – 1819) was a Scottish engineer trained as a tool maker—an area of expertise in which the Europeans had a distinct edge over other pre-industrial societies. The best clocks and telescopes were made in Europe as were some of the best firearms because Europeans were also experts at precision instrumentation and methods of precise measurement. Watt's skill in building a precision steam machine quadrupled the engine's efficiency. In addition to improving mining, his machines found uses everywhere—in pottery production as well as in powering hammers and blowers. In 1783 it was used to power steamboats in France. When the new engine was used to power the cotton spinning machines, worker productivity soared.

The first fossil fuel, coal, was powering the Industrial Revolution, and the coal mines were a source of innovation. The more efficient steam pumps allowed mining to go deeper and extract more coal. These deeper mines used coal carts on tracks with steam engines to pull the ore to the surface, and this combination became the genesis of the railroad. The railroads brought iron ore to the vicinity of the mines so steel could be made using coke smelting. Originally some of the best weapons had come from Sweden using Swedish steel. Luckily for the Free Society, easily accessible coal was found in England, and in addition, England was the location of much of the innovation. England retained its substantial lead in industrialization over others in Europe well past the 1860s.

The Industrial Revolution would not have proceeded as rapidly had the infrastructure of Capitalism not been in place. The merchant community and the banking system were already servicing the trade between Europe's different kingdoms. The protection of private property rights was increasingly recognized in nations dominated by the merchant community such as Holland and England. Europe's division into different nations and smaller political entities made the probability high these non-aristocratic merchants would be proportionally more concentrated in some countries. This occurred in the north of Italy, Holland, and England. The concentration of likeminded individuals also made the possibility of innovation more probable. In 1609 the Wisselbank was first opened in Holland. Receipts of deposit created a secondary market for cash equivalents. The well-known joint-stock company and stock market exchange also began in Holland. The bill of exchange, developed in Florence, Italy, was another such innovation in wide use.

The use of private property rights to encourage invention with the protection of a patent traces back to Florence. Patent law is a wonderful example of limited government power used as a stimulus to individual initiative. The first patent issued in Florence was in 1421. Venice would make it a regular part of their legal system, where, in 1474, a grant of monopoly was established giving exclusive patent rights for ten years. The idea would spread with Italian merchants to other parts of Europe or with those who visited Venice.

Elizabeth I would use patent rights to encourage tradesman to move with their craft to England. Lord Burghley at the behest of the queen, would target high priced imports and use this as a method to develop a domestic alternative. In 1561 a patent was issued to two Castilian merchants for the making of soap in England. In 1565 the first Scottish patent was issued to a Florentine for the making of salt. Under the dictators, the tradesman would not be required to reveal anything about the actual invention or technique, and if a business was not established, the patent would be revoked.

Only after the Glorious Revolution did the process proceed more as it was intended. In the past, a patent would be refused for political reasons since it might create competition with a friend of the crown. Patent petitions before the crown would highlight the social benefits of the new idea such as providing employment for the poor, as a means of getting the political cover to allow the crown to approve the patent. By contrast, Parliament restrained itself from abusing the process. When in 1732 a person attempted to renew a patent by a private Act of Parliament, he was soundly defeated.

The multi-state system also acted as a check upon excesses of the dictator. Any attempt to debase the currency was met with free market devaluation. Large tax increases would cause capital to flee to jurisdictions with lower rates. When talented minorities like the Huguenots or Jews were expelled from France and Spain, they would benefit another state willing to take in the new refugees. In nations with large merchant communities, demands against arbitrary actions would result in guarantees against abuses to private property. In 1575, when the Spanish crown defaulted on loans from Genoa, Spain could not pay its troops, and they sacked Antwerp. Spain could not get any more loans for many years. Had a single all-encompassing European empire been in place, the bankers in Genoa would have been in a much different situation. Merchants wanted predictability in their transactions, and this accounts for the gradual increase in the demand for lawyers outside of the criminal and spiritual realms from as early as the 1300s.

Adam Smith (1723 – 1790) was a Scotsman and held the Chair of Moral Philosophy at Glasgow University. As influential as any of the other Enlightenment philosophers, his major work, *An Inquiry into the Nature and Causes of the Wealth of Nations*, was a well-argued work against Mercantilism and in favor of free trade. The first part of his book traced two important Free Society themes: the development of the merchant community and the development of private property rights. In the second part, Smith stated his most famous insight, the so-called Invisible Hand of Competition between individuals who regulated the economy in the absence of feudal-minded Mercantilism. The king did not need to regulate, as competition would do it for him.

Competition in a free market would tend to fix the price near its "natural price" i.e. its cost of production. Any price above this will attract labor and capital, provided these inputs to production were free to move. The increase in supply would drive the prices down. The government's roll was to create the legal framework for commerce, the general law and order, the common defense, and necessary public works. As Adam Smith would say any "pretentions" by statesmen in the economic sphere were counterproductive.

Smith then turned to a discussion of the title of his book. He sought to answer what was the best policy to maximize the wealth of a nation. Again the Invisible Hand was at work. This time it came in the general desire of people to improve their lives. The most reasonable approach to this was to save a small portion of what one earned over a period of time. The businessman does this by investing in equipment improving the division of labor. This is the essence of Capitalism—the investment of profit in future capital assets.

Although writing at the dawn of the Industrial Revolution, Adam Smith did not predict the explosion of productivity made possible by powered machines as he merely observed what was already taking place. The division of labor produced a wealth of goods unavailable in previous generations, and he observed how a simple item like a coat was the work of a host of different individuals. The market for coats created this coordination of so many people—and not some government dictate. Efficiency was the wealth of nations—not the stored gold bullion in the king's treasury.[17] At the time, this efficiency extended to all levels of society as it drove labor costs up when businessmen hired more workers for further divisions of labor. Smith's vision, however, was not utopian—only optimistic. Until a nation reached its "full compliment" of capital, wages would rise. He did not believe any European country was close to its maximum. In the end, he did not advocate a transformation of society but a simple recognition of a process already in place and the steps necessary to encourage it. The maximization of the wealth of any nation was best achieved by the institution of free trade abroad combined with free markets at home.

Self-correcting negative feedback mechanisms are needed if the Free Society is to exist. Competition between nations and individuals restrains excesses of both taxation and prices and are examples of self-regulating

---

[17] One political difficulty for a free market system is the advantages to society are diffuse while the pain of failure falls upon the individual. An inefficient or obsolete business going under benefits society at large while losing one's job can be a personal disaster.

negative feedback mechanisms. If such mechanisms did not exist, governments would tax and regulate without bound.

11

Other civilizations did not develop like Europe because of their dictatorships.

The disunity of Europe made the Industrial Revolution and the Free Society possible, and although institutions like the Constitutional Monarchy with a strong parliament existed only in Europe, other advanced pre-industrial civilizations could have developed an Industrial Revolution of their own. Whereas the Hereditary Dictatorship came under increased pressure with industrialization, this did not guarantee a Free Society. The Industrial Revolution did not need the Free Society, but the Free Society definitely needed the Industrial Revolution to maintain long term viability.[18]

When compared to pre-industrial Europe four kingdoms of the world are generally considered to be advanced enough to merit consideration as to why an Industrial Revolution did not occur there: the Ottoman Empire, the Mughal Empire of India, the Ming and Manchu Dynasties of China, and late Feudal Japan.

The Ottoman Empire's practice of "the Cage" to prevent succession struggles made it a poor candidate for innovation. The future Sultans never received an education in statecraft while isolated in "the Cage." Because the dictators in this empire became weak, they could not be a force behind innovation as were the dictators of Europe. The ostentatious displays of wealth by each Sultan encouraged others to do the same, and the elites of society built large palaces and maintained extensive harems. All this diverted capital to demonstrations of current wealth over investment. The slave basis of society also discouraged innovation as many slaves were in positions of power and had little incentive to innovate. In addition, there was a culture

---

[18] A popular explanation for western advances compared to China and others is the western exploitation of native peoples. However the monetary value of this trade was never more than 10% of the total trade across Europe and with Spain much of the wealth was wasted in military adventures.

in the Ottoman Empire encouraging Islamic suspicion of new ideas as being heretical. The Ottoman's suppression of the Arabic language restricted access to the books that inspired the Renaissance.

In many ways the Mughal Empire was no better. Although not as highly centralized as the Ottoman Empire, the subjugation of the people was as pervasive. Like the Sultans, the Maharajas lived lavishly at the expense of the ordinary citizen. It was a pyramid society, and the rulers intended to keep it that way. The caste system also was an aid in keeping people in their proper place. Heavy taxes and arbitrary rule kept wealth accumulation at a minimum, and land owners were reluctant to make improvements for it proved they had money and risked government confiscation. With little commerce, each small city was a kingdom onto itself.

The rulers of China, however, took their Mandate from Heaven seriously and did their best to run an efficient pre-industrial society. Various comparisons between Western Europe and China show a high average energy usage as well as a male literacy rate for both around 10%. Like Western Europe, China had large urban cities and had an inventive spirit fueling innovations like the printing press and gunpowder. The large state-sponsored maritime expeditions in the late Ming Dynasty were proof of the high level of organizational skills and technology.

However, when China was at its cultural peak, the Ming and Manchu Dynasties had at best no reason to change, and at worst saw foreign ideas as a threat to their rule. The tribute ships were banned in 1480, and by the 1550s knowledge of large ship construction had been lost. The Manchu's had an official policy of coastal defense but fought no battles at sea. Most Chinese officials believed the four great books and five classics of Confucianism were all that was needed for effective rule.

The Emperor Qianlong in 1793 told British diplomats China had all it needed and he was not interested in clever toys of the west. Such pronouncements should always be taken seriously since rulers can be arbitrary. For example, it was said of the Ming Emperor Zhu Yuanzhang when his officials knew they would be meeting with him, they would say goodbye to their families as if it was their last goodbye. The official persecution of Buddhism at various times would also have a similar effect. In such an environment, it was dangerous to stand out because at any time the dictator might change his mind. Caution and conformity was the safest path to longevity.

Finally, one needs to ask a fundamental question: once European technological superiority was a demonstrated fact, why didn't China simply copy the Europeans? If China did not have the sufficient advancement to cross the Industrial Revolution's threshold on their own, then surely after having seen the Europeans do it, they could have copied their example. Their refusal speaks volumes about some other limitation; a limitation self-imposed by the dictatorship and best illustrated by the Japanese example.

In Japan, Tokugawa Ieyasu (1542 – 1616) was able to restore central government control after a warring states period. Sometimes called "centralized feudalism," the Tokugawa Era (1600 – 1868) was one of strict social order. Using a Neo-Confucian model adapted to Japanese social realities, each person belonged to a social class. The warrior class was at the top followed by the peasants who grew the food, then the craftsmen who lived in towns and made things with their hands, and finally, the merchants who, in the Japanese view, only moved items from place to place for sale. Tokugawa imposed death for anyone switching classes. Marriage between classes was also strictly forbidden.

A restoration of the ancient order did not tolerate the relatively new Christian faith. Strong measures against Christians were already in evidence when twenty-six Franciscans were crucified on a hill overlooking Christian Nagasaki in 1597. In 1616 all foreign Christians were expelled, and all Japanese Christians were required to renounce their faith under penalty of death. Most priests left, while those remaining were captured, tortured, and executed. A Christian peasant revolt (1637 – 1638) over discriminatory taxes was brutally suppressed, and 40,000 Christians were beheaded. By 1640, open Christianity had ceased to exist. For several centuries all Japanese, including children, were required once a year to officially renounce Christianity in the *fumi-e* ritual. This ritual, performed at the nearby Buddhist temple, forced each person to trample upon a picture of Jesus or the Virgin Mary proving their contempt for Christianity.

To further ensure foreign influences would not disrupt the new order, the Shogunate issued the *sakoku* edicts. Called the "closed country" edicts, they forbade travel abroad, and foreign books were declared illegal. The sizes of Japanese ships were severely limited. All contacts with foreigners, including Chinese and Koreans, took place at limited ports of entry. A western sailor who made it to shore after a shipwreck was to be killed in the surf before he put his foot upon dry land. The Dutch were the only western contact, and this took place once a year on an island outside of Nagasaki. A thorough search of the Dutch imports was made to prevent any Christian influences.

For over 250 years Japan lived in isolation. Then, after forced contact with Europeans, the Japanese dictatorship made the decision to modernize and began the *Meiji* Restoration. From the beginning of the *Meiji* Restoration in 1868 until the Japanese defeat of the Russians in the Russo-Japanese War (1904 – 1905), Japan modernized in a time span of less than 40 years.

The key to the puzzle is not complicated. When the dictatorship deems outside influences are a threat to their power, the dictator suppresses these influences. However, if the dictator sees backwardness or technological inferiority as the bigger threat, then he encourages development. China remained behind the west despite the western "toys" being superior to China's, because the dictatorship judged the threat of subversive ideas greater than the possibility of European conquest. In retrospect, the Manchu's decision was reasonable. Their Dynasty lasted into the early 20th century, and its longevity was comparable to previous dynasties. Although forced to endure humiliation at the hands of the European dictators, they never conquered China. At worst, the Chinese were forced to lease ports of entry to the Europeans, but the Europeans eventually gave back their leases when they had expired.

The Japanese dictators fared far better. They locked western influence out as long as was possible, and then, when it became apparent this strategy was no longer tenable, they reversed course and adopted western technology. In a blink of an eye historically, they were able to go from a feudal society to defeating a major western power. Free Societies should take note. Dictators have tremendous power to move their societies in new directions if they so desire.

12

The Free Society developed in Europe despite the best efforts of its dictators. This development was an unintended consequence of the fractured political landscape of Europe created by its warring states condition and the constant competition between different European dictators.

The failure of a single dictator to establish control over Europe, versus the rest of the world, allowed for free institutions to develop there. Since freedom is not man's natural inclination, only a long list of special circumstances allowed it to come into being. The barbarian invasions set the stage by destroying the old central authority in the West. When kings began to reassert their power a pan-national religious institution and popular assemblies fought back.

Scholasticism brought in the prior heritage of free society ideas from ancient Greece and Rome and incorporated this heritage into the body of the sacred texts for the pre-industrial societies of Europe. By the time of the Renaissance, Scholasticism made the discussion of democratic ideals acceptable, as they were part of the 'wisdom of the ages.' Renaissance Humanism added a new twist, Individualism, an important change in perspective needed for members of a Free Society. Throughout this entire process the more freedom-disposed merchant community, with its larger concentration in small city-states, grew in influence. The Reformation built upon the split of church and state while ushering in the balance-of-power wars, making the domination of Europe by a single dictator nearly impossible. The Free Society achieved its first major victory in the Glorious Revolution in England where a vibrant merchant community was isolated on an island and protected by a powerful navy.

With the innovations of Gutenberg, the drop in the cost of information combined with a lack of a central censor to create another critical development. The Scientific Revolution began as the Europeans discovered their ancient texts were wrong. The combination of the Scientific Revolution with the desire of European dictators for military advantages pushed discovery.

It is from the Capitalism developed by the merchant community and the discoveries of the Scientific Revolution that the Industrial Revolution was born. However, even at this advanced stage, the success of the Free Society depended upon an accident of timing. The Industrial Revolution began in England, the one nation furthest down the path to a Free Society, as industrialization was destroying the economic basis of the Hereditary Dictatorship. Fortunate, too, the Enlightenment was making arguments for a Free Society and proposing methods of government to make it a reality. The arguments of Locke, Montesquieu, and Smith were showing how negative feedback methods could counteract the positive feedback causing government to grow.

Sometimes this progress is attributed to reason alone, and though many in the Enlightenment thought this way, this thinking is incorrect. It was freedom at the root of this progress. It was freedom to worship, freedom to think, freedom to innovate that produced the "European miracle." Despite the improved standard of living resulting from these many developments, the real European miracle was freedom itself and the Free Society taking shape in England. The real miracle is the Miracle of the Free Society. While the key question is can Europe overcome the legacy of its many Hereditary Dictatorships to fully implement the Free Society on the continent?

The human race got lucky. A new approach to government had been invented, and it was now up to the Hereditary Dictatorships to adapt. It is possible this was all a product of implacable forces of development, and it all would have happened anyway, but history tells a different story. The confusion in Europe was only a necessary condition for the Free Society; the natural human tendency toward dictatorship needed to be overcome. This implies there exists a weaker human tendency toward democratic ideals, but it requires action. As Seneca, a Stoic philosopher in ancient Rome once said, "He who is brave is free."

The Experiment that almost Failed

Chapter Four

The American Revolution was not unusual. Peasant revolts, people voting with their clubs and pitchforks, dynasties losing their Mandate from Heaven, occurred with regularity in pre-industrial societies, but always a new king took over in the wake of the revolt. Machiavelli's comment in *The Prince* that men who take up arms to better themselves invariably find themselves worse off is unfortunately true most of the time. What was unusual when the Americans revolted against George III was the type of government the rebels established—Representative Democracy. This was an experiment never attempted on such a grand scale. Many peculiar and unique circumstances around its establishment helped to sustain the experiment. Had the experiment not been established at the dawn of the Industrial Revolution it would have been doomed to failure.

When the American colonies formed, several factors contributed to the young Republic's early success. The Republic benefited from the democratic traditions already established in each colony including functioning legislatures present in each colony at the time of the American revolt. Like England, it also benefited from a strong merchant community as well as the frontier, something uniquely American. The frontier tended to reinforce individualism a trait necessary for a Free Society. The extensive freely available land also acted as a check upon the formation of a pyramid shaped pre-industrial society. Finally, the Judeo-Christian tradition in America and its voluntary religiosity was an important part of the national character, and it did much to motivate the Americans to live up to their professed ideals.

The American Revolution nominally was about the power to tax but in actuality was a struggle between the Free Society in its infant stage in America and the forces of the Hereditary Dictatorship in the person of King George III. The American Revolution was a manifestation of the pragmatic, more religiously tolerant, side of the Enlightenment, and this democratic experience of the Americans was combined with the ideas of Locke, Montesquieu, and Smith. By way of comparison, the other daughter of the Enlightenment, the French Revolution, stood as a warning to those who wished to remake society via the monopoly of violence. These two different views of government guided man's future and produced dramatically different results. The first viewed government as something dangerous, needing hard limits to preserve liberty, while the second saw government as a tool to make a better world.

Despite the many lucky circumstances favoring the Republic, one contradiction remained. The contradiction of slavery, a ubiquitous feature of the pre-industrial society spawned by the secondary monopoly over the economy, had to be abolished or the American experiment would collapse. Eighty-five years after the American Revolution, the American Civil War was inevitable and almost broke America in two. It remains to this day America's most bloody war. However, it would impart upon America a tendency to see fighting for the freedom of others as a legitimate military and political end. This, combined with America's full embrace of the Industrial Revolution, would have important implications for the future.

2

The dominance of the English colonies in America left the Americans free to develop unmolested by other European powers.

European conquest of North America by the European dictators was a contest of competing claims and colonies. Spanish claims were based upon the Papal bull of 1493 dividing the New World between Spain and Portugal, as well as the exploration of Florida by de Leon (1513), the lower

Mississippi valley by de Soto (1539), and New Mexico by Coronado (1540). French claims were based upon the explorations of de Champlain (1608) and a colony in Quebec. The Dutch could point to Hudson (1624), colonies at New Amsterdam, and in Connecticut. Sweden had a small settlement in Delaware (1638). The English, too, had colonies at Jamestown (1607) and Plymouth (1620). The Anglican persecution of the Puritans who desired to "purify" the Church of England inspired many to settle in what was now called New England. Over 1,000 settlers arrived by 1630 in Massachusetts Bay. By the early 1640s, 20,000 had arrived. The religious conformity, high educational level, and basic desire to permanently settle and not plunder made this the most successful colonization effort in North America. Catholics, too, unhappy with their situation in England started moving to Maryland in 1633.

The English civil war and Interregnum left the colonies in a state of benign neglect. As long as they obeyed the trade restrictions of the Navigation Acts, Cromwell paid little attention to the colonies. Nevertheless, events in Europe impeded upon the colonies from time to time. When the Anglo-Dutch War of 1664 began, a concerted effort was made to eliminate the Dutch New Netherlands. The Duke of York secured an English charter claiming the entire Hudson valley. In the fall of 1664, Richard Nicolls captured New Amsterdam, later New York, Fort Orange, later Albany, and the Dutch possessions elsewhere. The Dutch had already eliminated New Sweden in 1655, and this was included in the English conquests. When monarchy returned to England in 1660, an effort was made to make the colonies serve the Empire and after the Glorious Revolution the pattern continued. By 1700, royal charters had replaced older charters of monopoly in Massachusetts, New York, New Jersey, Pennsylvania, and Maryland.

English policy toward immigration facilitated the population growth of its colonies.[19] France was by now the only other major colonial compet-

---

[19] Unfortunately the growth of the slave trade followed the increasing population and demands of commerce. Parliament in 1697 ended the monopoly of the Royal African Company resulting in worsening treatment of transported slaves and an increase in shipments. By the mid 18th century an estimated 70,000 forcibly left Africa each year. Most ended up elsewhere in the New World, while approximately 5% went to the English Colonies.

itor in the region, and it had strict laws requiring political and religious loyalty. England basically could have cared less. It is estimated by 1763 only 50% of the population was English in origin. The rest were Scotch, Scot-Irish, African, German, and Dutch. Toleration of religious differences was necessary to absorb the diversity of peoples and this toleration also aided in gaining new immigrants. Persecuted minorities from Europe came including Quakers, Huguenots, Mennonites, and Amish. War in Europe also encouraged new colonists, particularly from western Germany. Indentured servitude provided a means for the relatively poor to cross the Atlantic and England sent 50,000 criminals to Georgia for a limited period of time starting in 1732. By 1763 the English colonies had over two million inhabitants while New France had less than 100,000.

Gradually the European balance-of-power wars began to impinge upon the colonies.[20] King William's War (1688 – 1697) mostly impacted the colony of New York as France was planning an invasion of New York as a way to split the English colonies. France tried to form an alliance with Indians, but the Iroquois would have no part of it, and the plans were abandoned. The colonists sent a small naval expedition to Canada with little effect. When Queen Anne's War (1701 – 1714) broke out the Iroquois were neutral, and their neutrality kept New York safe, but the same could not be said for New England. The Algonquin Indians conducted numerous raids against New England towns and outposts. Any request for aid from England fell upon deaf ears, and the colonists organized counter-attacks on their own capturing Port Royal in Nova Scotia. By the time of King George's War (1740 – 1748) the colonial response was more organized. Under the leadership of Sir Peter Warren they captured the fortress of Louisbourg in 1745.

The colonists began to see how their interests were being subordinated to the British Empire when the Louisbourg fort was returned to France in exchange for the Madras in India. When the French and Indian War (1756 – 1763) began, the British and American interests were clearly different. Virginia and Canada were nearly at war already in 1755. Governor

---

[20] The names listed here are those the American Colonists used. They are more generally known as the Nine Year War, the War of Spanish Succession, the War of Austrian Succession, and the Seven Year War already discussed in a previous chapter.

Dinwiddie sent the young George Washington to the base of the Ohio River to request a French withdrawal. Instead he and his force of 200 militiamen surrendered near Fort Duquesne. When William Pitt became prime minister in 1757, he made a point to attack the French in North America. The year 1759 saw British victories at Fort Louisbourg and Fort Duquesne. In 1759 Niagara and Ticonderoga fell. The British captured Quebec on 18 September 1759, and Montreal fell in 1760.

In the past the British would make concessions to the colonists to gain their cooperation, but since the British did all the heavy lifting in the French and Indian war, they felt differently. The Treaty of Paris (1763) gave Britain sole control of all of North America east of the Mississippi River making it the dominant power in North America. However, it upset the colonists when the Proclamation of 1763 restricted their colonization efforts to east of the Appalachian Mountains. The Boundary Proclamation only proved how out of touch London was by demanding the return of those currently living past the boundary. In 1771 the Proclamation was modified to allow for settlement along the Ohio River between Pittsburg and the Kentucky River, but this too was a moot point as the colonists ignored the British restrictions and continued their western expansion.

3

Under the British policy of benign neglect the American colonies became a democracy training ground.

When originally constituted, the American colonies started as commercial joint-stock companies or proprietary companies. Charters of either type were always issued by the King. Originally this was colonization on the cheap. By contrast Spanish or French colonies came with the trappings of royal rule including an immediate colonial bureaucracy. When it became clear to London the colonies were too independent, the old charters were gradually replaced. By 1776, nine of the thirteen colonies had royal charters. The King appointed governors of the nine royal colonies, while the four others required royal approval. Each colony was required to have an elected lower assembly much like the House of Commons. After the acquisition of

Nova Scotia, the local British authorities established a governor and council as their form of government, and they were forced to establish an elected lower chamber. Local protests claiming the French Acadians knew nothing of representative government fell on deaf ears.

Since each colonial government had a governor as the royal representative and a royal council acting much as the House of Lords, there was constant tension between the governor and his council and the lower chamber elected by the people. These lower chambers took as their model the House of Commons. The members always had a keen awareness of the history of the struggle between the King and Parliament. The governor with his council acted as both chief executive and supreme judicial authority in the colony, but in rare cases, an appeal could be made to the Privy Council in London. One peculiar feature of colonial government was each colony had a written constitution. This was in stark contrast with Britain. The British government was ruled by tradition and specific documents like the Bill of Rights passed by Parliament in 1689. It never had an all-encompassing constitution. Thus the American Colonies represented the most advanced version of the Free Society. With the governor as the King's representative, each colony was a mini-version of a Constitutional Monarchy.

The appointed governors tended to act more like ambassadors—afraid to overstep their mandate from the crown—and in general they had no active political agenda of their own. The representative assembly, however, took every opportunity to expand its authority at the expense of the governor. All colonies, with the exception of Virginia, set the governor's salary. The assemblies demanded the power to raise or lower taxes, and once acquired, kept taxes low. This made colonial governments small, a tradition continuing after the revolution. As early as the 1680s, assemblies initiated their own legislation. They supervised the expenditure of taxes with their own treasurers. A majority of adult white males voted in representative districts, a method for selection of representatives not currently in use in Britain for Members of Parliament. In 1724 the Solicitor General in England ruled colonists could only be taxed by their own assemblies or Parliament. A governor in his frustration would remind the assemblies he had the power to dissolve them, but prior to 1763 it was never done. Governors had a choice to either fight with the assemblies and get unwanted attention from the crown, or simply live and let live. The American colonies had become a democracy training ground, and in addition had the blessing of being a colony of the European power furthest down the road to the Free Society.

4

As in Britain, America had a strong merchant community. In addition it had the unique frontier, which supported free institutions in a like manner. The westward expansion made America the dominant power in North America alleviating the need for a large standing army.

The merchant community, so dependent upon maritime trade and so important to the Free Society, was driven by shipping. Access to cheap wood enabled New Englanders to build ships 20% to 50% cheaper than in Europe, and by 1760 one third of the British merchant fleet was built in America. The British government encouraged this activity since all sources of wood products from America made them less dependent upon supplies from across the English Channel. During the same period New Englanders had become the most skilled whalers in the world. The surplus of the accumulated capital in trade then stimulated the manufacturing sector. The Board of Trade, the body responsible for regulation of colonial activity in this area, demanded of governors the details of colonial manufacturing. New Hampshire produced better linen than the Irish imported variety, and South Carolina refined its own sugar. Some industries received British subsidies for hemp products or for the development of naval stores. American economic growth outpaced Europe. In 1700 America was only 5% relative to England's economic output, but by 1775 she was at 40%. England had grown a healthy 25% over the same period.

The American frontier contributed to keeping the pre-industrial society in the colonies from evolving into a pyramid like shape. Over time land typically becomes gradually more concentrated as part of the positive feedback concentrating government power. This could not happen in the American colonies since the supply of new land was always available, and a peasant class working large estates could not form. This was the first time in human history large amounts of cheap land became available to the average man. Only in the South where slavery was used to work large tobacco plantations did the more traditional form of the pre-industrial society begin to emerge.

The frontier was a feature of America dominating her history for the next 200 years. It was common to see waves of immigrants coming from Europe driven by particular circumstances. The wave of Ulster Protestants and lowland Scots in the 1720s to 1750s is an example. They came in large numbers, driven by a ban on wool exports to England from Ireland, a new enforcement policy of tithes to the Church of England, and the expiration of Ulster plantation leases (1714 – 1718). Directed by colonial authorities, they founded towns like Blanchford, settled in Grafton county, New Hampshire and various counties in Vermont. Upwards of 500,000 souls left those specific areas in Europe to settle in specific areas in America.

The American frontier continued to march west after the American Revolution. The territorial expansion took place in several major jumps. The first was the initial grant of territory in 1783 extending to the Mississippi River. The second was the 1803 Louisiana Purchase. Since every major western river ran through Spanish territory, it was of serious economic concern to the Americans they have direct access to the Gulf of Mexico. Meanwhile Europe was engaged in the Napoleonic Wars, and Napoleon had dreams of a vast new French North America. By the treaty of San Ildefonso, France gained some Spanish New World territory in exchange for the promise of the Italian Throne to the brother-in-law of the Spanish King. The territory France acquired included a huge tract of land west of the Mississippi. However, as Napoleon was always short of cash, he offered America the territory for $15 million. The American President Jefferson (1743 – 1826) sent James Monroe (1758 – 1831) with instructions to pay $10 million to France to seal the deal. The treaty was signed in May 1803 at the price of $15 million or 13 cents an acre. The Mexican-American War (1846 – 1848) was the next major territorial expansion. With the purchase of Spanish Florida in 1819 and the small Gadsden Purchase in 1854, the continental United States or "lower 48" was complete. The final big jump was the American purchase from Russia of Alaska in 1867 called "Seward's

Folly" as Secretary of State Seward arranged for the United States to pay $7.2 million for the new territory.

The frontier kept America's pre-industrial society from forming into the classic pyramid shape partially due to policies adopted by the central government. Rather than retaining the land for its own purpose, perhaps renting the land to farmers as China did, America kept with its concept of a small government and gave the land away. The Homestead Act of 1862 was an important part of Lincoln's 1860 Republican platform, and it also represented continuation of a tradition already established earlier in the country's history.[21] Under its provisions, a farmer could get the title to 160 acres of public land after six months of occupation paying $1.50 per acre or nothing after five years. This accelerated the pace of westward expansion. Two states entered the Union during the Civil War: Kansas in 1861 and Nevada in 1864. The large scale ownership of land created a free market for the commodity, something not existing in Europe or any other major civilization at the time. The central government used this land for other developmental purposes. The Morris Land Grant Act of 1862 helped States create agricultural colleges with Federal funds raised from land sales. The shifting center of population of the United States showed how quickly the people moved west to settle the frontier. Baltimore was the center in 1790, but by 1840 it had crossed the Appalachians near Clarksburg West Virginia, and by 1890 the center of population, was in the Midwestern state of Indiana.

5

The novel approach to religion preserved civic virtue in a way not anticipated at the time of America's founding and highlights a larger point. Namely, both faith and reason tend to operate for the good in a Free Society but become corrupted in the service of the dictator.

The role of private religious convictions impacting the public life of the nation has a long history in America. There was the concern the new

---

[21] One might add this was a good wartime strategy. It was important to ensure the west was settled by free states as fast as possible not knowing the final disposition of slavery while the civil war progressed.

Republic would not have a large enough pool of public-minded individuals putting the good of the nation first. In past republics such public-minded individuals would come from the top levels of society as history recorded for the Roman Republic. As it turned out, public virtue would come from the bottom levels of society. This was important for a reason the founders could not foresee. The control of religion by the Hereditary Dictatorship was a source of values, but there needed to be another source of meaning and values in a Free Society. The voluntary religious devoutness from the bottom ranks of society fulfilled this role. The religious revival movement, the abolitionist movement, and the civil rights movement are three examples of this religiosity.

The best early example of a religious revival movement was called the Great Awakening (1730 – 1760) beginning on the American frontier when William Tennent (1673 – 1747) established his Log College for the instruction of preachers. Various preachers were identified with the movement including Gilbert Tennent (1703 – 1764) a graduate of his father's school, Jonathan Edwards (1703 – 1758), and George Whitefield (1714 – 1770). The younger Tennent was a Presbyterian Minister who so roused his congregations they called themselves New Light Presbyterians to separate themselves from the less enthusiastic. Edwards was from Massachusetts and called for a return to the religion of their fathers. Whitefield, an English Anglican cleric, was a speaker without equal in his inspiring oratory. The Awakening was advanced by strong emotional sermons and best selling pamphlets. As a movement it was the first colony-wide phenomenon and gave all colonists a sense they were all Americans.

When Europeans visited America they were always struck by the voluntary religiosity in the absence of government coercion. Alexis de Tocqueville (1805 – 1859) was a Frenchman of noble birth whose family had suffered under the French Revolution. His parents were jailed and his maternal grandfather guillotined, but Tocqueville was nonetheless personally drawn to democratic ideals. He saw them as inevitable and was interested in how these ideals could harmoniously be wedded to the societies of Europe. It was not *if* democracy was coming to Europe but *when*. He and his friend, Gustave de Beaumont, were sent to America to study its prison system in May

1831. He came to America when Andrew Jackson (1767 – 1845) became President and the so-called Jacksonian Democracy was about to start.

Tocqueville had come to American during the Second Great Awakening, another religious revival occurring in the first half of the 19th century, and he was impressed America had such intense fondness for religion. In his own country he saw piety without sincerity and the Church losing ground. Both Protestants and Catholics in America were more sincere and less legalistic in practice than in Europe. After his return to France in February of 1832, Tocqueville produced the required report in 1833. Then in 1835 he began publishing in parts his general observations of the country, *Democracy in America*. In his analysis, democracy in America was an encouragement to religion and not an impediment as many in Europe feared.

The second example, the Abolitionist movement, did not begin in America. Initially the voices for slavery's elimination were stronger in Europe. Charles de Montesquieu, the French Enlightenment philosopher, argued in 1748 since slaves were human beings no true Christian could be a slaveholder. Adam Smith, a Scottish Enlightenment philosopher famous for his theories in economics, denounced slavery in his *Theory of Moral Sentiments* in 1759. John Wesley, the founder of the Methodist Christian denomination, denounced the conditions of slaves in 1774. By 1792 the abolitionist movement could present petitions with 400,000 signatures to Parliament calling for its ban. On 25 March 1807, the British slave trade became illegal. The complete abolition of slavery in British colonies passed Parliament on 29 August 1833.

This strong religious foundation of the Abolitionist movement was continued in America, and hints of it could be found in early America. The Pennsylvania colony had many features later incorporated as part of the future American government. Under the Quaker William Penn, they had a written constitution, provisions for limited government, and guarantees of fundamental rights. The American Quaker Anthony Benezet wrote an attack upon the practice of slavery in 1754 and called for its abolition in 1772.

The American Quaker opposition to slavery never ended, as exemplified by Benjamin Franklin's (1706 – 1790) proposal to Congress for the abolition of slavery in 1790. While the Congress complied with the Constitution and ended the slave trade in January of 1808, they had already signaled their willingness to support slavery when they passed the Fugitive Slave Law of 1793. The abolitionist movement needed a leader in America, and he was William Garrison (1805 – 1879). His newspaper, *The Liberator,* first came out in January of 1831 calling for immediate emancipation at a time the southern states were making speaking or writing about abolition illegal. Garrison traveled to England and brought back George Thompson, a British abolitionist, to help organize the movement in America. In December of 1833, over sixty abolitionists including twenty-one Quakers, met in Philadelphia to found the American Anti-Slavery Society. As the movement grew, so did its opposition. When an abolitionist, Elijah Lovejoy was murdered in his Illinois home in November 1837, abolitionists across the country were shocked. A rally was organized in Faneuil Hall in Boston, called the Cradle of Liberty and the site of famous Revolutionary War speeches by Samuel Adams and John Hancock. After much debate Wendell Phillips, another famous abolitionist, gave a rousing call for both black emancipation and free speech.

The most famous of all the emancipation speakers was Frederick Douglas (1818 – 1895) an escaped slave who taught himself how to read and write. Garrison invited him to speak in Nantucket Massachusetts in 1839, and it was a turning point. Douglas would write his personal story in 1845 and travel the country spreading his emancipation message. Supporters raised the $1,250 demanded by his Maryland owner for his manumission to prevent possible capture by slave hunters in the North. He was then free of any legal return to the South, although he was never free from possible physical harm. The issue of slavery split many denominations including the Methodists and Baptists in the 1840s into Northern and Southern conferences. The 1840s saw another change. The clergy was beginning to speak out. It was a moral issue, and they were going to have their say.

Religious belief motivating social reform continued well into America's modern era. The civil rights movement of the 1950s and early 1960s had strong religious leadership from the Black community.[22] Martin L. King, Jr. (1929 – 1968) was the son of a pastor of the Ebenezer Baptist Church in Atlanta Georgia. He entered Morehouse College at the age of fifteen having not completed his senior year in High School. It was here on reading Henry D. Thoreau's essay, *On Civil Disobedience,* he first became acquainted with the ideas of non-violent resistance. He finished college at the age of 19 and entered the ministry like his father. On 8 May 1951 he received a divinity degree from Crozer Theological Seminary, and at the seminary he was profoundly influenced by the ideas of Mahatma Gandhi. Gandhi's ideas became the foundation of King's method to social reform. His Christianity was driving him also, and he finished a doctorate in systematic theology from Boston University in June 1955. He was by then a married man and the pastor of Dexter Baptist Church in Montgomery Alabama. It was from there he began to organize resistance to the segregation laws of the American South. He had hardly begun before his home was bombed on 30 January 1955.[23] Of the repeated acts of violence directed at him and his family he would say the more the outside pressure, the more the inner peace God gave him.

King was a masterful orator and skilled organizer. His leadership in the newly formed Southern Christian Leadership Conference was a focal point for organizing the protests. When a group of white Birmingham ministers wrote a letter to him while he was in a Birmingham jail to ask he tone down his activism, he responded. His famous reply was a passionate defense of Christian non-violent resistance to unjust laws. His method was to resist unjust laws openly, lovingly, and with acceptance of the penalty. This was all outlined in his *Letter from a Birmingham Jail.* King believed it was by God's love the movement would win. In his view, Jesus was an extremist of love. If people accused King of being an extremist then he felt he was in good company.

---

[22] The Jim Crow Laws of racial segregation were a perfect example of the tyranny of the majority and legislation based upon unjust powers. The African-American and the Native-American are good examples of how government power even in a democracy can be oppressive.

[23] As will be shown in a later chapter, the transition from the pre-industrial to the industrial society produces modern dictatorship movements. The collapse of the pre-industrial South and the rise of the KKK should be viewed in this light.

6

The successful American Revolution was made possible by both the armed citizenry and the balance-of-power politics of Europe.

The heavy cost of the French and Indian War led the British to impose taxes upon the American colonies. The American Revenue Act, commonly known as the Sugar Act, passed Parliament in 1764 and imposed a wide range of duties upon many goods including taxes upon imported molasses and refined sugar. As the assemblies had already claimed this power and had been exercising it for many years, this was bound to produce a conflict. Opposition to this tax motivated the Massachusetts House of Representatives to create a Committee of Correspondence to contact other American colonies. While the Sugar Act affected only maritime merchants, the Stamp Act passed in 1765 affected larger numbers of colonists as it imposed a tax upon all business paper, newspapers, pamphlets, and legal documents, even taxing playing cards. Violators were to be tried in vice-admiralty courts thus bypassing a jury trial. Petitions from several colonial legislatures reached London, including one from Virginia in which Patrick Henry argued without representation in Parliament the taxes were illegal. The proposal to meet in Massachusetts received acceptances from nine colonies, and this Stamp Act Congress drew up a Declaration of Rights and Grievances and sent it to Parliament. The Stamp Act was repealed after a vigorous Parliament debate including testimony from Benjamin Franklin, but unfortunately Parliament also passed the Declaratory Act simply stating Parliament did indeed have the power to tax the colonies.

A few years later in May 1773, Parliament passed the Tea Act to try to save the ailing East India Company by giving it a monopoly of the colonial tea trade. Several colonial cities prevented the ships from selling their cargo. In Boston, rebels dressed up like Mohawk Indians dumped the tea from the three ships into the bay. The British reaction to the Boston Tea Party was strong as the British viewed this as proof they had been too lax. In 1774 Parliament passed five colonial measures known collectively as the Coercive Acts. Passed to punish the Massachusetts Colony, the port of Boston was closed, their charter of 1691 was in essence revoked, and town meetings were banned. The Quebec Act passed at the same time expanded the territory of Quebec into the Ohio River valley, an area already claimed by Virginia, causing many Virginians to go over to the rebel cause. While the Coercive Acts stiffened colonial resolve, the Quebec Act gave the Canadian Catholics more rights than they enjoyed in Britain and kept them loyal to the Empire.

The First Continental Congress, composed of twelve colonies, met in 1774 to draft a response. In its Declaration of Rights and Resolves the Congress rejected the Coercive Acts, the Quebec Act, and all other Acts since 1763 as well as denouncing the use of the vice-admiralty courts and the stationing of British troops in towns. It created a Continental Association to boycott British goods. Nonetheless, the colonies stayed loyal subjects of the King blaming his incompetent ministers. They agreed to meet in May 1775 if Britain did not repeal the acts.

In March 1775 Parliament passed the New England Restraining Act a severe economic blow to the New England Colonies as it restricted trade to only Britain and the British West Indies. When General Gage ordered the capture of Samuel Adams and John Hancock at Lexington and the capture of possible arms in Concord, the actual armed revolt was about to begin. The famous ride of Paul Revere warned the minutemen of the invading British troops. Captain John Parker commanded a force of seventy Minutemen and met the redcoats on 19 April 1775. Only one redcoat was wounded and the British made their way to Concord where they met the stiff resistance of hundreds of armed farmers at Concord's north bridge. Having failed in both missions, the British made a speedy retreat. Harried by colonists from behind trees and walls, the retreat almost became a rout until they met a force of 1,400 fellow soldiers sent as reinforcements. The Battle of Lexington and Concord cost the British seventy-three killed and 213 wounded or missing. The minutemen suffered ninety-nine casualties in all. It was a small but significant victory for it proved the colonists, the citizen soldiers, could defeat the professional army of the British.

At first the initiative was with the Americans. The Massachusetts Provisional Congress appointed Artemas Ward commander of the militia, and he was able to raise 9,000 troops and begin the siege of occupied Boston. A force under Benedict Arnold (1741–1801) from Massachusetts and Ethan

Allen (1738 – 1789) from Vermont both had the same goal—the capture of Fort Ticonderoga on Lake Champlain. The combined force took the fort and its garrison on 10 May 1775. Colonel Henry Knox (1750 – 1806) moved the captured cannons and mortars to Massachusetts where they were used to force the evacuation of the British.

When Congress reconvened in May 1775, news of the Battle of Lexington and Concord had already reached the members. On the 10th of June they designated the forces surrounding the British in Boston the Continental Army, and on the 15th they appointed George Washington (1732 – 1799) the Commander-in-Chief of the Army. Thomas Paine (1737 – 1809) published his pamphlet *Common Sense* in January 1776. The pamphlet was read throughout the colonies and argued both against monarchy in general and King George III in particular.

When on 7 June 1776 Richard H. Lee of Virginia proposed a draft resolution of independence be written, a committee was formed with John Adams (1735 – 1826), Benjamin Franklin, and Thomas Jefferson plus two others. The committee appointed Jefferson with the task of writing the document, and with a few modifications, the American Declaration of Independence was adopted on 4 July 1776. After this Declaration it was impossible to believe the Americans were not going to establish a republic should they win the war. During the late 1770s each colony re-wrote its constitution as a free republic. If the Americans could win their revolution, they would establish the first major self-governing nation anywhere in the world.

The first British strategy to emerge was to split the colonies and then concentrate on New England and Boston. General Burgoyne was to march from Canada while General Howe was to march up from New York. Washington would be caught in a pincer maneuver, and the British could concentrate upon an isolated New England. Aiding in this effort was a third smaller force from Lake Ontario following the Mohawk River. Luckily for the Americans, the complete plan never took place as the other two forces proceeded as planned, but Howe, thinking he could end the war by capturing George Washington and the rebel capital of Philadelphia, marched south.

General Burgoyne marched south with 7,000 men in June 1777 from Canada down Lake Champlain and toward the Hudson River capturing Fort

Ticonderoga on June 30th and later Fort Anne to the south. While he was making slow progress toward his objective, the other pincer departed Lake Ontario along the Mohawk River toward Fort Stanwix. By August the 1,800 British force lay siege to the fort defended by 750 Americans. Two relief expeditions were sent to the fort. The first was defeated in the Battle of Oriskany, but the second under Arnold was successful, and the British retreated to Ontario. Of the original three pincers in the attack, only one pincer was left.

The Battle of Saratoga was two separate engagements. In the first, fought on 19 September 1777, the British attacked an American position on Bemis Heights. Riflemen under the command of General Daniel Morgan repulsed their attack. Since frontiersmen were usually good shots, these citizen soldiers concentrated their fire, on the British and Hessian officers, and Burgoyne's army sustained heavy losses. The second battle began on 7 October and, in a repeat, the British attacked American positions. As before the British were forced to retreat. Under the command of Arnold, the Americans pursued the British and surrounded them, and the entire British force surrendered on 17 October.

The Battle of Saratoga was a tremendous victory for the Americans. It proved to the world betting on the Americans was a long shot—but perhaps odds worth taking. Franklin was in Europe in the first part of 1778 making this case. The French agreed and made an alliance with the Americans in June. Spain would declare war on the British the next year. In 1780 the British declared war on the Dutch to forestall any Dutch support to the rebels. The Americans were gradually becoming a lesser concern of the British as they had to worry about a possible channel crossing and the loss of other colonial possessions. The Revolution was becoming tangled up in the balance-of-power politics of Europe, and thus all the Americans had to do was hold on.

The British approach shifted after Saratoga to a southern strategy. The British felt frustrated with their attempts to defeat and capture George Washington who they started calling the "sly fox." They hoped that, with the loyalist sympathies more pronounced in the southern colonies, the capture of major southern cities would rally the loyalists to the British cause. General Henry Clinton (1730 – 1795) who replaced Howe would implement the strategy. In November 1778 Clinton sent a force of 3,000 men to capture Savannah. By January 1779, British forces had captured Augusta. In December 1779 Clinton led an 8,000 man force into South Carolina and with a combined force of 14,000 captured Charleston on 12 May 1780. Leaving General Cornwallis (1738 – 1805) with his 8,000 men in South Carolina, Clinton then returned to New York hoping to confront Washington. Although the southern cities were secured with British troops, they faced constant harassment along their supply lines by American irregular forces another example of how important the citizen soldier was to the war's final outcome.

Determined to join forces with American loyalists, in April 1781, Cornwallis moved north into Virginia. With a force of 7,500 he made camp at Yorktown. The decision appeared a reasonable one as they constructed an elaborate series of redoubts and trenches, and they could be confident the British navy would ensure their resupply. Washington meanwhile was negotiating with the French about a possible attack upon New York. The meeting took place in Wethersfield Connecticut in May of 1781. The attack would include a French fleet sailing up from the French West Indies to combine with other French naval forces. The orders were vague and in August 1781 the French fleet arrived at Chesapeake Bay rather than New York. The New York attack was called off as Washington learned of Cornwallis's encampment. Washington left a sufficient force behind at New York to make Clinton believe he was still there, and with a combined force of 8,000 French and 11,000 Americans he put Cornwallis under siege. This was one of the few times the Americans had a solid numerical advantage over the British.

Out in Chesapeake Bay, the French fought against the British on 5 September 1781 in the Battle of Chesapeake Bay Capes. Although militarily a draw, the British ships were badly damaged. When the French Admiral Barras arrived from Newport Rhode Island, the British Admiral Graves was numerically outnumbered and sailed to New York for repairs as he apparently did not appreciate Cornwallis's situation. The French and Americans had gradually been carving away at Cornwallis's defensive position. Cornwallis became convinced of the hopelessness of the situation when Lt. Colonel Alexander Hamilton (1755 – 1804) and his men overran redoubt number ten on 14 October. On 17 October the British raised the white flag. At first the British tried to surrender to the French but the French sent them over to the Americans. Cornwallis surrendered to the combined French and American army on 19 October 1781, five days before a relief force of 7,000 sent by Clinton was about to arrive. The Americans received Cornwallis's sword, and although George Washington could not have known it at the time, the Americans had won their Revolutionary War. With major British troop concentrations in Charleston, Savannah, Wilmington, and New York, peace negotiations began, and in the Treaty of Paris (1783) the British recognized American Independence.

7

The new American experiment was an embodiment of the Enlightenment ideas of Locke, Montesquieu, and Smith.

The world had decidedly changed in the twenty years between the two Treaties of Paris. A large nation dedicated to some specific principles had won its Revolutionary War and was now free. One might think in some ways the Free Society had suffered a setback. How could a war between the only two large nations on the path to the Free Society be a positive step for freedom? But it was. Britain recovered quickly after the conflict. The merchant community did not support the war and neither did other supporters of the Free Society in Britain. After the war, Adam Smith was a welcome guest at 10 Downing Street, the residence of the Prime Minister, and his free trade ideas put an end to Mercantilism as Britain was on the verge of the Industrial Revolution. The Hereditary Dictatorships had hoped their support of America would hurt Britain, but instead, their situation was made worse by the war. Spain did not get Gibraltar has she had hoped, although Florida was returned. France was much worse off with huge debt and no territorial gains as French Canada stayed with Britain. Not only did Britain recognize her independence, but the Treaty of Paris (1783) also gave America domain over all territory east of the Mississippi River and north to the Great Lakes except for Florida and a small strip along the Gulf of Mexico.

When Washington resigned his commission before the Congress on 23 December 1783, he was already well aware his actions would set the tone for the new Republic. Most of the leaders of the revolt were familiar with the history of Athens and Rome, and Washington's actions were an attempt to imitate Cincinnatus, a Roman hero who was a model of virtue and public service. It also probably helped matters Washington did not need the commission to support himself. The Congress was meeting in Annapolis, and after his resignation he rode off to Mount Vernon where he planned to enjoy a comfortable retirement. The Articles of Confederation were first proposed in 1776, but not until 1781 did all colonies adopt the measure. The Articles were weak and left many issues unresolved for the young Republic.

Virginia and Maryland were in a disagreement over customs along the Potomac River. Washington volunteered to mediate the dispute and invited delegates to his Mount Vernon estate. When Congress ratified the agreement, James Madison (1751 – 1836) proposed a general conference be held by all the states to address these issues in a more comprehensive fashion. Only five states attended the conference at Annapolis in September 1786. Hamilton prepared the conference report and repeated the call for all states to attend a conference at Philadelphia to propose modifications to the Articles of Confederation. Congress approved the report and issued its own call for a convention. On 25 May 1787, delegates opened the convention and selected George Washington as president of the proceedings. The delegates agreed to keep the proceedings secret for twenty years to enable everyone to speak freely. It did not take long before they all came to the conclusion the Articles should be discarded, and they would write a new constitution from scratch.

The delegates were in basic agreement the new government would be divided into three powers—legislative, executive, and judiciary—and be strong enough to correct the weaknesses of the Articles of Confederation. It was said at the time the Declaration of Independence was based upon Locke, and the new constitution was based on Montesquieu using the checks and balances he proposed.

The Virginia plan introduced by Madison formed the basis of the discussion. It had a bicameral legislature with the lower house elected directly by the people and an upper chamber elected from the lower. It had a strong central government empowered to nullify state laws. To some of the delegates, it was the exact same thing they had rebelled against. An alternative, called the New Jersey plan, proposed a legislature with equal representation for each state. The Great Compromise, as it was called, created an upper chamber called the Senate composed of two representatives from each State and a lower chamber called the House of Representatives created by direct vote of the people. To make "no taxation without representation" a reality, the lower house had the sole power to initiate bills on taxes and appropriations. With a President elected by popular vote, although indirectly, the delegates created a strong executive position. With the slavery issue avoided, the Constitutional Convention concluded its work on 17 September 1787 and sent its report to Congress. Congress sent it to the States for ratification on 25 September 1787. It was then up to the people.

The debate on the Constitution was between Federalists who supported ratification and the Anti-Federalists who opposed it. Prominent revolutionaries were on both sides. Newspapers and pamphlets proliferated to make each side's case. Three important Federalists, Hamilton, Madison, and John Jay (1745 – 1829), argued for ratification in a series of newspaper essays, later published as a book titled the *Federalist Papers*. Anti-federalists like Patrick Henry, John Hancock, James Monroe, and Samuel Adams argued against ratification. The public sentiment generally favored a stronger central government, but the Anti-Federalists had raised important questions. How were the rights of the people and the States to be protected from federal power? The British had their Bill of Rights, but where was America's Bill of Rights? As part of the discussion a new element, individual rights, was added. What protected the minority from the arbitrary abuse of the legislative majority? People had rights even against their own representatives.

A public consensus emerged: a Bill of Rights, as amendments to the new Constitution, would be the first order of business for the new Congress. A cynic might argue these contentious Americans barely had adopted their Constitution before they started modifying it. This would be a concern if, for every political issue, the Constitution would be constantly amended—but this was not what happened. When the first Congress of the United States met, Madison drew up twelve amendments for consideration. Massachusetts would make their ratification of the Constitution legally contingent upon these amendments being submitted to the States.

Delaware was the first to ratify, while Rhode Island waited until May 1790. Ten amendments were ratified on 15 December 1791 and became law. A tacit assumption furthering the ratification of the Constitution was George Washington would be its first President. When he was sworn in on 30 April 1789, the experiment had begun.

Luckily for America no existential crisis would confront the new Republic. New Connecticut, which remained neutral during the Revolutionary War, entered the Union as Vermont in 1791 after New York and New Hampshire dropped any territorial claims. The new State of Kentucky entered in 1792, the first from the new territories out west. Washington, again following the precedence of Cincinnatus, refused to run for a third term, setting a tradition lasting for 140 years. Most importantly, a peaceful transition of power occurred when Thomas Jefferson from the opposition party became President in 1801. All the early signs had the experiment off to a good start.

The only part of the United States Constitution evolving over time more like the British model was the role of the judiciary. The Americans had inherited English common law, and it was a creature of gradual change through judicial rulings. The man to solidify the judiciary as the solid third branch of government was John Marshall (1755 – 1835) the Chief Justice of the Supreme Court for thirty-four years. A commanding force on the bench, Marshall handed down 1,100 rulings, 519 authored by himself during his tenure. He quickly established the supremacy of the Court in the Marbury versus Madison ruling in 1803. In this ruling the Court declared itself the final arbiter of state and federal legislation. In the event of a conflict between legislation and the Constitution, the Constitution was the supreme law of the land. The Court had the power to declare laws unconstitutional—a phrase not actually appearing in the Constitution. The Constitution had certain implied powers of which this power by the Supreme Court was one. The Constitution was something "organic," "capable of growth," and "susceptible to change."[24]

---

[24] Ultimately this could become a pernicious doctrine. A document difficult to amend by the popular will but easily changed with the interpretation of unelected judges could undermine the entire democratic process. Tocqueville would remark how everything in America would take on a judicial aspect to it.

The pre-industrial society did not trust the new kinds of property needed in the Industrial Revolution. John Taylor (1753 – 1824) was a Virginia Senator and convinced of the superiority of land over other types of property. In his 700 page book, *An Inquiry into the Principles and Policy of the United States*, Taylor attacked "artificial property" with banks as a major villain. He compared credit to the feudal powers of King and Church leading to the eventual establishment of a feudal society in America. The paper of banks and the stocks of companies were "fictitious" property. Southerners in particular, already further along in the creation of a pre-industrial pyramid type society, were most sympathetic to Taylor's ideas.

Fearful of a mob mentality after reading Burke's *Reflections on the Revolution in France* and a strong adherent of Adam Smith, Marshall would have none of it. In the 1810 Fletcher v. Peck ruling and many others he would defend private property and contracts. The Gibbons v. Ogden (1824) ruling prevented States from creating private monopolies. In 1819 Marshall issued three different rulings protecting private property rights. Sturges v. Crowninshield struck down state laws in bankruptcy because they violated private contracts. Dartmouth College v. Woodward established that a corporate charter was private and not subject to state legislative interference. McCulloch v. Maryland ruled the Congress had the power to create a national bank and a State could not tax such an enterprise. This last ruling infuriated John Taylor. In his view it enshrined artificial property in the Constitution and this is exactly what Marshall wanted. His determined defense of private property and contracts would make the legal environment in America well disposed to the coming Industrial Revolution.

8

The French Revolution is a prime example of the dangers of the concentration of government power. Despite the good intentions of the revolutionaries to use government power to make a just society, it ended in the dictatorship of Napoleon.

In some ways the American Revolution led directly to the French Revolution. The American war was costly and had left the French monarchy deeply in debt. The ideals of the American Revolution embodied the ideals of the Enlightenment, and the French public, including many nobles, were enthusiastic regarding the American cause. It was only natural French citizens would ask when the American ideals would see some light of day in France.

Had the situation in France not already been so desperate, their involvement with the American Revolution would not have been enough to push them over the edge. When Louis XVI (1754 – 1793) could not raise sufficient revenue to meet the demands of government, he called the Assembly of Notables for help. He was hoping for a relaxation of traditional tax exemptions, including ecclesiastical, so as to fix the financial situation. The Assembly refused, somewhat dishonestly, saying these changes required the Estates General. The Estates General was an ancient assembly representing each class, the aristocracy, the clergy, and the peasants, with 300 members for each. When they met in May 1789, the aristocracy had expected the results to be controllable since, with the clergy, they had a 600 to 300 majority. The King however, responding to appeals from commoners, increased the Third Estate's representation to 600. One could reason the King did this because the nobles had already refused him before and, with such a lopsided majority, it would happen again. Once the Estates General met they could accomplish nothing. In their frustration, the Third Estate declared itself the National Constituent Assembly on 17 June 1789 and took the Tennis Court Oath on the 20th of June to refuse to disband until France had a written constitution. When a rumor began to circulate the King was about to disband the new assembly, the crowds of Paris stormed the Bastille Prison on 14 July 1789.

The National Assembly worked through the summer without fear of dismissal and was the de facto national government for the next two years. Their first act, Decrees Abolishing the Feudal System, passed in August 1789. Peasants throughout the countryside were elated, but not reading the fine print about waiting periods and landlord compensation, they began to seize property. The Decrees also provided for all citizens to be eligible for all offices regardless of birth. The next National Assembly action was to pass the Declaration of the Rights of Man and the Citizen in late August 1789 providing for many of the same rights in the American Bill of Rights. The final reform waited until September 1791 when the Assembly passed the new Constitution. This new government was technically a Constitutional Monarchy, but the king's powers were weak. It was at this time a new legislative assembly of 745 was elected. The Tennis Court Oath was finally fulfilled.

The Constitutional Monarchy operating under the Constitution of 1791 lasted one year. The major issue was who had the power to declare war. After much debate, and with the King's reluctant assent, the assembly declared war on Austria in April 1792. Prussia soon became Austria's ally. The revolutionaries expected to march into the Netherlands and liberate them from Austria, but control of the revolutionary crowds became increasingly more difficult. The King was deposed in September of 1792, and a National Convention was elected to write a constitution for the French Republic. The French victory at Valmy against the Prussians on 20 September 1792 provided the revolution the needed breathing room. The King eventually was put on trial for treason and guillotined in January 1793. This First French Republic would operate in some form until ended by Napoleon in 1804.

The revolutionaries began to do something never attempted in human history. They attempted to completely remake a society along ideological lines. The Enlightenment had two branches, and they followed the more atheistic, rationalistic branch. Reason, as they perceived it, would be their only guide. Consequently, the French Revolution became famous for its atrocities. Science is neutral in the struggle between good and evil, while reason cannot arrive at the values upon which a society is to be based. At the core of every value system is an irrational acceptance of certain basic assumptions. The goals of the French Revolution could not be accomplished because they were impossible. The French Revolution's utopianism was an omen of the ideologically driven future dictatorships of the 20th century.

The revolution took many steps to remake society into a so-called more rational mode. The new calendar was a simple example. The old calendar was replaced with one of twelve equal months of 30 days each. These 30 days were divided in decades of 10 days like a week. There was no advantage to the new calendar except it did away with vestiges of the old regime. The revolutionary calendar took effect 5 October 1793 and Year I had begun. A few reforms were reasonable, such as the adoption of the metric system in the same year, but many reflected the personal preferences of a particular revolutionary. For instance, the Cult of Reason was a favorite of Jacques Hebert. A strident atheist, he and others took over the Cathedral of Notre Dame in November 1793 during their Festival of Reason, but Hebert fell into disfavor with a main revolutionary leader, Maximilian de Robespierre (1758 – 1794), and was executed in March 1794.

The Cult of the Supreme Being was Robespierre's personal choice. The first Festival of the Supreme Being was held on 8 June 1794, the same day Pentecost would have been celebrated by Christians. Robespierre saw such worship as critical to the promotion of private virtue. The famous painter Jacques David, sometimes called by historians the "Dictator of the Arts," made all the preparations. His artwork depicted the Supreme Being as the sun. The festival began at dawn and by noon, with the sun at the apex, the National Convention led by Robespierre proceeded out to participate in the ceremony. Mothers raised any small children high into the air toward the sun while all pledged allegiance to the Supreme Being as represented by the sun.

Their goals may have appeared rational, but their governance was irrational and violent. The famous French Terror, from which the word *terrorist* came into the lexicon, began in the fall of 1793. Twelve men were selected for the Committee of Public Safety including the leader Robespierre. The revolution already had experienced mob violence, but Robespierre would make it more systematic as an organized state enterprise. From his assent to power to his death in July 1794, Robespierre would be responsible for the deaths of 40,000 French citizens. The Revolutionary Tribunal sent 17,000 to their death in Paris alone, and an additional 12,000 were executed in the provinces by the Committee's representatives. Much of the Terror's focus was enforcement of the 23 August 1793 *levee en masse* proclamation, a desperate measure to save the revolution. This proclamation required all men ages eighteen to twenty-four to join the army. All married men were required to make munitions and transport them to the front lines, all women were required to make uniforms and tents, while children made bandages. It was the first total mobilization of a society for war. The arrest of suspects was made easier by the Law of Suspects, passed in 17 September 1793, allowing arrest on virtually no evidence and resulted in over 300,000 arrests over the next year.

The area of Vendee in western France south of the Loire River was particularly hard hit as it was a center of resistance to the revolution. A scorched earth policy was employed destroying crops and killing livestock, and an estimated 250,000 or 25% of the population perished. In one particular incident, 1,665 people were forced to stand in front of a ditch forming a large grave and were shot by cannon. In another, people were forced onto boats in the Loire, which were sunk, drowning them in "revolutionary baptisms." In an eerie echo of the future, revolutionaries discussed a plan to put people into mines to gas them to death.

The terror intensified with the passage of the Law of 22 Preairial of Year II (10 June 1794) forcing all jurisdictions to ship suspects to Paris. It also limited appeals, defenses, and allowed for group sentencing to speed up the process. In one case, all sixty people at once were found guilty. Since the only sentence of the Revolutionary Tribunal was death, the body count went up quickly. In the Thermidor coup, Robespierre was overthrown and guillotined on 28 July 1794.

Napoleon Bonaparte (1769 – 1821), the future dictator, was born on the island of Corsica and educated at the Ecole Militaire in Paris. He entered the French army as a second lieutenant in the artillery believing in the cause of the French Revolution, and as a captain was given the artillery command of the siege of Toulon in 1793. When the port city was captured using his plan, he was promoted to brigadier-general. During the Vendemiaire coup of 1795, he was asked to defend the National Convention. They had proposed the Constitution of Year III creating a strong executive called the Directory. Many in Paris and France perceived this as a usurpation of the right to vote and attempted to take over the Convention. Napoleon deployed artillery in the city streets firing grapeshot point-blank into the crowds, and his troops were able to secure the city after the crowds had dispersed. Napoleon's brutal use of artillery against crowds of civilians made the government grateful, and he was soon a divisional general with command of all interior forces in France. The Directory was replaced in November 1799 by the Consulate, a three-man body, and Napoleon became First Consul in December. Executive power was increasingly concentrated and Napoleon took advantage of the situation. He became Consul for life in 1802 and on 2 December 1804 crowned himself Emperor of France.

The chronology of the Napoleonic wars revolves around the many alliances formed to oppose France. There were seven coalitions in all with Britain at war with France for well-nigh the entire time. The First coalition (1792 – 1797) began when France declared war on Austria. The last coalition ended when Napoleon was defeated, barely, at the Battle of Waterloo on 18 June 1815. During this time he accumulated power to himself until he was the unquestioned dictator.

Napoleon Bonaparte was the first dictator in history to conquer Europe. Had he not invaded Russia in 1812, he may have held on to his conquests. Military technology had advanced to the point the other impediments keeping Europe in a permanent warring states condition were overcome. Although he eventually lost because of the disastrous Russian invasion, every dictator going forward would try to imitate his example. The balance-of-power reestablished in the Congress of Vienna after the Napoleonic Wars by the Austrian diplomat Klemens von Metternich (1773 – 1859) and others could not last.

The Congress of Vienna (September 1814 – June 1815) was an attempt to restore the balance-of-power in Europe, and proof the historical baggage of Europe prevented a complete embrace of the Free Society. It was also guided by lesser objectives such as the obvious containment of France and the restoration of displaced dynasties. Compensation for physical losses as well as compensation for lost territory was part of the agreement. The Kingdom of Holland was expanded with the addition of the Austrian Netherlands, and neutral Switzerland was restored. Austria was given possession of northern Italy including Venice having already ended as a republic when Napoleon invaded in 1797. Denmark would give Norway to Sweden. Both dynasties of Spain and Portugal would be restored. As an aside, Great Britain attached a declaration against the slave trade. However, there was one genie the Congress could not put back into the bottle. Napoleon had proved it was now possible to conquer Europe. The possibility of a single European dynasty was now a reality with all the implications for the Free Society this would imply.

9

The American South shows how a pre-industrial society tends to take on a pyramid shape.[25] It is yet another example of how the Free Society cannot permanently survive in a pre-industrial setting.

More than the North, the South resembled the structure of a pre-industrial society. As early as the 1780s, 8% of the landowners controlled over a third of the land in Virginia, and the average size of a farm in the South was always larger than a farm in the North. Had the Industrial Revolution not occurred, when the frontier eventually closed the North would have fallen victim to the positive feedback mechanism concentrating government power and gradually would have looked more and more like the South.

A military caste was also developing. At the beginning of the civil war the South had several military academies to the single West Point in the North. Two of the most famous, the Virginia Military Institute (1839) and the Citadel (1842) in South Carolina, survived into the modern era. Like other pre-industrial societies, the landed-wealthy looked down upon commerce as an occupation, but for the ambitious a military career was a socially acceptable alternative. Alden Partridge, a West Point graduate and former superintendent, along with several former students, established dozens of private military academies in the country with most of them in the South. The military tradition of the South would extend after the Civil War when military style education was implemented as part of the land-grant colleges.

The same concentration can be found in data regarding slave ownership. While the Africans were about one third of the total population and had grown in size from one million in 1800 to about four million in 1860, only about 5% of whites owned slaves. Within this group, approximately 10% of slave owners held title to about half of all the slaves. Slavery was heavily concentrated in agriculture with 95% of all slaves working in agriculture and 50% of these working on large plantations. The pyramid shape of the pre-industrial society was exemplified in plantation districts. These districts would concentrate in areas suitable to the cash crop in question, and the presence

---

[25] This is sometimes called the Planter's Aristocracy.

of these large plantations tended to drive land prices up and small farmers out. Many sold their farms and moved west while some whites ended up as tenant farmers on plantation land. The slave population in these areas would be high, in some cases 90%.

Slavery density was unevenly distributed within states and between states. South Carolina was completely dominated, more than any other state, by the plantation system. It had a slave population representing 55% of the state followed by Louisiana at 50%. At the other end of the spectrum, northern boarder states had smaller black populations. Delaware had only 1.4% of its population enslaved, and Maryland and Missouri also had small slave populations. Slavery was equally paltry in certain northwestern counties of Virginia, which would later form the State of West Virginia.

Other than cotton the South had several cash crops, and these, too, supported the plantation system. Tobacco was mostly grown in Kentucky, Tennessee, North Carolina, and Virginia, and while originally an export crop in colonial days, was increasingly used for internal consumption. Large factories turned the leaf into finished products of snuff, chewing tobacco, and cigars in areas like Lynchburg and Richmond Virginia. Rice was a major product of plantations in South Carolina and Georgia. Its production, more than any other cash crop, needed the plantation system as it was both expensive and labor intensive to maintain the levies and dikes needed to protect the plants. Only the extremely wealthy grew rice. Sugar cane was restricted to those areas having long growing seasons and abundant rainfall, which mostly meant southern Louisiana and small areas of Texas and Florida. Over 90% of America's sugar came from Louisiana.

In a typical irony of history, it was the beginnings of the Industrial Revolution perpetuating the pre-industrial society of the South. Nothing compared to cotton. As visitors to the region would remark—they could not travel far without seeing cotton farming. Its productivity was improved in 1793 with the invention of the cotton gin. Invented by a Yankee, Eli Whitney, on a visit to a southern plantation, it made it easy to separate the cotton lint from the seed. A slave, who before 1793 took all day to make one pound of cotton fiber, could now produce fifty pounds in the same period of time, and so its production spread rapidly all over the South. Its increase in productivity dovetailed nicely with the industrialization of the textile industry, and Britain became a huge importer of American cotton. Exports to Britain grew by 130% between 1840 and 1860. While Britain constituted 50% of the South's production, Continental Europe consumed 25% and the remaining 25% went to the United States. US consumption was increasing more rapidly than Europe and grew 184% over the same period.

10

The American experiment was almost lost in the American Civil War. This war fixed in the American mind the idea fighting for the freedom of others was a legitimate military objective. With slavery abolished, the American Republic became the first Free Society.

The consequences of a successful separation of any group of States from the Union would have been a severe blow to the Free Society. It was always important for the Free Society to avoid a large standing army. The establishment of a militia in each state as well as the individual right to bear arms was both American law and tradition going back to the same right enunciated in the British Bill of Rights. An armed people and a small professional army were seen as the solution to possible abuses by a strong central government. The American experience with the British occupation validated this view. If the nation broke apart into multiple strong nations in North America, a strong standing army would become a necessity. Britain being an island had avoided this problem because it had a powerful navy to protect its freedom from foreigners. When the United States began to dominate North America, it created the same situation. With weak neighbors to the north and south, it became an island continent free of the need for a large standing army.[26]

The contradiction between the American Declaration that all men are created equal and the reality of American slavery was about to be resolved. The actual secessions began after Abraham Lincoln (1809 – 1865) was elected President, but before he took the oath of office. His simple election was enough to prompt the Slave States to leave. This was principally due

---

[26] By contrast Latin America was divided into numerous competing nations. The standing armies of each country would perpetually be involved in their politics.

to three factors: the Republican Party opposed the expansion of slavery into the territories, the Republican Party was dominated by abolitionists, and Lincoln had made numerous anti-slavery statements. His most famous quoted the Bible (Mark 3:25) "A house divided against itself cannot stand" when he was running for the Senate in 1858.

The first significant blood was spilled at the Battle of Bull Run (21 July 1861). Near Washington DC, it started out as a closely fought contest until a Union retreat turned into a rout. McDowell, the Union general, was soon replaced by George McClellan (1826 – 1885). The blockade got off to a better start as the improvements to mobility made possible by steam and the longer range of shell guns had reversed the advantages shore defenses normally had over a sea assault. Part of the Union strategy was to capture key coastal port cities. In North Carolina, Union troops captured Fort Hatteras in August 1861. In September, Ship Island, Mississippi was taken. The Union forces took Port Royal Sound (7 November 1861) and captured Forts Walker and Beauregard. The Union would continue to capture Confederate coastal areas for the entire length of the war.

Union General Ulysses S. Grant (1822 – 1885) with 20,000 troops and a fleet of gunboats attacked Fort Henry along the Tennessee River, and it fell on the 6th of February 1862. After he shifted his attacks to the Cumberland River, and captured Fort Donelson on the 16th, 13,000 Confederates surrendered to Grant. Kentucky was already in Union hands by this point, and General Buell of the Union was able to move out of Kentucky and toward Nashville. When Grant was promoted by Lincoln for his victories, William T. Sherman (1820 – 1891) fell under Grant's command, and this was a partnership that would work well for the Union throughout the war. In the South's midsection, Grant attacked Confederate General Beauregard in the Battle of Shiloh (11 April 1862). It was the largest battle of the war to date. Over 50,000 Union troops attacked 45,000 Confederates.

Robert E. Lee (1807 – 1870) was now in command of the South's army outside of Richmond. In June, Lee and McClellan met for the first time in a series of attacks launched by Lee. The largest and last engagement was Gaine's Mill (27 June 1862) where 57,000 Confederates attacked 34,000 Unions. Lee's victory convinced McClellan incorrectly Lee had numeric superiority in the entire Virginia theater, and McClellan ordered a retreat. In August, the Confederates maintained the initiative in the Second Battle of Bull Run (30 August 1862), and McClellan responded by engaging Lee at Antietam (17 September 1862) where Lee was outnumbered 75,000 to 36,000. Antietam, Maryland was in Union territory, making it vital for the Union to achieve victory. It would become the bloodiest single day in the entire Civil War with over 23,000 casualties on both sides. Lincoln used the slim victory to issue his Emancipation Proclamation (22 September 1862).

The Emancipation Proclamation was a short, lawyerly statement. Come 1 January 1863, any slave held in a State in rebellion against the Union would be free forever. Some of this was happening already. In May 1861, General Butler from the Massachusetts militia was at Fort Monroe where fugitive slaves escaped and crossed into Union lines. Butler maintained, as contraband of war, they should not be sent back. Butler's decision went all the way up to the Secretary of War for a final determination, and Butler's decision became Union policy. Lincoln was offering the South one last chance to keep their slaves as the Republican Party platform had maintained in 1860. The Republicans only wanted to restrict slavery in the territories. If the South stayed in rebellion, what they feared the North might do in the future would come true in January. When January came, a second proclamation was issued, and it not only freed slaves, but allowed service in Union military forces.

The Union was checked by Lee in the east but continued to make progress in the west in 1863. Lee struck first at the Battle of Chancellorsville (3 May 1863). Out west, Grant had put Vicksburg, the key to control of the Mississippi River, under siege. A force of 30,000 Southerners was surrounded by 70,000 Union soldiers. The Union victory at Liberty Gap (28 June 1863) made a Union assault against Chattanooga their next objective.

Lee, encouraged by his recent success, made preparations for an invasion of Pennsylvania and began his invasion with 80,000 men and 300 main artillery pieces. Lee and Meade met at Gettysburg Pennsylvania on 1 July 1863. The battle has long gone down in American history as one of its most famous. Fought before the 4th of July, the American National Holiday of Independence, the American experiment was only eighty-seven years old, and its future was in doubt. A decisive victory by Lee in Union territory might have had the political impact to end the war. However, Lee was repulsed and retreated while Meade's Union army, badly mauled, did not pursue. Casualties for the three days of combat totaled an astonishing 20,000 plus for each side. In the west, Vicksburg surrendered to Grant on 4 July. This was clearly the turning point of the war.

With the South split in two, Grant began to assemble a large force in November to begin a push into the South's center toward Dalton, Georgia. Sherman with 17,000 men, Thomas with 35,000, and Hooker with 20,000 forced the Confederacy to evacuate Tennessee, and Chattanooga was securely in Federal hands. About the same time, 19 November 1863, Lincoln gave the Gettysburg Address to dedicate a national cemetery at the site of the battlefield. It was a short stirring speech clearly reminding the nation what it was fighting for—the Free Society.

The first part of 1864 was characterized by major but temporary thrusts on both sides. Meanwhile Grant was appointed by Lincoln to command all 147,000 troops in northern Virginia including the 99,500 under Meade and 19,300 under Burnside. Sherman was put in command of all Union forces from the Appalachians to the Mississippi, a force over 100,000 strong. Lincoln's military decisions set the stage for the final defeat of the South.

In Virginia, Grant began a long series of attacks hammering Lee. His first meeting with Lee was the battle in the Wilderness (6 May 1864) and Spotsylvania (19 May 1864). Sherman began an advance into Georgia on the 7th of May. Rome, Georgia fell to Sherman on 18 May 1864. There were no more glorious charges as both sides built fortifications and tried maneuvers to outflank each other. Grant fought Lee at Cold Harbor and Petersburg, while Sherman was beginning to encircle Atlanta on the 17th of July and had put the city under siege by the 28th, and a series of relief attacks from the Confederates failed. The Union conducted several major cavalry raids into Alabama. Atlanta fell on 2 September 1864. At the same time Lincoln was winning his reelection, Sherman began his march to the sea. He took a month to reach Savannah mostly unopposed. Lincoln's Inaugural Address in March 1865 was conciliatory. On 9 April 1865, Lee surrendered to Grant at the Appomattox Court House, west of Richmond, with military operations continuing against holdouts into May.

The American Civil War was pivotal for many reasons. It remains the worst war the Americans have ever fought. Despite much larger totals of men underarms in later wars, the 620,000 Americans who lost their lives has never been equaled. In the South, approximately 25% of the white male military age population was dead. The overall fatalities, as a percent of the thirty-six million population, was comparable to that suffered by either Great Britain or France in the wake of World War I. It was a harbinger of the new destructive power science and the Industrial Revolution would bring to the battlefield. It also made America the first authentic Free Society with the ratification of the 13th amendment to the constitution in 1865. Without king or slave, America had cut the last cord tying it to the pre-industrial society.

It was remarkable the South in their foolish arrogance thought they could win the war. The ratio of military age men between North and South was over four to one. The ratio of factory production was even more lopsided at ten to one. Cotton may have been king, but it was not a god. British companies began stockpiling cotton as soon as it looked like the South might secede. They increased production in Egypt and India, and before the war ended the North was exporting cotton to Europe. Much better would have been to fight at the times of the Compromises of 1820 or 1850 because by 1860 it was simply too late.

The South was also blind to the political context in which they fought the war. The abolitionist movement began in England, and Britain had abolished slavery in 1833. After Lincoln's Emancipation Proclamation, Britain's entry into the war on the side of the South would have produced vigorous internal opposition in England. The Union Navy also took pains to not provoke the British with a strict adherence to British rules of blockade warfare. During the course of the war, there were few incidents to incite British public opinion.

The American Civil War was also remarkable for something else: fighting for the freedom of others. Since the Revolutionary War, the Americans had always seen themselves as part of a new wave of history. When, for example, the 1848 revolutions swept Europe, Americans saw this as only natural as they believed the Europeans were only following the American example. It is easy to sympathize with someone, but to pick up a gun and charge into enemy fire is an entirely different matter. The ideals of the Free Society had penetrated deep into America and allowed abolitionism to overcome racist attitudes in the worst war ever fought. The idea of fighting for another's freedom would be a major theme in America's future.

11

The freedom unleashed in the American experiment made America the most powerful nation on earth.

To survive the Free Society had to become strong, and to be historically significant it had to be victorious on the battlefield. America became a major power by fully embracing the Industrial Revolution and completing the settlement of the frontier.

The Civil War was barely over when the first transcontinental railroad was completed in 1869. Before the automobile, the Americans had a love affair with the railroad. As early as 1840, America had an estimated 3,000 miles of track compared to Europe and Britain's 1,800. By 1883 two other transcontinental routes connected Atlantic to Pacific. The growth in track miles was explosive and reflected both industrialization and settlement. In 1869 the total track miles amounted to 46,000, but by 1909 it was over 238,000. Government policy encouraged this expansion. By laying track, a company would gain title to the public lands on either side and large fractions of the new western states were owned by the railroad companies. 25% was the highest slice in the states of Minnesota and Washington, while 12% of the large state of California was initially in railroad hands. Local governments got in the act too, encouraging the railroad to come its way. Donations of land or paying for the price of a surveyor could completely change a town's future. In New York, $30 million was spent by local governments toward railroad expansion.

Other examples of industrialization showed the same trend. Steel production rose in a twenty-year period from 1.3 million tons in 1880 to ten million tons by the turn of the century. One of the other markers of industrialization was urbanization while farming was an occupation in decline. In 1870 only 26% of the population lived in urban areas but by 1910 it was 46%. In 1870, along with fishing and mining, 54% of adult males were involved in farming. This number declined to 34% in 1910.

The population of America was increasing too. In 1865 America was a nation of thirty-six million souls. In 1880 it had risen to fifty million, and by 1915 it was over the 100 million mark. One might think this would put a strain on the economy or the flood of new immigrants from Europe might create a pyramid type society, but the opposite happened.

The Industrial Revolution produced a steady increase in the standard of living and made America an economic powerhouse. The per capita GDP in constant 1860 dollars started at $147 in 1878 and rose to $268 by 1908. To illustrate how powerful America would eventually become, one only needs to look at the year 1941. It was the year America entered World War II, and by this time she was the largest economy in the world. Her production of steel, aluminum, oil, and motor vehicles each exceeded all other major nations combined. Within a year her military output exceeded the total Axis military production. America would eventually produce 70% of all Allied military equipment, and by the end of the war her GDP would double.

12

The experiment that almost failed was made possible by a remarkable set of circumstances. It was a nation founded on the ideas of Locke, Montesquieu, and Smith.[27]

The United States of America is the best representation of the Free Society. The Free Society in England was made possible by a set of favorable circumstances, and America was nurtured by its own. Chief among these was the founding of America by the one colonial power already developing into a Free Society. America would inherit all the culture and institutions of the mother country favoring freedom. This—combined with periods of benign neglect to foster American independence, a set of written colonial constitutions, and an immigration policy making America a haven for

---

[27] Like a "bell-curve" societal happiness is maximized when government power is kept small while at the same time avoiding anarchy. The extremes of anarchy or authoritarian rule make for a miserable existence.

Europeans desirous of freedom—gave the colonies all the necessary ingredients for a Free Society to grow.

Culturally, the frontier bred a different type of individual who did not always look to the government for solutions. In many cases, the government was simply not present, and a spirit of individualism was necessary for simple survival. The lack of landed nobility combined with a general availability of land tended to keep the nastier elements of the pre-industrial society at bay. The American approach to religion was also different. It was much more a bottom-up approach than a top-down imposed structure and this remained a unique feature of the country to the present day.

Once the new nation was established, it kept the same immigration policy and new citizens kept arriving, making America the predominant power on the North American continent. Thus, the new institutions of the young country did not come under any immediate external pressure, and there was no need for a large standing army.

Many things the Americans simply did right. The framers of the Constitution kept their word and passed a series of amendments—the Bill of Rights. The first President, George Washington, did not become a president for life but stepped down after two terms. The states gave up their territorial ambitions and allowed new states to enter the Union. There was a peaceful transition of power to the opposition party in 1801. Chief Justice John Marshall husbanded the evolution of the Supreme Court into a fully equal third branch of government and also was instrumental in protecting private property rights needed for the subsequent Industrial Revolution.

Despite all of these advantages the experiment in pure self-government was almost destroyed in the American Civil War. Slavery was simply a contradiction too big to ignore though it was ignored initially to unite the colonies into a single nation, and it was ignored in the two compromises of 1820 and 1850. When it finally came to war, the two previous compromises had allowed the North to become the more powerful adversary. Had the war been fought in 1820, it was likely the South would have broken away. The Northern cause to fight for the freedom of others was something unique in the annals of warfare, and it would have a lasting effect upon the American psyche.

It was from this a powerful free nation was created. The four large jumps in acquired territory created the net effect of forming an 'island' with all the advantages flowing to a Free Society. As America became the third largest nation on earth, its vast resources combined with the Industrial Revolution to make this new nation into an economic powerhouse as well. The best ideals of the Enlightenment had taken root in an experiment not weighted down with the historical baggage of European nations. Virtually every single item favoring a Free Society—including a strong merchant community, the citizen soldier, popular assemblies, checks and balances, island-like isolation protected by a navy, and the near absence of the secondary monopolies— was present in America.

The French Revolution, also a product of the Enlightenment, but so different from the American Revolution, was a harbinger of things to come. For the first time a utopian vision of the future motivated people to remake their society, and the entire society was mobilized around this single purpose. It was a concentration of government power unlike anything in the past. Terrorism by the government on a new scale crushed dissent. The future utopia inspired armies under command of the dictator to explode out of France. Like the famous novel about the period, *A Tale of Two Cities*, the real tale was the contrast of two revolutions—the American and the French.

Section III

The Rise of the Modern Dictatorship

"If you want a picture of the future, imagine a
boot stamping a human face–forever"

1984 by George Orwell

Civil War in the West

Chapter Five

B ecause industrialization had destroyed the agricultural basis of the old
societies, the Hereditary Dictatorships had to adapt to the requirements of the Industrial Revolution. The second phase of human civilization,
the industrial phase, had begun. As the wealth of the Industrial Revolution
made wars more expensive, and the Scientific Revolution made the battlefield
ever more deadly, adaptation was also a military necessity. As each kingdom
confronted this new reality, a struggle ensued between the ideals of the Free
Society and the new form of dictatorship—the Modern Dictatorship. The
Free Society, long dead for two millennium and now revived in a pristine
form free of king and slave, had to fight to stay alive. The Great Western
Civil War (1914 – 1945), the seminal conflict of the 20th century, fought in
two phases, was a war about the survival of freedom.

The term Modern Dictatorship is more accurate than Totalitarianism.
Totalitarianism implies something new and completely different. In reality
this was the more 'natural' form of human government using the wealth
and techniques of the Industrial and Scientific Revolutions in the service
of the dictator.

The 20th century produced three types of Modern Dictatorships: Fascism,
Communism and Khomeinism. Fascism took over in Italy, Japan, Spain, and
Germany. Devoted to extreme doctrines of nationalism and racism, it was
militaristic and aggressive. The dictator of Germany, Adolf Hitler (1889

– 1945) and his brand of Fascism called Nazism, was particularly violent. Communism was the form of the Modern Dictatorship taking over in Russia, China, and many places in the Third World. Communism's appeal was based upon building a just society devoted to equality. Notwithstanding the pretty words, Russia's dictator Joseph Stalin (1878 – 1953) and China's dictator Mao Zedong (1893 – 1976) would rival Hitler in their brutality. The third type, Khomeinism, first appeared in Iran in 1979. The dictator, Ruhollah Khomeini (1902 – 1989), combined elements of Fascism, Communism, and the religion of Islam, to form this third version of the Modern Dictatorship. Because the Islamic World is transitioning from the pre-industrial to the industrial, this form of the Modern Dictatorship has a magnified appeal for Muslims in the Middle East, the Islamic World in general, and to some in the Free Societies.

Two principal methods, one major and one minor enabled the Free Society to survive the 20th century. The major method was the victory by the Free Societies in the Great Western Civil War. It was the bloodiest set of conflicts in human history with the true unbounded monopoly of violence on full display thanks to the Scientific and Industrial Revolutions. Only the massive industrial might of America and her willingness to fight turned the civil war into a victory for the Free Societies over Fascism and ended the European king's Age of European Domination (c. 1450 – 1945). For now, this issue is settled in the West with freedom's victory.

The minor method, which enabled the survival of the Free Society, involved the interactions of the Free Societies in the West and those people in other nations disposed to the ideas of freedom. When nations were occupied by British or American troops for extended periods of time, democracies tended to emerge. The long-term occupations of Germany and Japan have left in their wake solid industrialized democracies. India is particularly instructive as it had both Fascist and Communist movements but turned instead to the Free Society as the British troops left and the colonial era ended. Across the globe there is a strong correlation between British or American troop occupation and the eventual development of a Free Society.

Finally, given this worldview, what does the future hold? To answer that question one must look to the Cold War. After the Great Western Civil War, which left most of Asia dominated by Communism, a new struggle—the Cold War—began. This struggle had the potential to exceed the previous one in devastation thanks to the invention of the atomic bomb. Luckily, it ended in another triumph of freedom due to the dogged determination of the American Republic and other Free Societies. The Cold War is an example of a permanent feature of the industrial age: the constant struggle of democracies and dictators. The natural human affinity for dictatorship will create new dictators and new Modern Dictatorships in the future. Only by constant vigilance will the real oddity of history, the Free Society, continue to exist.

2.1

The Great Western Civil War was a war to determine if the Free Society or Dictatorship would be dominant in the West.

Only the Hereditary Dictatorship of Germany did not lose the Mandate from Heaven due to industrialization, and it became the most powerful industrial nation in Europe. World War I, the first phase of the Great Western Civil War, was another war to dominate Europe; like Spain, the Hapsburgs, and France of the past, it was Germany's turn. Had it not been for the wealth of the American Republic and its willingness to fight, the Free Society would have lost the civil war.

Contrary to what is commonly believed, the First World War (WWI) was a war the dictators wanted to fight and not some accident everyone wanted to avoid. There exists a common misconception war is something people and governments try to avoid at all costs. In this view most wars are big accidents, but nothing could be further from the truth. Government is the struggle for power and war is simply an extension of politics by other means.

As Gottlieb von Jagow, the German Foreign Secretary during the crisis of July 1914 starting WWI, said later—the German government wanted the war. The Germans in particular wanted to fight because they wanted to finish what they started in the Franco-Prussian War (1870 – 1871). Otto von Bismarck (1815 – 1898) had tricked France into declaring war first in July 1870, leaving her diplomatically isolated to fight alone. The Prussians took only six weeks to force a French surrender while Paris held out for several months more. Prussia formed the new German Empire on 18 January 1871, in Versailles, when the King of Prussia was crowned Kaiser Wilhelm I, Emperor of Germany. In the subsequent Treaty of Frankfurt (May 1871) France was forced to give up Alsace and a part of Lorraine while otherwise maintaining her independence.

When WWI began there were two alliances. The Triple Alliance consisted of Germany, Austria-Hungary, jointly called the Central Powers, and Italy who joined with them in 1882. The Triple Entente was the alliance between France, Russia, and Britain formed in 1907. The German goal was to split the allies of the Entente by provoking a war with only France or Russia under favorable circumstances. Given the general instability of southeastern Europe, the Balkans was a natural area to find a provocation.

Austro-Hungarian elites had already convinced themselves an expansion of their empire would cure internal stagnation and decline. Russia, the other major dictatorship, believed she had recovered from the defeat in the Russo-Japanese War (1904 – 1905) and the failed revolution of 1905. However, her two Balkan humiliations of 1909 and 1912 made it difficult to ignore the crisis and back down. The Kingdom of Italy was a Constitutional Monarchy with a highly stratified society and divided by regional differences. In the recent past she had fought both Austria and France.

France became a Republic in the aftermath of the defeat in 1871 and though cautious wanted to recover the lost territory of Alsace-Lorraine. She did not want to be tricked a second time into isolation and made every effort to keep Britain, now a Free Society, onboard. Britain was concerned about rising German power and the German's serious naval building campaign. These two Free Societies, France and Britain, had robust opposition parties wanting to avoid war at all costs.

When on 28 June 1914 a Serbian nationalist murdered Archduke Francis Ferdinand, the next in line to the Austro-Hungarian throne, both the Germans and Austro-Hungarians had what they needed. On 7 July, the Austrians had received word of the so-called blank check or unconditional support from Germany in regards to any decision they made. They drew up demands amounting to a Serbian surrender but instructed their ambassador to Serbia to break off diplomatic relations no matter how the Serbians responded to the demands. After the ultimatum was issued on 23 July, to everyone's surprise, Serbia accepted it all save for one item, and Kaiser Wilhelm II, the son of Wilhelm I and current German dictator, assumed there would be no war. However, the Austria-Hungary Empire, proceeding with their plan, broke off diplomatic relations and declared war on the 28th of July 1914. Britain issued its own ultimatum to respect the neutrality of Belgium on the 29th. The other major powers responded quickly with Russia mobilizing on 30 July and Germany mobilizing the next day. Italy declared neutrality saying the Triple Alliance was a defensive treaty only. Germany declared war on Russia on 1 August and on France on 3 August. Because of Belgium neutrality violations, Britain declared war on Germany on the 4th.

When the Germans attacked, they attacked with a plan that had always included the violation of Belgium neutrality. Their immediate objective was the capture of the railroad center in Liege. Called the Schlieffen Plan, it contemplated a decisive right flank by the German army crashing through Belgium and into France, with a huge swing down on Paris and finally to the encirclement of the French army. France's own Plan XVII called for some defensive forces opposite Belgium with the majority of the forces poised to retake parts of Lorraine. Because the draft rates were higher in France, when Germany attacked with 1.7 million troops, France defended her country with about 2 million.

Initially in the Battle of the Frontiers (20–24 August) the Germans had the upper hand. The French lost 75,000 and 260,000 other casualties while the German losses were light. However, the German supply situation deteriorated rapidly once they left the railheads and the German soldiers were forced to requisition their own food while their horses simply died along the road with their artillery in tow. With telegraph infrastructure badly damaged, the Germans began to use radio in the clear to issue orders, and the French learned of the German troop movements. This was a blow to the possibility of German tactical surprise.

The French met the Germans at the River Ourcg outside of Paris in the Battle of the Marne (5 – 8 September). The Germans were having the better of the fight when they suddenly decided to pull back because they were over-stretched against the British Expeditionary Force (BEF), having sent two army corps to the eastern front on the 31st of August. The Miracle of the Marne, as the French called it, would mark the furthest German advance toward Paris until the German offensive in 1918. Within three months, trenches stretched from Switzerland to the English Channel.

In the east it was the Russians who would strike first. The Russians had the largest army and committed twenty-one divisions against the German's thirteen, and fifty-three divisions against the thirty-seven of Austria-Hungary. The Russians initially made progress but after a series of missteps found themselves surrounded in the Battle of Tannenberg Forest (24 – 31 August). Samsonov, the commanding general, committed suicide, and the Russians lost 92,000 as prisoners, 50,000 dead, and 500 major guns. The Germans only lost 15,000 and regained the initiative with the arrival of the two corps from the western front.

Though new allies joined, the strategic situation remained constant, and the war became a hopeless stalemate. The Ottomans joined the Central Powers in September 1914, and the Bulgarians also entered on the side of the Central Powers, which contributed to Serbia's defeat. This was offset by Italy's entry into the war on the side of the allies in May 1915. Japan had entered the war on the side of the allies too so as to grab German possessions in the Pacific. In 1916 Portugal joined the allies while Romania joined the Central Powers. Even poison gas, first used in the Second Battle of Ypres, was not decisive. Submarine warfare could have been decisive but political considerations prevented its effective use. Massive attacks like the one at Verdun did not end the stalemate. Only events in Russia and America in 1917 had the potential to determine the outcome.

Although their impact would not be felt until 1918, the events of the year 1917 gave hope to both sides. The Central Powers saw favorable events unfold on the eastern front. When in March 1917, the Tsar of Russia was deposed and a democratic form of government came to power, there was hope the Russians would press for peace but they continued the war. Because of this, in April the Germans sent a Russian revolutionary, Vladimir Lenin (1870 – 1924), to Russia where he was able to take over the government in November. By March 1918, the Russians and Germans signed the Treaty of Brest-Litovsk freeing up Germany's eastern front. One million troops rushed west to begin a new offensive.

On the allied side, the American president, Woodrow Wilson (1856 – 1924), was fruitlessly trying to mediate an end to the war as late as February 1917, calling his plan Peace Without Victory. In retrospect, this would have been a disaster for the Free Societies as they would have been war weary trying to avoid a new conflict, while the Germans, having learned from their past mistakes, would be eager to settle old scores.

Two German actions pushed the Americans to war. With fresh armies from the east, the Germans made an all out push for victory and resumed unrestricted submarine warfare in February. The second, called the Zimmerman Telegram, was a secret offer made to Mexico. Arthur Zimmerman, the German Ambassador to Mexico, offered Mexico the territory it lost in the Mexican-American War, if Mexico attacked the United States. The Germans hoped this would keep the Americans occupied long enough for Germany to complete their new offensive in France. The British had decoded the secret telegram and released it on 1 March 1917. On 2 April the Americans had declared war on Germany, and American troops began to arrive in large numbers by January 1918.

So after years of bloody stalemate, the Central Powers and the Triple Entente both prepared for a major confrontation in France in the spring of 1918. As the Germans began their offensive over 140,000 American troops had arrived and many more were on the way. The Germans, having failed so many times in a direct assault, tried small-arms infantry tactics to open holes in the enemy trench system while flooding troops through the gaps. The new method worked well and the Germans were back, only forty miles from Paris. But as in the first Battle of the Marne, the Germans lost the Second Battle of the Marne, but this time with help from the Americans. As the Germans were being pushed back many in their high command knew this was defeat for Germany. Eventually, the Americans poured upwards of 500,000 men into France.

The price of victory in WWI was ten million military dead and an estimated six million civilians—higher than any other war in human history. The only consolation was the war prevented a European empire under German domination and numerous Hereditary Dictatorships fell in the wake of their failure to conquer Europe. The monarchies of Germany, Austria-Hungary, Russia, and the Ottoman Empire were no more having lost both the war and the Mandate from Heaven.

However, the stated goal "to make the world safe for democracy" as President Wilson said, was a failure. The chaos in politics during the pause in the Great Western Civil War caused most European countries to turn to Fascism or authoritarian dictators as a means to restore order. Fear of Communism combined with some actual subversion from Communist Russia was a prime motivation. Strongmen like Horthy seized power in Hungary in 1920 while others did the same in Poland (1926), Lithuania (1926), Latvia (1934), and Estonia (1934). Meanwhile, the Hereditary Dictatorship made its comeback in Albania (1928), Yugoslavia (1929), Bulgaria (1934), and Romania (1938). In Portugal the new dictator ruled from 1932 to 1968.

The victory was only a temporary reprieve. In place of the Hereditary Dictatorship, a new form was emerging, a form as horrible as the war itself. The Modern Dictatorship was taking root in Russia, and would soon spring from Germany and elsewhere. The Free Societies had won for now but the Great Western Civil War was about to enter its next, more deadly, phase.

2.2

In the second phase of this civil war, WWII, the Free Society confronts the Modern Dictatorship for the first time.

The Second World War (WWII) was the most devastating war in human history. As the prime mover in this war, the dictator Hitler did everything in his power to grow his new empire—the Third Reich. In 1936 he reoccupied the Rhineland in violation of provisions in the Treaty of Versailles (1919), and in March 1938 Austria was annexed. In his boldest move yet, he demanded in 1938 portions of Czechoslovakia bordering Germany, called the Sudetenland and populated mostly by Germans, become part of his Reich. The Free Societies of Britain and France finally began to resist his constant string of demands. Trying to avoid war they signed the Munich

Agreement on 29 September 1938 assuming all parties to the Munich talks were acting in good faith. Hitler gave his personal assurance to the British Prime Minister, Neville Chamberlain, this was his last territorial demand. Chamberlain returned to England paper in hand and proclaimed "peace in our time"—making himself perhaps the biggest fool in history.

Hitler quickly moved to carve up Czechoslovakia by first getting Slovakia to declare independence. Then with nothing left to the country but Bohemia and Moravia, he threatened the leaders with devastation of what was left if they did not agree to a peaceful occupation. On 15 March 1939, Czechoslovakia was gone. The British and French protested but did not act. By the end of March, Britain gave Poland an unconditional pledge of support and in April started a military draft.

Hitler was now making demands regarding the Danzig corridor. This was a narrow area connecting Poland to the sea and split most of Germany from a small area to the east. Hitler first needed to determine what the Soviet Union under Stalin would do in the event of a German invasion of Poland. Joseph Stalin was the dictator of the Soviet Union Empire with Russia as its major constituent, and Hitler needed to make a deal with Stalin. Hitler understood Germany would be much more powerful if she could avoid a two-front war.

Stalin's Foreign Commissar Molotov had been in contact with the Germans secretly as far back as May 1939. Molotov also invited the British and French to Moscow on 23 July. When they arrived, Molotov asked them to provide proper credentials, which did not arrive until August the 21st. It was the same day Molotov asked the German Foreign Minister Ribbentrop to Moscow, and Ribbentrop signed a Non-Aggression pact with Molotov within hours of landing. The British and French were sent home, and the peace agreement was proclaimed to the world a few days later. If Hitler was the kindling for World War II then Stalin was the match.

The German invasion of Poland began on 1 September 1939. Both Britain and France declared war on the 3rd. Poland was no match for the Germans, and the Germans were at the gates of Warsaw by the 10th. When Stalin attacked Poland from the east on the 17th, it was clear there were secret protocols to the Non-Aggression pact. It was a tremendous treachery since a Russo-Polish Non-Aggression Pact had been in place since 1932, but it was also a shock to the world because of the stark ideological differences between Nazism and Communism. Other secret protocols gave Estonia, Latvia, and Lithuania to Stalin. He took advantage of this in 1940 by invading all three. Stalin also made demands on Finland. The Russo-Finish War (1939 – 1940) was an embarrassment for the Russians because initially their troops performed poorly. Given the difference in size between the two belligerents, it was only a matter of time before Russia won. Finland and Russia signed a treaty with the territorial concessions Russia wanted on 12 March 1940.

On 10 May 1940, the same day Winston Churchill (1874 – 1965) became the British prime minister, France was invaded by Germany. France was prepared, but only prepared to fight the last war. The Germans, the losers in WWI, were forced to make hard choices to come to terms with why they lost. Their response was to embrace tank warfare—blitzkrieg—using large tank formations, well in front of the infantry and assisted by airpower. The tanks punched through enemy lines, attacked positions deep in enemy territory and encircled the enemy from behind. France's response to its experience in WWI was to build a massive string of fortifications called the Maginot Line along the French-German boarder, though, for political reasons, the Line was not extended along the Luxembourg or Belgium boarders.

Hitler would now do what the Germans could not in 1914. He would split the defenders in two. Pressing through the forest of the Ardennes in southern Belgium, Panzer tanks under the command of General Guderian made it to the objective of Sedan in a few days—punching a hole through the French 9th Army. The tanks poured through the hole and made a dash to the coast on May 22nd to encircle the BEF and Belgians. The British, in full retreat, used Dunkirk for evacuation, and the First French Army was trapped at Lille. The Belgians surrendered on the 28th of May and by 10 June, the Germans had crossed the Seine north of Paris. Soon they had overrun all of France with Italy joining in the attack by invading southern France. Not since the days of Napoleon had the British found themselves in such a desperate situation. Luckily for them, most of the BEF had made it back to England via Dunkirk, and the British fought on throughout 1940 and 1941 above England in their own skies, in the Atlantic in a repeat of WWI, and in North Africa.[28]

However two events in 1941 would change the character of the war permanently. They were both surprise attacks by different dictatorships, which initially gained them success but in the long term destroyed them. Again, the question of American and Russian involvement was the key to the outcome of the war. On 22 June 1941, Hitler invaded the Soviet Union, and on 7 December 1941 the Empire of Japan attacked the United States.

Stalin should have known Hitler's attack was coming as Churchill sent him a warning in April. A group of Russian spies in Lucerne Switzerland known as the "Red Trio" with the leader code-named "Lucy" knew the exact date of the invasion. So, too, did the spy Richard Sorge in Tokyo. Sorge informed Stalin on 1 June of the size of the attack, and on 15 June that the 22nd would be the date. On the day of the invasion 3.4 million Axis forces faced 4.7 million Soviets. Stalin was loath to cause an incident with the Germans, so no Soviet general was allowed to mobilize his troops. The leadership of the officers had been degraded as many good ones were swept up in the purge of 1937. Consequently, the German Operation Barbarossa got off to a terrific start.

Initially Stalin would not believe the reports, but eventually the double-crosser of Poland realized he had been double-crossed by Hitler. The Russians were in full retreat, and by October 1941, the German army—the Wehrmacht—had exceeded their gains of World War I. Large numbers of Russians surrendered at Minsk, Smolensk, and Kiev. In October, the Wehrmacht launched Operation Typhoon to push on toward Moscow. Stalin's defense of Moscow held because twenty fresh divisions arrived from the east. Sorge had told Stalin in September the Japanese were not going to attack, taking advantage of Russia's weak position, preferring to expand elsewhere in Asia. Stalin had learned his lesson and took advantage of this new intelligence by moving troops from the east to face the Germans. Sorge was eventually discovered and executed in 1943.

---

[28] A low point in the history of democracy, less than a dozen democracies existed worldwide. Of these only Britain and the United States were historically significant.

There were many factors including the winter weather contributing to Hitler's inability to take Russia. Germany was not on a total war footing while obviously the Soviet Union was. The Germans had not prepared for a long war and thought this would be a repeat of France in 1940, but Russia was simply a much bigger country. She had much larger reserves of manpower, and the distances to conquer were longer. Russia was also less developed than France and did not have the same extensive road network. The Germans were defeated in their attempt to take Stalingrad in February 1943, and lost the initiative after the largest tank battle in history, the Battle of Kursk, which took place from July to August. Stalin was able to liberate Leningrad from its seventeen-month siege in December.

Early on Sunday morning 7 December 1941 at 0615, 214 Japanese warplanes flew south toward the Hawaiian Island of Oahu in the Hawaiian Territory. At Pearl Harbor, the Americans had 8 battleships put out of action along with 8 other capital ships. In the surprise attack sixty-five aircraft of 231 were destroyed at Hickam Field.[29] A 1760-pound bomb quickly sank the USS Arizona, and Rear Admiral Kidd went down with 1,106 other sailors out of a crew of 1,511. The USS Oklahoma took five torpedoes and sunk equally quickly trapping 415 souls inside—a few tragically lingered alive inside until Christmas. The reason for this attack was the American embargo of oil and other goods to Japan because America was opposed to the Japanese war against China. Franklin D. Roosevelt (1882 – 1945), President of the United States, asked for a declaration of war before a joint session of Congress on the 8th and was able to sign it that day.

After Hitler's declaration of war on America on 11 December, Roosevelt then could politically implement a Germany first strategy. However, he needed the Japanese checked militarily before he could implement it. Meanwhile, with the Far East militarily stripped to support Europe, Japan had free reign to grab what she wanted. In the immediate aftermath of the Pearl Harbor attack, Japan grabbed Guam, Wake Island, the Gilbert Islands and invaded the Philippines. The Dutch East Indies, the economic area most of interest to them, was attacked in January 1942, and by mid-February,

---

[29] Far from being a rarity, a surprise attack is a common way wars begin.

Singapore had fallen. June 1942 saw the end of American resistance in the Philippines. May 1942 also saw the conquest of Burma, which turned out to be the most westward Japanese expansion.

The Americans knew the Japanese had a big strike planned in June but they did not know where. The Japanese in the spring tried to decide if their next objective would be Australia or Midway Island north of Hawaii, and when the Doolittle Raid hit Tokyo on 18 April the action made the Japanese decide in favor of Midway. Based on intelligence reports, the Americans positioned its three carriers fifty miles north of Midway with 233 planes. Four carriers and 272 planes led the Japanese attack force, while the Midway invasion force was 600 miles behind. The Japanese lost all four carriers while the Americans lost only one. With another carrier in the Pacific under repairs from a torpedo attack, the Americans were now in an excellent position to check any Japanese attack upon Hawaii or California. The German first policy could go forward.

From the Russian victories at Stalingrad and the American victory at Midway, the Axis fortunes gradually declined. The air campaign by the Allies against the Axis powers, a completely new innovation in warfare, had opened up a third front against the Axis taking up to 30% of the German industrial production. The D-day invasion on the 6th of June 1944 was conducted within a few days of the promise made to Stalin about opening a second front in Europe. In the Pacific, the Battle of the Philippine Sea (18 – 20 June 1944) destroyed much of Japan's naval aviation, while the Battle of Leyte Gulf (late October 1944) destroyed what was left of the Japanese navy.

In April Mussolini tried to escape to Switzerland, was captured, and was quickly executed. Germany was overrun, and on 7 May 1945 Hitler committed suicide. The dropping of the atomic bombs by American B-29s caused the Japanese to unconditionally surrender and accept the Potsdam Declaration on 14 August 1945.

The cost of WWII exceeded the horror of WWI. Over twenty million military and an estimated forty to fifty million civilians lost their lives. The total of the entire Great Western Civil War was thirty million military dead on both sides and close to sixty million dead civilians. Roughly 100 million had been sacrificed on the altar of dictatorship with the Fascist version of the Modern Dictatorship taking the majority of the share.

America's position at the end of the Great Western Civil War was one of unchallenged dominance. She alone possessed the atomic bomb with a long-range aircraft to deliver it. Her economy was the largest in the world, and her homeland was free of the devastation suffered by other major powers. With light casualties compared to others, unmatched technological superiority and a large intact army and navy, she had no equal. At no time in human history had a single nation had the power to conquer the world as did America, and it is a great testimony to Free Societies America's only goal was rapid disarmament.[30] From a peak of around 40% of GDP, military spending would fall to near 3% within a little more than a year. The American and Russian occupation of Europe also signaled the end of the European dictators' Age of European Domination (c. 1450 – 1945).

3.1

The transition from the Hereditary Dictatorships to the Modern in the 20th century shows how quickly democracy was abandoned in times of crisis. This is a testament to the attraction of dictatorship in human affairs. Losing the Mandate from Heaven in the past resulted in a new king, but it now produced an entirely new category of dictatorship—Fascism—in the nations of Italy, Japan, and Spain.

The person to coin the term Fascism and to become the first Fascist dictator was Italy's Benito Mussolini (1883 – 1945). He used the ancient Roman symbol, the *fasces*, as the symbol of the Italian Fascist Party. The symbol, a bundle of rods capped with an axe-head, represented the many small groups he brought together into one strong organization. He became Prime Minister in October 1922 and used the position to consolidate power. He was able to attract army veterans from World War I, members of the lower middle class who feared socialism would lower their status, and many peasants who feared they would lose what little land they had

---

[30] Democracies do not demonstrate the hyper-aggressive tendencies of dictatorships. A world dominated by democracies should experience wars far less frequently.

to collectivization. Centers of power in Italian society were also afraid of the Communists and socialists. By claiming he supported the monarchy, Mussolini gained the support of the aristocracy. He garnered the implicit support of the Catholic Church by opposing all anti-clerical measures. In a speech in 1925 he said he wanted a total transformation of Italian society via Totalitarianism. By this he meant using the entire resources of the state, as was done during the total mobilizations of nations in World War I, for the transformation.

The Japanese transition from a pre-industrial society to the Fascist version of the Modern Dictatorship was a gradual affair. The Meiji Restoration saw rapid Japanese industrialization. The Constitutional Monarchy, modeled on the Prussian constitution, had several unusual features making the transition easier. The cabinet was isolated from the *Diet*—the elected legislature—while top army and navy officials had direct access to the emperor. The constitution was ideal for the founding fathers or *genro* of the Restoration to guide the nation but left a power vacuum as they grew old and died. It was into this vacuum the Fascists moved.

Japanese society was rife with Fascist ideals, and the army became a strong advocate of these ideals through organizations like the Reservist Association and the National Youth Association. The Japanese concluded from the economic disasters of the 1930s a third way between the extremes of liberal capitalism and Communism was needed, and this was where the Fascists and the army positioned themselves. This type of positioning was a common Fascist tactic worldwide.

Political violence was not unknown to the Japanese, and the public saw this violence as an unfortunate part of the process. The Fascists exploited this acceptance of violence to their advantage. The second *Diet* elections of 1892 saw twenty-five people killed and many injured. When, in 1932, the nation's finance minister and prime minister were assassinated, it was clear civilian control of the government and particularly the army was slipping away. It was the third prime minister killed in ten years.

A failed coup by Fascist elements paradoxically strengthened those who called for social order. When Prime Minister Konde made a speech in 1940 on the occasion of his second cabinet, he spoke about the collapse of the old European order. This necessitated the abolition of political parties and establishment of a 100 million person unity under the emperor. Eventually General Hideki Tojo (1884 – 1948) would lead the cabinet as the closest thing to a dictator in the Japanese version of Fascism. Using the emperor as a figurehead, they were repeating a historic pattern creating a Fascist *Shogunate*.

The Spanish Civil War was a contest between Communists combining with other left-wing groups against the Fascists. The Fascists would bring General Francisco Franco (1892 – 1975) to power and provide a testing ground for the new weapons and tactics used in the second half of the Great Western Civil War. The crisis in their constitutional monarchy had begun with a major military defeat in Spanish Morocco in 1921, the last major Spanish colony. By 1923 the Spanish Parliament was unable to accomplish anything in factional fighting, so the King supported a military coup led by Miguel de Rivera. He thought he was a Spanish Mussolini, but in reality he ruled only as a strongman uninterested in social transformation. Economic difficulties and poor health forced his resignation.

The new Parliament, democratically elected, pushed a far-left agenda. Championing simple things like eight-hour workdays and forced early retirements from the army, they rapidly made enemies of important centers of power in the country. They abolished the nobility and abolished religious orders within the Catholic Church. In agrarian reform they forcibly purchased land from large estates and gave it to small farmers.

When the new parliament lost the elections in 1933, riots broke out all over Spain with two opposing groups organized into different Fronts. The Communists, socialists, liberals, and anarchists called themselves the Republicans or Popular Front. The conservatives with the monarchists—but not the Fascist *Falange* Party—called themselves the Nationalists. In the elections of 1936, the Popular Front won with 4.2 million votes to the Nationalists Front of 3.8 million, and as before, the left-wing Popular Front governed in an openly provocative manner. They exiled Franco, the leader of the *Falange* Party, to the Canary Islands. When another *Falange* leader was assassinated, open civil war began.

Franco returned from exile to lead the Nationalists now including the Fascists. Mussolini, Hitler, and Stalin all sent aid to their respective sides in the civil war. Italy sent 50,000 soldiers including 950 tanks and some aircraft plus warships. Hitler provided his most modern aircraft and 16,000 military advisors. Stalin sent equal numbers of tanks, some aircraft, and 5,000 advisors. He also used the *Cominterm*, an international Communist organization, to organize brigades of volunteers from over sixty countries to join the fight. About 40,000 people came, including the famous Lincoln Brigade from the United States. Like many civil wars, there were atrocities on all sides.

Franco's superior leadership ability, combined with the Republican's constant infighting, led to a Nationalist victory. In Barcelona in 1937 the anarchists, socialists, and Communists fought each other in open combat. By April 1939, Franco had crushed all opposition.

Three nations, Italy, Japan, and Spain had transitioned to Modern Dictatorships.

3.2

A particularly evil form of Fascism called Nazism became the Modern Dictatorship in Germany.

Unlike Franco, the future dictator, Adolf Hitler, came to power relatively peacefully when he was appointed German Chancellor on 30 January 1933. He did not yet have sufficient power to transform German society since only three other Nazis joined him in the cabinet, and the German President Hindenburg had granted him limited emergency powers. In typical Hitler style he was quick to use all the powers granted to him calling for new elections after being in office only two days. The combined vote in the 1932 elections for Nazis and Communists constituted a majority of the vote by the German people. A majority voted for a Modern Dictatorship of some form, and this did not bode well for the future.

A few days before the new elections, on 27 February 1933, the Parliament building, the Reichstag, burned to the ground from an apparent arson, and Hitler blamed the Communists. As did many Fascist and Communist Parties, Hitler had a private army of thugs to do his bidding—the Storm Detachment (SA) and the Elite Guard (SS). They both were sent on a campaign of violence and intimidation taking over town halls, police stations, and newspapers. Nazism was arriving at the local level before it arrived nationally.

When the new Reichstag met after the 5 March elections, their popular vote had risen from 33% to 44%—well short of the two-thirds needed for constitutional change. However, Hitler had expelled all Communists from the Reichstag and this action got Hitler nearer to the required two-thirds. He then made a deal with a minor party to get the two-thirds vote. On 23 March, the Reichstag passed the Enabling Act, an example of how democracy without limited government can be used to act contrary to the Free Society.

By 14 July it became a criminal offense to organize any other party other than the Nazi Party, and when new elections were held in November, only Nazis were on the ballot. When the SA leader Rohm became increasingly radical and violent, Hitler moved against him as Rohm was alienating the army, the group Hitler most desired to dominate. In July of 1934, in the so-called "Night of the Long Knives" the SS eliminated the SA leadership. The timing was partly motivated by President Hindenburg's health. When he died a few weeks later, Hitler became the German President and took on the title of Fuhrer—'Leader' in German. He required each member of the armed forces to swear a personal oath of obedience to the new Fuhrer, thereby completing the transition to the Modern Dictatorship in Germany.

3.3

The Modern Dictatorship confronts Russia, and Communism, another form of the Modern Dictatorship, overcomes Russia.

In Russia, the center of Orthodox civilization, the fall of the Tsarist dictatorship resulted in a civil war. However, Lenin became the first dictator of the Communist version of the Modern Dictatorship.

In March 1917 the Hereditary Dictatorship of Tsar Nicholas II lost its Mandate from Heaven to spontaneous food riots and troop desertions. A provisional government was formed under the leadership of Prince Lvov in Petrograd, the Russian capital, while a rival workers council, termed a Soviet, formed in Petrograd and elsewhere. The new government continued to fight the unpopular war and resist peasant attempts to take over land from their landlords.

The Germans, seeing an opportunity, allowed Lenin to leave exile in Switzerland and to return to Russia. In July Kerensky, a true socialist, took over control of the provisional government but continued the unpopular policies. Lenin was the leader of the smaller faction of the Communist party in Russia he called the Bolsheviks—literally meaning majority—and he led an uprising against the provisional government. The government issued arrest warrants causing Lenin to flee to Finland.

When General Kornilov, head of the Russian army, attempted a takeover of the Provisional government in August, Kerensky asked Lenin and his Red Army for help. This action saved the capital and the government, but it brought Lenin back into the country, and it put the Bolsheviks in charge. Lenin then moved to seize control of other Soviets already in control of other cities. He began to seize landlord property, which made the Communists popular in the countryside. When he seized complete control of the government in November 1917, Kerensky fled and lived as an exile for the rest of his life.[31]

Lenin, correctly reasoning a civil war was looming, moved to end hostilities with the Germans and signed a separate peace treaty with them in 1918. The Russian Civil War (1918 – 1922) began as a series of struggles with different revolutionary groups. During 1918, Lenin worked with Tsarist forces to defeat other socialist revolutionaries. The major part of the civil war then began between Tsarist forces called the White Russians and the Red Army under Leon Trotsky (1879 – 1940). The European powers, America, and Japan all sent troops to Archangel and Murmansk in the north, the Crimea and Caucasus in the south, and Vladivostok in the east. Despite foreign intervention on the White Russian's side, the Red Army was eventually victorious in 1920, and by then all foreign troops were gone. The Communists were then free to crush socialist peasant armies and end the civil war by 1922.

The Russian Civil War was incredibly destructive with the Reds and socialists losing approximately one million each while the White Russians

---

[31] It is commonly called the October Revolution because the Russians had not fully adopted the Gregorian calendar.

lost a similar amount. Eight million people in total lost their lives in the conflict of which five million were civilians who died due to rural destruction, atrocities, and terror on all sides.

When Lenin died of a stroke in 1924, a struggle for power began. All the Communist Party officials feared Trotsky because he was a dynamic speaker and had the loyalty of the army. An ideological struggle broke out between Stalin's "Socialism in One Country" and Trotsky's "Permanent Revolution." In the XIV Party Congress, Stalin's version was adopted and Stalin would continue to consolidate his power eventually having Trotsky expelled from the Politburo—the ruling council—in 1927. When Trotsky was forced to flee Russia by 1929, he left Stalin as the dictator. This made the transition to the Modern Dictatorship complete in Russia.

3.4

The fate of the Chinese civilization was the same as Russia. The fall of the Manchu dictatorship resulted in a civil war and the Communist dictator Mao won.

Though it would take several more years to consolidate their power the Qing or Manchu Dynasty (1644 – 1912) officially began with their capture of Beijing in 1644, but they were as conservative as the Ming Dynasty believing foreign ideas were dangerous. The Manchus had their heyday of power in the 18th century but by the end of the 19th century had seen a long slow decline. Unequal treaties, forced upon them by different European powers, began with the First Opium War (1839 – 1842) followed by many others. Their Mandate from Heaven was also eroding in a series of internal revolts, the Taiping (1850 – 1864), the Nien (1851 – 1868), the Muslim (1855 – 1873), and the Tuncan (1862 – 1878). China further suffered from a series of natural disasters, seen by the general public as further proof the Mandate from Heaven was lost. When the Chinese secret society of the Righteous and Harmonious Fists, dubbed the Boxers by the Europeans, began a rebellion with Imperial support, it was distinctly anti-European and anti-Christian. The rebellion lasted from 1900 to 1901 until an alliance of Western powers occupied Beijing and this last failure caused many educated Chinese to believe the Dynasty needed to end.

The end came when a two-year-old boy became emperor in 1908. In 1911 military units rebelled, and by 1912 his Regent officially abdicated for the boy. At first the prospects were bright as a western-educated Christian, Sun Yat-sen, became President of the new republic, but like Chinese history of the past, the country entered a warring states period. The military chief, Yuan Shikai, seized power and proclaimed himself emperor in 1915 while various other warlords seized power in different areas across the vast country. Sun first looked to the west for military aid, but finding none turned to the Soviet Union for assistance in 1923. Under Commandant Chiang Kai-shek, the Russians helped organize the military and established a military academy.

Upon Sun's untimely death in 1925, Chiang became commander of the army, broke with Russia, and slowly subdued the warlords—capturing Beijing in 1928. Chinese Communists attempted to establish a Soviet style republic in 1931, but were forced by Chiang to abandon the area in 1934. Desperate to find a sanctuary, the Communists began their famous long march of 6,000 miles, losing almost 70% of the original 90,000, to an area safe from Chiang. Mao Zedong was to emerge as a prominent leader in the march.

Chiang followed a policy of attacking internal enemies more than the external Japanese enemy. Kidnapped in 1936 by the Communists, he agreed while in captivity to focus on Japan and was allowed to return in time to help the Nationalists fight a new wave of Japanese aggression in July 1937. The number of Communists was initially small, but by the end of World War II they had grown to over a million strong under the command of their leader Mao.

Once the Japanese left China and mediation attempts by the United States failed, full civil war broke out in 1946. The Nationalists were nominally in control of the major cities while the Communists dominated the countryside. By 1948 the Communists were gaining the upper hand and soon took Beijing. In October 1949 Mao proclaimed the People's Republic of China, and in February 1950 a fifty-year Friendship treaty was signed with the Soviet Union. The remainder of the Nationalists fled to Taiwan establishing a separate government, while the rest of China made the transition to the Modern Dictatorship.

3.5

Like the more industrialized areas of the world, the Third World was making the natural transition to the Modern Dictatorship.

Latin America would have transitioned to Communism, but interference by the United States caused a stalemate. In Latin America, one did not ask what countries had strong Communist movements, but what countries did not. Argentina, Bolivia, Brazil, Chile, Colombia, Cuba, El Salvador, Guatemala, Nicaragua, Peru, Uruguay, and Venezuela—all had Communist movements of some sort.

Cuba is the prototype Communist Revolution and the most successful of all those in Latin America. Batista, the long-time power broker and military dictator of Cuba, used the military and the secret police—the 'Tigers'—to maintain control. Although the economy grew, there was a large disparity between the cities and the countryside. Batista was also notorious for being corrupt as were many in his regime.

On 26 July 1953, a group of students attacked the barracks in Moncada, Cuba. The attack failed and the surviving students were imprisoned including Fidel Castro (1926–).[32] Originally sentenced to 15 years in prison, he was shortly released, and fled to Mexico where he formed the 26 July Movement (M26). Returning to Cuba in 1957 Castro began his guerrilla campaign, and on 7 Nov 1958, his fellow revolutionary, Ernesto "Che" Guevara, marched on Havana. The dictator Batista, suffering under an American arms embargo, fled in January 1959.

As soon as Castro seized power on 8 January 1959, mass executions, 600 in all, began in the two main prisons: the La Cabana and the Santa Clara. A master at playing the American press, Castro told the *New York Times* he wanted to return to his village and practice law. By 15 February 1959, the Prime Minister Cardona had resigned, and in the spring of 1959 the

---

[32] When left blank this indicates the person was alive when this book was written.

revolution picked up steam when Castro suspended the constitution and began to rule by decree. Collectivization also began in May when the army seized hundreds of large estates.

One by one prominent Cuban officials fled. In January 1960, Jorge Zayas, the editor of the anti-Batista newspaper *Avance* went into exile. The year 1960 also saw the mass exodus of ordinary people, many from the middle class, getting out before it was too late. By the end of 1960 prominent opposition leaders, still trapped, were being arrested and shot.

Castro used the failed Bay of Pigs invasion as an excuse for increased repression. The Catholic Church had been supportive of the revolution and backed several priests who fought with the guerrillas. When Castro declared the "Falangist priests must go," 131 priests were expelled from the country. Devout Catholics were refused a university education or a civil service job.

Castro turned to his brother, Raul, to run the internal security apparatus. The DGCI, popularly called the 'Red Gestapo,' first began by infiltrating groups opposed to Castro and soon had every aspect of Cuban society under watch—for example, Section #3 kept watch on sports, film, and artistic events while Section #6 did wiretaps. One new innovation of Castro was the Committees for the Defense of the Revolution (CDR) who had a representative in every neighborhood. Looking for any counterrevolutionary activities, neighbor would report on neighbor. 100,000 people were taken in for questioning in March 1961 based upon lists created by the CDRs, and thousands went to detention centers run by the Red Gestapo.

Outside of Castro and his brother, the most famous revolutionary to the outside world was Che. Che, more than anyone else in the revolution, was a proponent of exporting the cause to other "oppressed peoples." He had an intense hatred for the United States with his stated goal of "Two, three, many Vietnams." By 1963 he was in Algeria and later in the Congo exporting revolution, and in 1966 he turned his attention to South America. He was captured and executed in Bolivia in October 1967.

A window into the mindset of the regime can be seen in the Military Unit of Production Assistance (MUPA), formed in 1964. In 1967 it was closed down under international pressure, but it was Castro's first attempt to create a large slave-labor system where camps lumped together all elements potentially dangerous to the regime. Religious figures such as the Bishop of Havana and Jehovah Witnesses could work alongside pimps and prostitutes. Military style discipline was used while conditions in the camps were poor, prisoners malnourished, and prisoners expected to build their own shelters.

The Cubans were the original 'boat people,' escaping from the prison island as soon as the Communists gained power.[33] The largest exodus was the Mariel Crisis in April 1980 beginning when thousands of Cubans went to the Peruvian embassy to try to get exit visas and the crowd quickly spiraled out of control. Eventually Castro was forced to allow 125,000 people to leave from a country of only 11 million. Taking advantage of the situation, Castro released common criminals as well as mental hospital patients. He was never able to completely stop the exodus despite desperate actions such as using Cuban helicopters to drop sand bags on the makeshift boats. In 1994 an estimated 7,000 people lost their lives in attempts to escape. Across the many years of the regime, an estimated 20% of the Cuban population escaped into exile.

In the wake of the American defeat in Vietnam, the Americans were in no mood to defend anyone's freedom and neglecting their military, turned inward. This gave the Communist Modern Dictatorships, mostly the Soviet Union, a free hand to expand their influence particularly in Africa. At the peak, 8,850 Soviet advisors were in numerous African countries as were 53,900 Cuban troops. Cuban and East German internal security specialists helped train their counterparts in the new fledgling dictatorships. Three particular countries received the bulk of the Soviet help: Angola was under the control of the Popular Movement for the Liberation of Angola (MPLA), Mozambique was ruled by the Mozambique National Liberation Front (Frelimo), and Ethiopia was under the brutal Ethiopian Worker's Party (Dergue).

In 1974, a power vacuum was left in Angola when left-wing officers came to power in Portugal and the Portuguese army was swiftly withdrawn. Different liberation groups, who had fought the Portuguese, formed a

---

[33] The term "boat people" refers to the large number of refugees who used boats to escape the Communists of Vietnam. Millions fled while the UN estimated approximately 300,000 died at sea.

coalition government. The planned November 1975 elections never took place as open warfare broke out between the various factions. By October 1974 the Soviets were backing the MPLA and the coalition government was gone by next August. Near the end of 1975, the Soviets and Cubans had 7,000 advisors in the country while South Africa began to support UNITA one of the other revolutionary groups—with an originally Maoist orientation.

In December 1979 the new MPLA Workers Party signaled a closer alliance with the Soviets and Cubans while a smiling Raul Castro looked on as the Congress of Luanda created the new workers party. The MPLA was ready to make the change since they had already purged their party of 'deviationists' earlier in August. The MPLA had control over the coast, the oil, and the diamond producing regions. UNITA controlled the interior, especially areas that had experienced forced collectivization. All foreign troops were removed in an agreement signed in New York in December 1988 in the wake of the Soviet collapse. The foreign troops left, but the civil war did not.

Likewise, when the Portuguese left Mozambique, an anti-colonial movement called Frelimo, took power. While receiving aid from both the Soviet Union and Maoist China, they began a campaign of forced collectivization in the 1970s. When they signed import exchange agreements with Eastern Block countries, Frelimo agreed to support the Zimbabwe African National Union (ZANU) fighting the white minority government in Rhodesia. As in Angola, a resistance movement formed against the Marxist collectivization and was supported first by Rhodesia and later South Africa, and this resistance was joined by people who had escaped Mozambique's reeducation camp system. The death penalty, officially abolished by the Portuguese in 1867, was reinstituted in 1979 for crimes against national security and crimes against the people. The combination of civil war and collectivization forced the people to pay a heavy price. UNICEF estimated 600,000 died in the civil war period from 1975 – 1985. After the Soviet Union collapsed, Mozambique toned down its ideology to encourage foreign investments.

The most brutal Communist regime in Africa was the one in Ethiopia. The dictator, Mengistu Haile Marian, head of the Dergue, proclaimed a socialist republic in December 1974 and abolished land ownership in

March 1975. The government ordered 50,000 students to the fields as part of a forced collectivization. Mengistu conducted his first terror campaign against other Marxist groups in 1976 by proclaiming a campaign against imperialism, feudalism, and bureaucratic capitalism. All military ties to the United States were terminated by April 1977, and this accelerated massive Soviet and Cuban aid. The general terror in 1977 and 1978 claimed a large number of victims and, as in China, the victim's family would be forced to pay for the execution.

Like all forced collectivization, Ethiopia's resulted in starvation with an estimated 200,000 to 300,000 people dying as a result of Mengistu's policies. They did not request outside aid so desperately needed until after a September 1984 celebration of the regime's accomplishments organized by the North Koreans. Reporting anything negative about the regime would get one expelled, as Doctors without Boarders were in 1985. As with the other Communist regimes in Africa, it soon ran into trouble with the collapse of the Soviets. Mengistu fled to live in Zimbabwe.

3.6

Islamic civilization is currently engulfed in the crisis of transition. It is transitioning to Khomeinism—yet another form of the Modern Dictatorship.

Islamic civilization is divided geographically into a western and eastern half with the crisis of transition caused by industrialization most acutely felt in the western half. The Iranian Revolution of 1979 represents the first of what it likely to be many transitions from pre-industrial societies to this version of the Modern Dictatorship—Khomeinism. Iran stands out as one of the few countries experiencing two revolutions in the 20th century. The first in 1905, established a constitutional monarchy limiting the Hereditary Dictatorship's power. Lasting to 1921, it was overthrown when a military coup returned the Shah to power.

The internal affairs in Iran were always a concern to the outside powers of Britain and Russia who reached an accord in 1907 as to their respective spheres of influence in Iran. When World War II began, the same two powers occupied the country to ensure Iran's oil resources were under the control of the Allies. After the war, America and Britain pressured the Soviet Union to remove its troops before the Shah Mohammed Reza Pahlavi (1919 – 1980) was returned to rule. When a left-wing Parliament attempted to nationalize the British oil companies, the American Central Intelligence Agency (CIA), along with British help, returned full power to the Shah. The Americans were implementing their policy of containment and they perceived the left-wing government as a potential Soviet ally. It is an unfortunate byproduct of this policy the Free Societies would support many disreputable figures in the Third World. America and Britain had formed an alliance with Stalin to defeat Hitler in the Great Western Civil War and were taking the same approach in Iran. The Shah, restored to absolute power, adopted a policy of forced modernization. When he encountered resistance to the changes by both Marxist and Islamic groups, the Shah established the secret police (SAVAK) in 1957.

The White Revolution, as the forced modernization was called, produced a sharp reaction. Ruhollah Khomeini (1902 – 1989) went into exile in 1964 for his anti-government activities, and the guerrilla group Mujahedin-e-Khalq (MKO) was formed in 1965. The land reform part of the dictator's program inadvertently produced large numbers of displaced peasants who congregated in urban areas and by 1979 Tehran had 1.5 million persons living in slum conditions. These individuals along with many others had reason to resist the secular modernization and perceived the dictator as an American puppet. The situation became particularly heated when Khomeini's son died of a heart attack since many blamed the death on SAVAK.

Because Shiite Muslims have a forty day mourning period, demonstrations forty days after a martyr's death could produce more martyrs, and the American government warned the Shah to be tolerant of human rights and avoid a crackdown as the protests grew in October 1977. Demonstrations intensified in January 1978 when in the religious center at Qom protestors denounced a government insult to Islam. Once those opposed to the regime saw the government could not or would not stop the demonstrations—thanks to American pressure for tolerance—the demonstrations continued to grow. The Shah left in January 1979 and the army declared itself neutral in February. The demonstrators had won.

The date 11 February 1979 is considered the beginning of the Islamic Republic as the dictator Khomeini returned from exile. The American Embassy, as well as its diplomats, was captured on 4 November 1979, and the selective release of classified American documents fueled the anti-American propaganda. Khomeini was able to combine classic Marxist attacks against Third World imperialism with new Islamic attacks against an amoral, decadent west. American diplomats were held hostage for 444 days. A new ideology upon which to base a Modern Dictatorship had been born—Khomeinism. Iran had made the transition from a pre-industrial society to the Modern Dictatorship.

4

There is a high correlation between the occupation of a nation by British or American troops and the likelihood of a Free Society. The British or American soldier has historically been the best ambassador of freedom.

In many areas of former British colonization—India, Australia, New Zealand, and eventually in South Africa—the Free Society emerged victorious.[34] Free Societies also took hold in areas occupied by the American Army in the Philippines, Japan, West Germany, Italy, and South Korea. The Free Societies' victory in the Great Western Civil War made this secondary route to a Free Society possible in central Europe and other non-European areas of the world. Other areas in Asia, were a mixed bag owing in part to the American defeat in Vietnam. Parts of Europe such as Switzerland, the Netherlands, and the Scandinavian countries, who had already become Free Societies on their own, benefited from the explosion of democratic governments.

---

[34] The historic end to apartheid under Nelson Mandela was in part made possible by the collapse of the Soviet Union. With the Communists in a weak position, moderates on both sides had less to fear in reconciliation.

The largest of these new Free Societies was India, and much of the credit to a peaceful transition can be given to the Indian people under the leadership of Mohandas K. Gandhi (1869 – 1948). India represents the most peaceful non-European transition from the pre-industrial society to a Free Society anywhere in the world.

Gandhi was born to the merchant caste in India in the Gujarat region on the west coast. At the age of thirteen he followed the Indian tradition of arranged marriages, and after finishing high school he went to London to study law, returning to India a new lawyer in 1891. He was asked by a firm in India to represent them in a lawsuit in South Africa. Once the legal proceedings were concluded in May 1893, Gandhi remained in South Africa for the next twenty years campaigning against the unjust laws imposed on Indians by the British.

Gandhi considered himself to be a loyal British subject, expecting the British to live up to their own moral code he learned while in London. During two conflicts first against the Boers (1899) and later against the Zulus (1906), he organized Indian students as stretcher-bearers and medics. Inspired by the American Thoreau and the Russian Tolstoy, he formulated his concept of non-violent resistance against unjust laws. In 1907 he called this struggle *satyagraha* or the power of truth.[35] It was about this time he also became increasingly religious and vowed *brahmacharya,* which included chastity within marriage and as well as other disciplines of self-control. He was freeing himself of money, pain, and pleasure to pursue his cause, including the patience to endure suffering. He led strikes and protests resulting in beatings and imprisonment, and soon, he along with 2,500 other Indians, would be in South African jails. The struggle eventually ended on 30 June 1914 when a pact was signed between Gandhi and General Smuts, the future president of the Union of South Africa, representing the British Empire.

Leaving South Africa, Gandhi made a stop in London where he organized Indian students in ambulance squads for World War I. Back in India,

---

[35] As George Orwell would point out, non-violent resistance only works in certain situations. It may work if your enemy wants to turn you into a slave. It does not work if your enemy wants to turn you into a corpse.

he spent several years reacquainting himself with his native country, and when he met the Nobel Prize winning poet, Rabindranath Tagore, who called him Mahatma or 'Great Soul,' the name stuck. In April 1919 he organized the first national day of fasting and prayer, *hartal*, to begin a non-violent resistance to British rule.

As one might expect, the British had asked for Indian help during World War I and India sent 1.2 million troops. It was mostly Indian troops who liberated Mesopotamia from the Ottoman Empire. After the war when the British began to renege on their promises of Indian autonomy, the cause of Indian nationalism grew. By 1920, the Indian National Congress voted to follow Gandhi's method of non-violence and non-cooperation with the British embracing self-reliance. Gandhi would spin his own cloth with an antique spinning wheel, and it would become his symbol—eventually becoming part of the Indian flag.

When in 1922 the campaign extended to the refusal to pay taxes, the British dramatically increased the number of arrests. When a mob killed 22 policemen, Gandhi suspended the campaign saying God had warned him the Indian people were not ready to conduct a sincere non-cooperation campaign. He was sent to prison for six years, and unrest continued while the Indian Communist Party was formed in 1924. One could have easily expected India to go the way of China, but Gandhi's opposition to Communism because of its advocacy for violence was a major impediment.

When the Congress met in December 1929 it approved a new campaign of civil disobedience. The Salt March was a symbolic gesture to dramatize self-reliance as part of a general boycott of British goods. Large crowds and much publicity followed Gandhi on his journey as he walked 230 miles to the ocean from his headquarters to the sea to collect salt. The British arrested 90,000 people including Gandhi attempting to stop the boycott.

Released from jail, Gandhi attended a September 1931 conference in London with numerous other Indian representatives to discuss with the British the 'Indian problem', but the Indians could not agree on a unified position. Arrested after he returned and released in 1933, he focused on internal Indian society and its discrimination against the lowest caste, the untouchables. Meanwhile the British granted some autonomy and held elections with a much larger group eligible to vote than ever before resulting in a massive National Congress Party victory with 70% of the votes cast.

In 1939, Gandhi resumed the non-cooperation campaign. With the Japanese conquest of Southeast Asia, the British were keen to get India's help and sent a delegation in 1942 to India. The British proposals were rejected, and the non-cooperation campaign continued. Gandhi, and 90,000 others were arrested, and over 1,000 protesters were killed.

The British became increasingly convinced they could not hold India. This was emphasized after WWII with the trial of soldiers who fought on the Axis side. Prominent Indians defended these soldiers and much of the public was on their side. Despite both native Communist and Fascist movements within India, a Free Society emerged in 1947 when the British granted independence. Extremists hate the Free Society, so it should come as no surprise Gandhi was murdered by a Hindu fanatic in January 1948.

5

The Cold War is an example of the constant struggle between democracies and dictators. This struggle is a permanent feature of the industrial age.

The dictator always seeks constant expansion of his power through military conquest, and the Modern Dictatorship is no exception. Although the Great Western Civil War established the Free Society in Western Europe and eventually in Japan, a worldwide struggle resulted after Modern Dictatorships established themselves in other civilization centers. Called the Cold War, it was a struggle of close to fifty years between the Free Societies and the Communist version of the Modern Dictatorship. During this polarized time the world was divided into a Free World, the Communist Block, with the rest called the Third World. The Americans took the fighting for other's freedom seriously, calling their president the "Leader of the Free World." The Cold War was a window into what the future now looks like and into what will be many more protracted struggles between the Free Societies and Modern Dictatorships.

The Cold War began as Stalin imposed Communism on Eastern Europe. Beginning with Romania in 1945, followed by Bulgaria and Albania in 1946, each proclaimed themselves Socialist Republics. Since 1940 the Nations of Estonia, Latvia, and Lithuania had been part of the Soviet Union and remained so after Soviet troops reoccupied their countries as the Germans retreated. With corrupt elections, two different Marxist parties gained control of Hungary in 1947, and this surprise victory of Communists in Hungary plus the Communist opposition to the Marshall Plan helped defeat the Communists in elections in France in 1948. The Italian Christian Democrats were also victorious in 1948 elections in part with help from the CIA. Stalin was afraid the same thing would occur in Czechoslovakia, and the Communists staged a coup seizing power in February 1948. Poland also fell the same year. The guerilla resistance fighter Tito had his own power base and became the Communist dictator in Yugoslavia.

Germany would be the thornier problem. Since all allied powers occupied the capital Berlin, and no formal agreement had been reached about travel by land through Soviet occupied Germany, Stalin began the Berlin Blockade (June 1948 – May 1949) as a means to consolidate his hold on Germany. Because the Free Societies had disarmed so suddenly, Stalin could take what amounted to an act of war knowing the Americans would only use the atomic bomb in the event actual shooting started. Since the Germans tried to relieve the encircled 6th Army at Stalingrad by air and failed, Stalin had reason to believe the blockade effort would work. But the demands of a civilian society and a military at war are much different while airlift technology had also advanced. The Berlin Airlift, a massive supply effort by air to the city of Berlin, broke Stalin's blockade. By April the Communist East Germany as a separate entity was created, and Stalin lifted the blockade the next month. Stalin's efforts awakened the West to the danger and the North American Treaty Organization (NATO) was formed in April 1949.

It is surprising, after their Munich experience, the Free Societies would act so blindly. The Polish government in exile was already at odds with the Kremlin over the massacre of Polish army officers in the Katyn forest and because Stalin had refused to help during the Polish Warsaw uprising in August 1944. These indicators of Stalin's intentions should have opened Western eyes. The Soviet treachery when they invaded Poland on 17 September 1939 was obvious, and later the Soviet installation of a Communist government in Romania in March 1945 was a clear violation of Yalta's Declaration on Liberated Areas. Not all Westerners were naïve. Churchill warned an Iron Curtain was falling across Eastern Europe in a speech on 5 March 1946. He was ignored as he had been in the 1930's when he warned about Hitler.

The long-term policy of the United States when confronting the Communist Modern Dictatorships was first expounded in a *Foreign Affairs* article published in July 1947 and signed "X." The author was George Kennan (1904 – 2005), the former deputy in charge of the American mission in Moscow. Kennan argued for a policy of containment. The article was a summary of a similar but longer dispatch he had been asked to write from Moscow about why the Russians refused to cooperate on such issues as the World Bank. This policy of containment attempted to answer how to confront the Soviets in an age of potential total nuclear war.

The Cold War was not always cold. It became a shooting war in four major instances: the Korean War, the Vietnam Wars both I and II, and the Soviet invasion of Afghanistan. In many other cases it was a war fought with surrogates or conducted in secrecy. Its history was rich with many crises like the second Berlin crisis or the Cuban Missile Crisis. It was a story full of intrigue such as the Rosenberg spy ring passing atomic secrets to the Russians. It was a period of a massive nuclear arms race. It had the two power blocks racing to be the first to put a man on the moon. Two particular struggles, the American involvement in Vietnam II, and the Russian invasion of Afghanistan are most relevant to the thesis presented here. The American loss in Vietnam II weakened the desire by the Americans to fight for the freedom of others. The Russian invasion of Afghanistan was the final strain pushing the Communist dictatorship over the edge, losing its Mandate from Heaven.

America, attempting to implement the containment policy, was gradually taking a lead role in this effort as the European powers retreated back to Europe. This led to the Second Vietnam War with America as a major participant. It was during the John F. Kennedy (1917 – 1963) administration the groundwork for large American involvement took shape with American advisors already in Vietnam as part of the containment strategy. After North Vietnam was lost to the dictator Ho Chi Minh (1890 – 1969) following the French defeat in Vietnam I, the Americans desired to keep South Vietnam free.[36]

In March 1964, McNamara then the American Defense Secretary, returned from Saigon with a report on a deteriorating situation. The Communist guerillas recruited from the south, the Viet Cong, now controlled 40% of South Vietnam. The American President Johnson (1908 – 1973) made it official American policy to keep South Vietnam free. The North Vietnamese on the other hand wanted to show to the South how America was a paper tiger. The 7 February 1964 bombing of Americans in a Saigon theatre was but one provocation.

On 4 August 1964 the National Security Agency (NSA) intercepted North Vietnamese radio communications calling for an attack upon Americans ships off the coast. The destroyers Maddox and Turner Joy were informed. Later they reported being under attack. There is considerable doubt if they actually came under attack, as they never received any live fire hitting either ship. The engagement took place only on radar under unfavorable atmospheric conditions. Johnson had been looking for something to help get Congressional approval for the war. He did not want to repeat the situation the American President Truman had found himself in with Korea. Truman had fought the Korean War as a police action without any formal authorization from Congress. Johnson used the Gulf of Tonkin Resolution as his authorization.

The manner in which this war was fought made it the most unusual of any American war. McNamara was in charge and kept the Joint Chiefs of Staff (JCS) as uninvolved with any policy decisions as he could. While he was Secretary of Defense, the JCS did not attend the weekly Tuesday meetings at the White House where war strategy was discussed.

---

[36] The dictator Ho was a popular figure. In America some would argue as the "Washington of Vietnam" a popular vote should be taken to allow him to be elected. The better comparison was the dictator Hitler. He too was popular but "one man, one vote, one time" is not democracy.

McNamara was implementing the flexible response strategy developed earlier in the Kennedy administration under which America would gradually increase the pressure on the North until the cost of liberating the South was too high. The practical result of this strategy was to produce a war of attrition. Since the North derived much of their legitimacy from Vietnamese nationalism and anti-colonialism, it was doubtful they would ever respond to only pressure as the Americans had hoped. The North was fighting a total war, while the Americans were fighting a limited war.

By mid 1967, while the American public continued to be told it was winning, the war was actually a stalemate. The Communists attempted to end the stalemate with complete tactical surprise on 30 January 1968 called the Tet Offensive. Initially successful, in the end it was a military disaster for the Communists despite American reporting back home painting Tet as an American defeat. By the end of March, Johnson told the American public he would not seek a second term and he was halting bombing north of the 20th parallel. Negotiations began in Paris, and in October all bombing of the North had ended.

The newly elected President Nixon (1913 – 1994) was determined South Vietnam would not fall to the Communists. He expanded the Vietnamization of the war—a term the South Vietnamese always resented because they had been fighting with the Americans from the start. Nixon drew up a timetable for the withdrawal of American troops, and an eventual agreement was signed on 27 January 1973, but in the aftermath of the Watergate scandal Nixon was unable to enforce the agreement with American airpower. He resigned in August 1974, and a majority anti-war Congress was elected in November. The desire to fight for the freedom of others had its limits, and the Americans were simply not going to spill any more blood in Vietnam. The new Congress became stingy with aid to the South, but the Soviet Union gave North Vietnam fresh promises of aid. In December 1974 the North attacked, and by the 30th of April their tanks rolled into Saigon.

The Soviet invasion of Afghanistan was preceded in April 1978 by a Communist coup. By the time of the Soviet invasion in December 1979, the atheistic policies of the Communists had left Afghanistan in full civil war. In the first phase of the invasion, 100,000 Soviet troops occupied all major cities and towns. In this period 1979 – 1982, they attempted to back up the Communist government. When it became clear stronger measures were needed, the Soviets in essence waged war on the countryside from 1982 – 1987 making no attempt to win any hearts and minds. Devastating the countryside they never controlled more than 20% of the entire country. It was total war against the people of Afghanistan. Because of this brutal policy, the resistance only grew with Sunni groups supported by refugees in Pakistan and Shiite groups doing the same in Iran.

Promising to restore America's military and economic strength, Ronald Reagan (1911 – 2004) became President of the United States after the 1980 elections. He put a new twist on the long term American policy of containment. The Americans would now actively put pressure on the Soviet Union to hasten the eventual collapse foreseen in the original policy of containment. It was a strategy to win the Cold War. With Margaret Thatcher (1925–2013) as the British Prime Minister providing the same anti-Communist foreign policy in Great Britain, Reagan began assembling a formidable team to implement the new strategy.

The first part of this new strategy would be to support resistance movements fighting the Soviets and their allies. This meant supporting those fighting Cuban troops in Angola and those fighting the Sandinistas in Nicaragua. It would also mean supporting the government in El Salvador against a Communist insurgency. Two particular movements would provide the biggest potential pressure: Poland and Afghanistan.

The Polish Solidarity movement withstood the initial crackdown of 1981 – 1982 and was able to continue to resist thanks in part to about $8 million a year in aid, advanced communication equipment, and intelligence data. Some of the support was funneled through the Catholic Church now headed by a Polish Pope—John Paul II (1920 – 2005), and it is highly likely the assassination attempt against the Polish Pope in May 1981 was ordered by the Soviet Union. Afghanistan resistance support was provided by the Americans through bases in Pakistan while non-native foreign fighters were supported by Saudi Arabia and other Muslim states. The Americans went so far as to supply advanced technology like shoulder fired anti-aircraft stinger missiles to the Mujahedeen fighters to nullify the Soviet advantage in airpower.

The increased pressure on the Soviets was matched with an arms buildup in America. The Americans had neglected their military in the aftermath of Vietnam and had already begun to increase defense spending prior to Reagan's presidency. Although the increase was large by comparison to the 1970s, historically they were modest compared to the 1950s. In the Eisenhower era, spending on defense amounted to nearly 10% of GDP, while Reagan's spending would peak out at only 6.5%. However since the US economy was larger than it was in the 1950s, this would buy a lot of hardware.

Reagan's ability to gain allied cooperation also added to the pressure on the Russians. Saudi Arabia held down oil prices with increased production, which hurt Russia's ability to earn hard currency. Reagan sold American grain to the Russians forcing them to expend more hard currency. He also discouraged the Western Europeans from building pipelines to export Soviet energy supplies to Europe and banned the export of American pipeline equipment. Only one out of several proposed pipelines was eventually built, further limiting Russia's ability to earn hard currency. Reagan was able to get German cooperation in stationing Pershing II nuclear missiles on German soil over vocal domestic opposition.

When Mikhail Gorbachev (1931–) became Communist Party Chairman in 1985 he had a massive problem on his hands. He attempted reforms to the Communist system through campaigns called restructuring—Perestroika, and openness—Glasnost. When Gorbachev was not forth coming about the Chernobyl nuclear disaster in 1986, Russians learning of the details from western sources became disenchanted with his reforms. After a West German teenager flew a small aircraft from Helsinki to land in Red Square in 1987, Gorbachev now looked impotent. Party opposition grew to his reforms, and in a move reminiscent of Louis XVI he fought the Party by increasing popular participation in government. Gorbachev, with the war in Afghanistan at a stalemate and more interested in reforms at home, ordered a withdrawal in 1988.

When Gorbachev's reform efforts spread to the members of the Warsaw Pact, the Soviets began to lose their grip. Solidarity was legalized in April 1989 and before the end of the year Poland had a non-Communist president, as opposition to Communism grew in Hungary and East Germany. After massive anti-government demonstrations in Leipzig, a new government promised elections and lifted the travel ban to the west. Immediately large numbers of people tried to enter West Berlin, and the infamous wall was opened. Soon it was being dismantled by the crowds. Reagan had challenged Gorbachev to "tear down this wall" in a famous 1987 speech in Berlin. Now the Germans were doing it without Gorbachev's consent. One by one the Communist dictatorships in Eastern Europe fell.

All eyes were now on the Soviet Union. Under pressure from the newly elected Soviet Congress, Gorbachev released the secret protocols of the Hitler-Stalin Pact, which began World War II. The three Baltic States had their proof of an illegal incorporation into the Soviet Union and began to secede. By May of 1990, all three had declared their independence. Gorbachev sent troops into the Baltics in January 1991 killing a few nationalists, but his half-hearted measures only inflamed nationalist passions.

In his gut Gorbachev was not a dictator or revolutionary but a bureaucrat. He was a man of position papers growing up in a privileged position within Soviet society, and he did not understand what it meant to be the dictator of a brutal Empire. Others did however, and attempted a coup against him in August 1991.

At the time Boris Yeltsin (1931 – 2007) was a democratically elected President of Russia, and when news of the coup broke, he rushed to the Russian White House to oppose it. The building was surrounded both by troops and pro-democracy demonstrators. He was able to persuade the troops to switch sides in a famous speech while standing upon a Russian tank. He outlawed the Communist Party in November. When the Ukraine declared its independence from the Soviet Union in December, the Soviet Union ceased to exist. Gorbachev was the leader of a non-existent country, and the Cold War was over.

6

The natural human tendency toward dictatorship cannot be undone. With the advent of industrialization, Modern Dictatorships replaced the Hereditary Dictatorships of the world. Only the industrial power of America allowed the Free Societies to triumph in the West. This ended the European dictator's Age of European Domination (c. 1450 – 1945) and set the stage for the constant struggle of democracies and dictators.

As technology spreads and the world industrializes, each kingdom will confront the crisis of the pre-industrial society. The first to industrialize was Western civilization and was the first to experience this crisis. The Great Western Civil War (1914 – 1945) plunged the world into the worst period of warfare in human history where upwards of 100 million people died—the majority of whom were civilians. During the second phase of this war, the Fascist form of the Modern Dictatorship fought against an alliance of the Free Societies and the Communist form of the Modern Dictatorship. Only the contribution of America with its military and industrial might was decisive in the Free Societies emerging victorious. Nothing is intended to minimize the courageous sacrifices of the Russian or Chinese people or of the other Free Societies, but had Hitler survived or had Stalin alone defeated Hitler, the world today would be a much darker place.

While the more industrialized societies of Italy, Japan, and Germany turned to Fascism, most of the rest of the world turned to Communism. The first to do so was Tsarist Russia. Weakened by her participation in the first phase of the Great Western Civil War, her Hereditary Dictatorship fell, allowing the new dictator Lenin to seize power, make a separate peace with Germany and consolidate his rule. After Lenin died, Stalin became the new dictator until 1953, and despite Communism's destructive economic policies, the empire Stalin created lasted until 1991. The other major power to transition to Communism was China, proclaimed the People's Republic of China in 1949, when Mao became dictator of the most populace country in the world.

In other parts of the world, Communism spread in Asia, Latin America, and Africa. Communist governments took power in North Korea, Vietnam,

Cambodia, and Laos. In Latin America many movements made attempts to establish dictatorships, but interference from the United States prevented this in all but Cuba. Still in power today, Fidel Castro became dictator in 1959, and at the height of his power he had over 50,000 Cuban troops in Africa. Meanwhile, the transition to Communism in Africa was much more successful taking place in Angola, Mozambique, and Ethiopia. Ethiopia in particular exhibited some of the more horrific aspects of Communism including mass starvation.

The one major exception to this near universal pattern was India as its transition was mostly peaceful and democratic. As a former British colony, India, like America, adopted the best ideas of their colonial rulers. It also helped the British were not resorting to the more brutal measures of other European colonial powers. Nonetheless the credit goes to the people of India and the non-violent protest methods of Gandhi.

The one area of the world currently in the transition phase is Islamic civilization where the western half of Islam is particularly hard hit. Best described as Khomeinism, it represents another type of Modern Dictatorship. A new Totalitarian ideology exploiting the religion of Islam, it has features similar to both Fascism and Communism. The first government to fall was Iran in 1979, and the region continues in turmoil with uprisings in Tunisia, Libya, Egypt, Yemen, and Syria with the possibility of a Modern Dictatorship ever-present.

With Stalin as one of the victors at the end of the Great Western Civil War, the stage was set for another struggle between the Free Societies and Modern Dictatorships. The struggle set as rivals the Free Societies led by the United States against the Communist Block led by the Soviet Union. The Cold War began almost as soon as WWII was over and lasted until the Soviet Union collapsed in 1991. It included the four major 'hot' wars of Korea, Vietnams I and II, and Afghanistan, and also many lesser conflicts by surrogates and proxies. American military might combined with her willingness to fight for the freedom of others turned the worldwide struggle against the two 'isms' (Fascism and Communism) of the 20th century into victories for the Free Societies. The Cold War stands as an archetype of struggles in the future—the constant struggle of democracies and dictators.

Notwithstanding the tremendous changes due to the Scientific and Industrial Revolutions, the way government is conducted has not changed. Government remains the struggle for power to establish a monopoly of violence, and the governments naturally resulting from this struggle are militarily aggressive abroad and oppressive at home. The dictators of Europe are now gone and the Age of European Domination (c. 1450 – 1945) is over. Today, the Free Society, that aberration and freak of history, has its best chance of survival. This period in history beginning in 1945 is unique and represents the best opportunity yet for freedom to escape the fates of Athens and Rome.

The Perfection of Man

Chapter Six

The three incarnations of the Modern Dictatorship—Fascism, Communism, and Khomeinism—are similar to the Hereditary Dictatorship because they are founded on the monopoly of violence and use this to create the secondary monopolies already discussed. However, there is a new innovation on this monopoly: the Terror. It is unprecedented in history and helps governments murder large percentages of their own population. The death toll from the Communist Terror alone was nearly 100 million. Adding this to the depravations attributable to Fascism, these governments easily killed 200 million people in the 20th century. But because of the monopoly of violence's unbounded nature, there is now an existential danger. The Modern Dictatorship's quest to perfect man and build a utopia will mean the redesign of the human being. Whereas the Hereditary Dictatorship dominated the society figuratively in its body, soul, and mind, the Modern Dictatorship's domination of the physical human being will some day be literal.

To achieve this domination, another major innovation of the Modern Dictatorship is the new religion—the Utopian Vision. The Utopian Vision is the key element in sustaining the power of the Modern Dictatorship. It is the modern version of the secondary monopoly of religion found in Hereditary Dictatorships. The Party is the new priesthood and secret police the new military caste. Now, with the enormous wealth of the Industrial Revolution and the scientific principles at its disposal, nothing can stand in the way of the perfection of man.

This new religion exploits the human tendency toward hysteria—an innate human characteristic. Creating hysteria is a central part of the Modern Dictatorship's hold on people. The critical role of the scapegoat is often part of this hysteria, and its importance to the success of the Modern Dictatorship cannot be over emphasized. Hate, too, is a powerful emotion if it can be made to serve the dictator. Auschwitz, one of man's most infamous crimes, was made possible by hate of the scapegoat in an atmosphere of hysteria. All three types of Modern Dictatorships in Germany, Russia, China, and Iran exhibit these characteristics.

Using the secondary monopoly over the intellect, the Modern Dictatorship is a master of propaganda and subversion. The main purpose of propaganda is to gain new recruits, and the most effective propaganda is often based upon a plausible lie repeated over and over again. Because they are open and these lies are effective at gaining followers, the Free Societies are vulnerable to this propaganda.

The one Hereditary Dictatorship successfully navigating the transition into the modern era was the nation of Germany. Germany made this transition thanks in large part to one man—Bismarck—who stands out as a warning to all Free Societies because all forms of dictatorship are dangerous.

2

Historically four distinct types of Modern Dictatorships have developed. Those of the 20th century were Fascism, Communism, and Khomeinism. The fourth was the extreme rationalism of the French Revolution. One new possibility is offered as the ultimate abstraction of what all Modern Dictatorships aspire to attain.

Fascism is a form of the Modern Dictatorship based upon extreme nationalism and racism. It views the people in its state as superior to others, and in certain instances, a superiority based upon biology. In most cases, the dictator of this state is seen as the personification of this superiority. Both *Il Duce* and *Der Fuhrer* mean "leader" in their respective languages. Because much is done internally to glorify militarism and bloody self-sacrifice, such a state naturally lends itself toward territorial expansion. In Italy the Fascists formed a paramilitary organization with black-shirted uniforms called the *squadristi*. The Italians would use anything they could to recall the grandeur and power of ancient Rome. A Fascist funeral was full of religious imagery and speeches about self-sacrifice.

In Germany the arguments were similar. The Germans were descendants of a superior Aryan race. They had been corrupted and needed to take steps to purify themselves. The Nazi Party also glorified militarism and created its own paramilitary group, the Storm Detachment, headed by Ernst Rohm. Joseph Goebbels the Nazi propaganda minister, would stage elaborate funerals of Nazi members killed by Communists portraying them as martyrs to a great cause. Many Fascists were admirers of the philosopher Nietzsche (1844 – 1900) who's loathing for decadent western culture and longing for the new source of values, the *übermensch*, was a key ingredient of his philosophy.

In Japan, Dr. Nagai Hisomu, along with many others, promoted eugenic ideas and the need for racial purity. Nature via natural selection had a mechanism to keep the species healthy. Modern civilization had short-circuited the process, and it was up to the state to correct the situation. Asia needed to be a self-sufficient economic block under Japanese leadership. For many in Japan it was a 'violation of nature' for whites to dominate Asia.

Communism is a form of the Modern Dictatorship based upon extreme class warfare and envy of the wealthy. The ideas behind Communism are a direct product of the philosopher Karl Marx (1818 – 1883) whose theories predicted a utopian society evolving from the advanced capitalistic societies. Lenin would later add a twist saying a small band of dedicated revolutionaries would be needed for the last evolutionary step. Its symbol of the hammer and sickle represented the two main groups—factory workers and peasants—who would rise up to transform society. Communism, Marxism, and related class warfare ideologies have a more seductive attraction than Fascism as they purport to create a classless society with all needs fulfilled and everyone living in equality as well as an end to poverty and war.

While classic Marxism saw the Communist societies developing in advanced industrial countries, Mao saw a new path to utopia. According to Mao and Maoism, the future utopia would come from rural peasant revolts, thus springing directly from the pre-industrial society. This approach became useful as a way to galvanize revolutions against the European colonial powers in wars of national liberation. Russia, a relatively backward country, would turn out to be the most industrialized of any to experience a Communist revolution. No major industrialized country fell to a Communist insurrection while many pre-industrial societies did, and this made Mao's explanation more accurate. Communism continues to have a great appeal in the Third World.

Khomeinism is a form of the Modern Dictatorship that has kidnapped Islam and put it into the service of the dictator. Khomeinism includes all sects of Islam, both Shiite and Sunni. When the first elected Iranian president, Bani Sadr, was removed from office in June 1981, the Revolutionary Council under Khomeini had total power. The Islamic Republican Party (IRP) and their internal army the Revolutionary Guards were used for enforcement. In 1981 – 1982 they conducted mass arrests and summary executions of 7,700 persons.

In 1983 the IRP launched a campaign against deviant Islamic religious views establishing the IRP as the official interpreter of Islam within the Islamic Republic, while the legal system was brought into conformity with their version of *sharia* law. Shiite jurists approved by the Party prepared all criminal and civil codes. All government ministries and security forces had special offices staffed with Party approved clergy to ensure compliance. Teachers, along with students, were purged for not being sufficiently Islamic. Strict dress codes were enforced requiring women to observe the *hejab* while Christians and Jews were forced into a second-class status. The members of the Baha'i faith, the largest religious minority in Iran, were persecuted as infidels with nearly 200 Baha'i leaders executed and another 800 imprisoned by 1985. The Iranian dictator Khomeini took the title *Imam* normally used to refer to the *Twelfth Imam,* who was only to return in "the end of days." Khomeini was communicating a clear messianic message as part of his ideology.

Another important aspect of the ideology was its view of women. While in exile Khomeini had denounced the Family Protection Act passed under the Shah. According to Khomeini, all divorces under the act were null and void, and those women remained married to their ex-husbands. Later, his regime would support women protesters wearing the traditional *chador* shouting, "Death to foreign dolls" a reference to the women who refused to cover up by wearing the *chador*. The clear implication was such women were traitors aligned with foreign enemies of Iran.

Because of their hostility towards Jews, Khomeinism is sometimes called Islamo-Fascism. Its joy of brutality has strong Fascist overtones, and the public hanging of a girl from an industrial crane as a public reminder against adultery is a recent example. It is not a truly racist doctrine, however, since anyone can in theory join the movement, and thus it is technically not Fascism.

Khomeinism is also seen in various Sunni groups as well.[37] The Taliban in Afghanistan and Hamas in the Gaza Strip are not the only Sunni examples. Groups like the Moro Islamic Front in the Philippines and the Jemaah Islamiah in Indonesia are two other examples. All these groups wish to control every aspect of society under a rigid interpretation of *sharia* law. They see themselves as part of a global mission to convert the world to Islam via holy war—*jihad*. The combination of Nazi-like anti-Semitism and Marxist-like pronouncements about imperialism and the decadent west are evident in their propaganda. The Sunni Hereditary Dictatorship in Arabia ruled by the Saud Dynasty practice a rigid interpretation of *sharia* law in part to undermine a possible revolution. Although this will only delay the inevitable being a Hereditary Dictatorship they are doomed to eventual extinction. The industrial age has made the Hereditary Dictatorship obsolete.

In some cases the Khomeinist groups are not attempting to take over any particular country. Instead they practice *jihad* against the non-Islamic nations directly. As they are weak militarily, this usually means they attack the weakest of targets—unarmed civilians. The most spectacular of these kinds of attacks was on 11 September 2001 against targets in the United

---

[37] The recent upheavals in the Arab Middle East are reminiscent of the revolt in Iran. Based upon the discussion here one should not be too optimistic.

States. Almost 3000 were killed. This was the worst loss of life in any attack on American soil, exceeding those lost at Pearl Harbor. The Khomeinist group al-Qaeda was responsible for the attacks under the leadership of Osama bin Laden (1957 – 2011).

Given the failure of the Germans to create their *übermensch*, the Soviets to create their new Soviet Man, and the Chinese to create the new Socialist Man, it is reasonable to speculate about other potential Modern Dictatorships. What might the most extreme Modern Dictatorship do if it came to believe human nature was standing in the way of utopia? Possibly, it would develop a Utopian Vision based upon genetic manipulation of the human race. The technology available today exceeds anything the dictators of old could dream of, and there is every expectation this technology will only get better. Hitler, Stalin, and Mao, the three great dictators of the 20th century, had all the power of a modern state including secret police, torture, and death camps to force their will upon their respective countries. However, in the end no amount of education, propaganda, or coercion was enough for them to change human nature. A future dictator, concluding failure came from human nature, could manipulate technology to create a new type of human to better align with this dictator's Utopian Vision. The ultimate abstraction of dictatorship, such a society would combine the technology of *Brave New World* with the brutality of *1984*.[38]

3.1

The Terror is a new manifestation of the monopoly of violence. It puts the Party on an equal footing with the army. It is the consequence of the monopoly of violence's ubiquitous and unbounded nature.

The Party, whether it's the Communist Party or the Nazi Party, is much more than an ordinary political party in these dictatorships. They are the keepers of the orthodoxy and the dictator's direct representatives. They act as a government within the government to ensure ideological purity. They replace the priesthood found in the Hereditary Dictatorship but are much

---

[38] No doubt the foreign policy would be one of genocide in an attempt to wipeout inferior (read original) humans.

more powerful because of the secret police. The secret police as an army of the Party has put the new 'priesthood' onto an equal footing with the old warrior class. Trotsky, head of the Red Army, would have ordinarily taken over the Soviet Union except for the denunciations by the Party, but as Stalin controlled the Party, he became dictator. Each Modern Dictatorship has a secret police to implement the Terror. The Nazis had the Gestapo and the East Germans had the Stasi. Non-compliance with the orthodoxy could be met with a variety of methods.

Stalin's concentration camps, the Gulag Archipelago, were a vast system of labor concentration camps used to murder millions of people. This system was the largest and most extensive system of its kind in the world, and its records are now available to the public. By the early 1930s 140,000 prisoners were working for the State Political Directorate, the GPU. When the GPU was reorganized in 1934 and renamed the People's Commissariat for Internal Affairs, the NKVD, it took charge of all camps and prisoners in the Soviet Union. By July 1935, the new organization had 965,000 prisoners who were mostly confined to the harsher work camps. 240,000 having received sentences of less than five years were in the less severe work colonies. The operation of these camps was entirely economic in motivation with separate divisions for hydroelectric, railway, and roads.

This new modern form of slavery was used to complete the canal from the White Sea to Baltic in 1933. Once the Canal was complete, many prisoners were sent to start work on the Stalin Canal connecting Moscow to the Volga. A new railway route parallel to the Trans-Siberian railway was another project. In 1932 the gold mines in the Koylma region were developed and thirty-five percent of all gold mined in the Soviet Union came from this region. The gold was used to buy equipment from the decadent west to further industrialization. In June 1935, the dictatorship launched a new project to develop nickel production in Norilsk north of the Arctic Circle. By 1941 the slave numbers had grown to nearly 2 million, and much of the rapid industrialization in the early Soviet Union can be attributed to this slave labor system.

The Great Terror was known as the Reign of Ezhov or Ezhovshchina since Nikolai Ezhov was the head of the NKVD. It began in the summer of 1937 when a special Politburo directive with a four-month time frame went out to all local authorities. A special troika was to be created to speed trials headed by a regional NKVD chief. As in previous purges, each area was given a quota. Those Russians who showed hostility were shot while the rest were to be deported to the camps or the interior. In a short period of time, 260,000 were arrested and 72,000 shot. The categories were eventually expanded to include socially dangerous elements or former tsarist civil servants. To show Stalin their revolutionary zeal, many districts exceeded their quota.

The original four-month time frame was expanded to over a year and an additional 200,000 were rounded up as the Great Terror slowly grew to include other groups. New initiatives from the Politburo or NKVD attacked minorities to include Poles, Turks, and Germans for subversive activities. Hundreds of thousands more were arrested. In addition, there were special targeted lists of individual people signed by Stalin himself or other Politburo members. These lists would eventually contain 44,000 Party officials, leaders of industry, and leaders in the military. The last category turned out to be particularly damaging to the regime weakening the armed forces. Three out of five army marshals, eight of nine admirals, thirteen of fifteen army generals, and fifty of fifty-nine Army Corps generals were all executed. If a person was on the list, it was likely they would be executed as 39,000 executions attest. Five members of the Politburo, ninety-eight of 139 members of the Central Committee, and ninety percent of the Party leadership in Leningrad were all arrested. Records now publically available shows 1,575,000 were arrested in the years 1937 through 1938—eighty-five percent were found guilty and fifty-one percent were executed.

In China, Maoism took a different approach to the Terror. In addition to a camp system called the *laogai,* mass movements of citizens were used to further Party objectives. The All-China Federation of Democratic Youth had a membership of eighteen million in 1953. Other organizations had similar forced mass participation including the All-China Federation of Trade Union (ten million) and the All-China Democratic Women's Federation (seventy-six million). These societies would be periodically swept up in social campaigns. The Resist-America Aid-Korea campaign and the Five-Anti Movement of 1952 are examples. The Five-Antis were bribery, tax evasion, fraud, theft of government property, and publication of state economic secrets. When the largest of these campaigns, the Cultural Revolution, began in 1966 with incorporation of large numbers of students in the Red Guard, the pattern had already been established. This last movement was formed to combat Anti-Maoists. It in reality was Mao's way of holding on to power.

The Cultural Revolution was the largest mass mobilization of people in the history of the Chinese dictatorship, and it killed anywhere from one to three million people. The Cultural Revolution Group (CRG) was its steering committee and they determined the peasantry, the military, as well as the nuclear weapons programs, would be protected from the coming Terror. The peasants had yet to recover from the Great Leap Forward, so this revolution mostly took place in urban areas.

At the front of the movement were the Red Guards, a paramilitary organization of young people ages fifteen to twenty-two. Stalin had used the Great Terror to rid the Soviet Union of people who grew up before the revolution and replaced them with people who knew only Stalin. The people in the Red Guards knew only Mao and being urban were spoiled by traditional Chinese standards. Mao had been forced to concede some power after the blunders of the Great Leap Forward. He wanted his power back, and the youth indoctrinated in his cult-of-the-personality would be his means.

The Terror started in June 1966, when a call for struggle was read over the state-controlled radio. All the stereotypical characteristics of youth gangs were in evidence. They tended to idealize Mao, but questioned all authority at local levels. They intimidated all who questioned their attacks upon the Anti-Maoists. The younger members tended to be the most violent and sadistic as a way to prove their worth much like any other gang initiation. The Red Guard units went to the universities, to the Party members, and to the factories to correct their deviances. Armed with Mao's *Little Red Book* and full of slogans, they beat and intimidated their elders. Many officials were sent to the hospital and class enemies were commonly humiliated. The Reds were reminiscent of the Nazi brown-shirts of a past era. Professors were forced to wear clownish outfits or had black ink smeared on their heads.

This was symbolic since a person blacklisted in their personal file had severely limited opportunities. A professor whose name meant "horse" was forced to eat grass. Enemies would be marched through the streets as objects of public humiliation. In rare cases body parts of the victims would be put on display as symbolic meat because they were Anti-Maoist animals.

During the campaign against the "Four Old-Fashioned Things" as it was called, many cultural artifacts and historic buildings were destroyed. The destruction of old ideas, old culture, old customs, and old habits could be interpreted to mean almost anything. When the rumor started the Red Guards were about to come to a town, people hid anything of value, and the local officials, knowing full well what was about to happen, would station army troops around historic landmarks they thought worth keeping. Religious institutions were particularly hard hit. Buddhist monasteries were sacked and ancient manuscripts burned. In one attack, the sets and costumes of the Beijing Opera were burned. Bourgeois trappings like makeup, high heels, and jewelry were a problem to be fixed on the spot. When the Red Guard came to town it was best to remain inside, though this would not always help as counterrevolutionary homes were often invaded more than once by different units because the coordination was so chaotic.

At the same time, the picture of Mao was everywhere and these photographs took on the status of an eastern orthodox icon. A person could be stopped at any time in the street and asked to recite a saying of Mao.

In one sweep through Beijing, 1,700 were killed, 33,000 homes raided, and 84,000 individuals blacklisted were expelled. In Shanghai, 150,000 'black' homes were raided, and thirty-two tons of bourgeois gold confiscated. In the Ministry of Security 1,200 were executed, sixty percent were arrested from the Communist Party Central Committee as were seventy-five percent of the Party Secretaries in the provinces. 142,000 teachers, 53,000 scientists and engineers, 500 medical professors, and 2,600 artists were attacked for Anti-Maoist tendencies. In Shanghai, 10,000 persons classified as intellectuals were killed. The more prominent the individual the more likely the Reds would have a little fun with him or her as they taught a lesson. In one case, a crane held up the mayor of Shanghai from the back of a truck for all to see while he was beaten.

By mid-1968, the army was restoring order, and the Red Guards were disbanded. Many Red Guards were forced out to the countryside to start a rural life with upwards of twenty million displaced in this manner and many sent to reeducation camps. For those who refused to disband heavy artillery including airpower was needed to retake cities while universities, the center of the Cultural Revolution, were taken with armed assaults. Public executions began to rise, and the push for Party control led to some of the worst purges since the 1950s. And all this time, playing one side off against the other, was Chairman Mao. He used both the Red Guards and their suppression as a way to keep power. When he finally died in September 1976, Deng Xiaoping began the post-Mao era. Mao's closest confidants, the Gang of Four, were all in prison within a month of his death.

3.2

All dictatorships are militarily aggressive. The messianic nature of the Modern Dictatorship makes it more aggressive than the Hereditary Dictatorship.

The Modern Dictatorship is militarily more aggressive than any type of dictatorship in history. When it is stronger than its neighbors, it attacks in open military operations. For instance, the Italian invasion of Ethiopia was completely and totally at the whim of the dictator Mussolini. He was Italy's Minister of Foreign Affairs, Minister of War, Minister of the Navy, and Minister of the Colonies. On 3 October 1935, his war of aggression against Ethiopia began, and in only three days he captured Adowa, the site of an embarrassing defeat for the Italians in 1896. Sanctions imposed by the League of Nations were incomplete and inconsistent. They did accomplish one important thing—unifying the Italian people. The government asked for gold to help with the economic sanctions and the response was overwhelming. Benedetto Croce gave his Senator's gold medal and the Queen Elena gave her gold wedding ring.

In December the Ethiopians counter-attacked winning back some territory, but this only strengthened Mussolini's desire for a quick victory. With over 250 aircraft, the Italian military bombed villages and dropped mustard gas on hapless tribal warriors. The Ethiopians had little unity of command with many local warlords fighting uncoordinated, individual battles.

Mussolini had amassed the largest army in Africa's history for his colonial adventure, and the next phase of the offensive began on the 20th of January 1936. A force of between 350,000 and 400,000 troops attacked with a large contingent from Eritrea and Somalia. Nearly 30,000 vehicles and the 250 planes joined in the offensive. In early March his troops swept through Tigre, and soon they took Lake Ashangi and Gondar. The capital, Addis Ababa, fell on the 5th of May. The short campaign had cost 3,000 Italians and 1,600 colonial troops.

The Italian rule of Ethiopia was mostly brutal. When Mussolini's Viceroy Graziani escaped assassination, 5,000 people were rounded up and shot along with two Bishops of the Coptic Church, and all foreign missionaries were expelled. Imitating the ancient Romans, Mussolini embarked upon an ambitious building campaign to bring Ethiopia into the modern world. He built 3,000 kilometers of new roads with a few hospitals and schools for propaganda purposes. As an economic venture it was a pointless drain on Italian resources, but worth the effort to the dictatorship because now Mussolini was seen by the world as a great military captain.

When the Modern Dictatorship is militarily inferior to its adversaries it attempts to expand by subversion preferring this to attacking in open military operations. The Communist version of the Modern Dictatorship falls into this category since their ideological economic policies kept them weak. Only Korea, Vietnam I & II, and Afghanistan, the major hot conflicts in the Cold War, were exceptions to this rule. The spread of Communism was chiefly by revolutionary movements from within the target country supported with outside help. In most cases, the outside support was across the border providing sanctuary for guerrilla fighters. Diplomacy was also important as the Communists attempted to isolate the country under attack.

Malaya was one successful counterinsurgency operation and a Communist failure because the guerillas lacked a sanctuary, and they recruited from an ethnic minority. In Malaya after World War II, a strong Communist insurgency was threatening the country. During WWII the British supported insurgents fighting the Japanese, and hundreds of Party members trained at a British army school in guerilla tactics. The Communists through the *Min Yuen,* or Masses' Movement, had penetrated all major cities and towns. Their only weakness was recruitments coming from the Chinese ethnic minority. Numbering between five and ten thousand, the guerillas' initial campaign of terrorism and sabotage appeared winning.

The British eventually would be successful in their counterinsurgency efforts by separating the guerilla minority from the general Malaya population. There were one-half million Chinese migrants who worked in the mines and on the plantations, and the British expended a large effort to resettle them into fortified villages. The new housing weakened the Chinese support for the movement, and they were closely watched to prevent them from providing any supplies to the guerillas.

With the many disadvantages of the *Min Yuen*, it demanded ten years to completely defeat the guerillas. The British forces included 40,000 regular forces plus another 100,000 paramilitary police. In an almost comical episode attesting to the difficulty in defeating fanatics dedicated to a cause, a battalion was involved in a nine-month campaign backed with modern aircraft to eliminate what turned out to be only thirty-five guerillas.

When the Modern Dictatorship is yet weaker, violence does not stop being an important element in their movement. Khomeinism has taken root in an area of the world economically weak and unlikely to produce a Nazi Germany or Soviet Union. Being weak, it resorts to terrorism. The attacks by the groups Hamas and Hezbollah against Israel are a good example of terrorism by Modern Dictatorship movements in today's world. They are capitalizing upon the techniques of terrorism coming out of the Arab-Israeli conflict.

A short recap of Arab terrorism around the year 1970 shows how any group of fanatics, motivated by hate, can cause chaos despite being militarily weak. On 23 July 1968, three Arab terrorists captured an El Al flight from Israel to Rome and traded the twenty-one Israeli passengers for a release of Arab prisoners. Three days later an El Al plane was attacked on the ground in Athens. The list of further incidents is shown in the table below.

List of Arab Terrorist Attacks

February 18, 1969	El Al for Tel Aviv	Zurich airport	Attacked
August 29	American TWA	Skyjacked	Landed Damascus
November 27	Two El Al offices	Hand grenades	Athens/Brussels
December 21	American TWA	Skyjacked	Failed
February 10, 1970	El Al attacked	Munich	1 killed, 8 wounded
February 21	Swissair	Mid-air explosion	47 killed
July 22	Greek airliner	Skyjacked	Landed Cairo
September 6	Four Jets	3 Skyjacked	3 blown up at airport
All 1971	2 Airliners	Skyjackings	Failed
February 23, 1972	Lufthansa 747	Skyjacking	Diverted to Yemen
May 8	Jet from Vienna	Skyjacked	1 killed
May 30	Israeli Airport	Attacked	28 killed
August 26	El Al Flight	Mid-air explosion	No one hurt

In one of the most infamous attacks in all the history of terrorism, a group attacked the Olympic Games compound in Munich. On 5 September 1972 two Israeli athletes were killed and nine were held as hostages. The captors demanded they all be taken to the airport where a gun battle broke out between the terrorists and the German police. The hostages were killed and the terrorists captured. The last skyjacking of the year occurred on the 29th of October with the capture of a Lufthansa plane. The passengers were exchanged for the terrorists of the Olympic attacks!

If the Modern Dictatorship is strong, they attack. If they are weak, they subvert. When they have not yet attained the monopoly of violence, they terrorize.

4

The ruinous economic policies of Communism should not be used to judge all Modern Dictatorships. Modern Dictatorships are capable of managing the secondary monopoly over the economy despite the difficulties presented by the Industrial Revolution.

The pre-industrial societies' monopoly of agriculture proves dictatorships can perform economically within certain constraints. When the task is narrowly focused, it can perform well. However, centrally directing a complex industrial economy has thus far eluded the dictator's grasp. For Fascism and Khomeinism, there is not sufficient data to make a conclusive judgment regarding their long-term economic viability. Certainly Fascist Spain did not collapse economically. However for Communism there is a wealth of examples. The basic victory of the West in the Cold War was due to the poor economic performance of the Soviet Union. Many Communist dictatorships have had similarly poor economic track records. Some in Asia, most notably China, have recently abandoned central planning, and as a result, produced solid economic gains. By 2005, China passed Japan as the second largest economy in the world. It is likely China will equal American economic output well before the turn of the next century.

Communist Modern Dictatorships provide numerous examples of economic disasters caused by forced collectivization of farming. The Ukraine famine in the Soviet Union during 1932 and 1933 killed millions, but nothing is more infamous than the Great Leap Forward in China. It was a huge economic disaster for China and shows how the Modern Dictatorship, motivated by the Utopian Vision, can implement its ideology in defiance of any adverse consequences. Millions of peasants were forced into communes to work group plots of land. This is a common Communist practice because one of the salient characteristics of Communism is the abolition of private property. Factories are worker owned, and farmers jointly own the farmland. In China this would also include certain unviable ideas of the dictator Mao, such as the implementation of backyard furnaces to produce steel.

By November 1958, the Communist Chinese Party (CCP) Central Committee announced the creation of 26,000 People's Communes with ninety-eight percent of the farming population collectivized. Not surprisingly, rice output plunged from 200 million metric tons in 1958 to 107 million in 1961. While in the West there was not mass starvation during the Great Depression, in China tens of millions perished due to the Great Leap Forward. She could have asked for foreign aid to save her people but this would mean Mao was wrong. Millions died due to Mao Zedong's pride and his desire to keep power. Adding insult to injury, the steel produced in these backyard furnaces was of poor quality and useless. Because of these policies, Mao has the ignominious distinction of murdering more people than any other dictator in history.

The German rearmament stands in contrast to the poor track record of Communists and shows how Modern Dictatorships can be economically viable. Winston Churchill tried to warn Britain but was largely ignored. From the beginning of the 1930s until war actually began in 1939, the German state completely rearmed, and their U-boats stand as an example. The British rationalized to themselves if the overall ratio of naval vessels between Britain and the Germans was three-to-one, they should not be concerned about German naval developments.

Germany was originally banned from having any U-boats after the WWI, but to not provoke a confrontation, Britain agreed Germany could build U-boats up to sixty percent of the British number. What this meant as a practical matter was, for all types of ships in the German navy, the naval rearmament proceeded as fast as they could build ships. The agreement did not impede their production in any meaningful way. When the war began in 1939, the Germans had nearly reached equality in U-boats at seventy-five percent of the British total. The situation in front line aircraft was worse. By 1936 the Germans had exceeded the British by fifty percent in total deployed aircraft because their workers were more productive. The Germans had slightly more men engaged in aircraft production with 110,000 to the British 90,000, and with this small advantage they produced between two to three times as many aircraft. A comparison with the French is more striking. French aircraft production was around 1,500 aircraft in 1933, fell to fewer than 1,000 in 1936, and back to the 1,500 level in 1939.

German production was under 1,000 in 1934 and rose continuously until it was over 4,000 by 1939.

There are many who argue a Modern Dictatorship with free economic institutions will capitulate to demands for freedom and democracy. The Tiananmen Square Massacre (4 June 1989) was the dictator's response to the desire for Chinese democracy and is a refutation of this argument. It is proof the Modern Dictatorship can manage this more troublesome aspect of industrialization. Deng Xiaoping (1904 – 1997) became dictator, the new Red emperor, after Mao's death and instituted the four modernizations—agriculture, industry, technology, and military. Much like the Meiji Restoration of Japan, the dictator commanded a new direction for the nation. Rapid industrialization and modernization began and continues today. China by hosting the Olympic Games in 2008 repeated what Hitler did in 1936 and the Soviets did in 1980, legitimized the regime.

The desire for democracy in Tiananmen Square was not the first example of protest. After Mao's death in September 1976, Deng used liberalization to criticize those allies of Mao who supported the Cultural Revolution. The Gang of Four was criticized on the Democracy Wall. This protest lasted from the winter of 1978 to the spring of 1979. Former members of the Red Guard with Deng's tacit approval posted comments, but not all comments were welcome. Wei Jingsheng (1950–) posted a fifth modernization: Democracy. He was quickly sent to prison and not released until 1993. After taking up the cause of democracy again, Jingsheng was back in prison by 1995 and eventually exiled to the United States in 1997. The dictators in the modern era would need to balance the needs of industrialization with the needs of maintaining power like the European dictators of the past who supported the Scientific Revolution.

The springtime is a traditional time for protest in China. Many times it is conducted by students prior to the end of the semester. The government had long organized student protests during this period to commemorate the 4 May 1919 student uprising. April 6th also took on special significance, as this was the traditional date of the fall of the Gang of Four. On 17 April 1989, in the wake of the reforms in Eastern Europe, students marched to Tiananmen Square in Beijing to demand reform and remained to occupy the square. Demonstrations also took place in front of the symbol of Party power, the Zhongnanhai building. The students continued to occupy the square up to the 70th anniversary of the 4 May uprising. They began hunger strikes and were anticipating the arrival of Gorbachev on the 15th. By the 15th, 3,000 students were on hunger strikes. A march on the 16th had participation from the propaganda organs like the People's Daily and normally state controlled groups like the All-China Federation of Trade Unions. By the 17th, banners were proclaiming Deng must go. Martial law was declared on the 20th as troops poured into Beijing. The authorities demanded the students leave for security reasons on the 22nd of May while upwards of 200,000 people crowded into the square. In the early morning hours of 4 June 1989, troops supported by tanks attacked the square. Several thousand people, many who were not students, died as the square was cleared out.

One is hard-pressed to find any Communist economy matching the Free Societies' economic growth. Under Fidel Castro, Cuba became one of the poorest countries in Latin America. Communist currencies were always worthless, and this is why Ronald Reagan's strategy of denying Russia hard currency was so effective. The Communist devotion to central planning and the abolition of private property stands out as one of the greatest stupidities in modern history. It is a testament to how powerful the Utopian Vision can be when despite failure after failure, it was attempted in different countries again and again. This should not be used, however, as proof Modern Dictatorships must be economic failures.

5.1

The important relationship between the Utopian Vision and the Modern Dictatorship is parallel to the role religion played in the Hereditary Dictatorship. The Utopian Vision provides meaning and values, and it is a significant threat to the Free Society.

As the Hereditary Dictatorships collapsed in the West after 1918 and lost the Mandate from Heaven, a 'Crisis of the West' was produced. A rising nihilism swept Europe as a reaction to the huge human cost of WWI. Europe, prior to the war, perceived itself as the pinnacle of human civilization. The

Scientific and Industrial Revolutions were proof of this superiority. When these Revolutions were later seen as a key part of the disaster, everything came into question. The widespread pessimism was expressed in the influential book, *The Decline of the West,* by Oswald Spengler (1880 – 1936). Martin Heidegger (1889 – 1976), one of the most recognized philosophers of the 20th century, built a philosophical system to respond to this crisis of meaning and values. Nietzsche's philosophy was used in much the same way because he proposed an alternative to traditional Christian ethics. It was not surprising Hitler was widely perceived as Nietzsche's *übermensch*: the one to provide values. Heidegger helped reinforce this perception of Hitler by stating Hitler was the *übermensch* in comments made in 1933. Since the Utopian Vision is a source of values, Fascism's Utopian Vision filled the crisis of values in the wake of the German defeat in 1918.

The variety of future Utopian Visions should be as diverse as the traditional religions found in past Hereditary Dictatorships. One example already identified is the long-term threat of the Modern Dictatorship modifying the human being. No doubt variations on Utopian Visions already identified, Communism, Fascism, Khomeinism, and extreme Rationalism, are likely to reappear. The Utopian Vision has several aspects making it hard for many to resist. It usually contains a view of impending disaster motivating hysteria, a villain to hate, a certainty to victory, and a utopia in the future. The radical environmental movement has within it certain aspects capable of forming a Utopian Vision and is used as an example.

The Modern Dictatorship needs the specter of impending disaster to produce hysteria. The old adage "desperate times call for desperate measures" aptly sums up the thinking. Ecoside is the willful destruction of the environment with its implied negative impact on humanity, and in the extremist view is the path the human race is currently on. The loss of habitat and the attending loss of large numbers of species are viewed through the prism of lost ancient civilizations. Mass starvation and ecological collapse are an obvious certainty. It is easy to find predictions of this in the 1970s, for example, stating the current population at the time, 150 million for the United States, was unsustainable being thirty percent over the "proper" amount. The impending Ecocatastrophe requires immediate and radical action. Arguments typically make long lists of the current problems including air pollution, water pollution, pesticides, soil erosion, thermal pollution, and noise pollution. The reader is overwhelmed as the narrative describes a complete breakdown in the world's ecology.

If a future famine is not sufficient motivation, it is because one needs to take the mind to a new level of consciousness. A shift as profound as the Copernican Revolution is needed. Previously man gave up his geo-centrism (the belief the earth was the center of the universe) and now, in this second revolution, man will give up his anthropocentrism (the belief mankind is unique and special above all other species). The eventual death of large percentages of the human race is not the problem as this is a guaranteed certainty, while the real crime is the loss of habitat and the mass extinction of other species. The loss is a modern holocaust one only needs to open one's eyes to see. This ideology, called Deep Ecology, is the motivation behind such groups as Earth First. Mankind needs to be dethroned—the humans are but one of many species. All religions must give up the lie of man's cherished place in God's eye. Viewing the world as a pile of resources to use is wrong. Anthropocentrism must give way to biocentrism. All life is equally valuable with plants, animals, and the ecosystem all having rights.

Along with the need to create hysteria, the Modern Dictatorship needs to rally the emotion of hate against a scapegoat. The scapegoat of the Jew, the Capitalist, the Multi-national Corporation, and the Infidel are a few examples. For radical environmentalism it is technology and civilization itself. Nature is smart because in nature the ecosystem becomes better with increasing complexity. Humans on the other hand cannot manage complexity. The more complex a human system becomes, the worse it functions, and the more likely it is to fail. Amazingly, many of the individuals who make such arguments are often highly educated technologists.

In the novel, *Monkey Wrench Gang,* by professed anarchist Edward Abbey, eco-terrorists approvingly attack technology targets in the southwestern United States. Like Lenin's band of revolutionaries giving the eventual collapse of Capitalism a little push, the eco-revolutionaries give the technological society their own push. Excess human population and civilization's harmful technology are the new Infidel. This ideology can also take on Marxist-like pronouncements since in the Free Societies corporations and profits drive technology. It can likewise take on a feminist bent by comparing Mother Earth to a female figure full of life being defiled by modern man and technology.

The Utopian Vision needs a sense of inevitability to its final victory. By being the next wave of the future it motivates people to self-sacrifice and makes the ordinary man a hero. The Marxists score particularly high in this area since their entire worldview sees human history driven by the impersonal forces of class struggle and individual behavior entirely determined by economics. The utopia will come it is just a matter of time. Science is often invoked to lend respectability to these views with the certainty that two plus two is always four, and science is also used to silence dissent since it is assumed only a fool would question science.

A future utopia is the final element the Modern Dictatorship needs to inspire a mass movement. The more beautiful the vision the more willing followers will be to commit acts of fanaticism. There must be something to replace the coming disaster. The Communists have a strong utopia postulating a future free of poverty and war. Khomeinism, too, has the society here on earth living in harmony under God's laws with the ultimate reward of heaven. For the radical environmentalist it is Ecotopia. In the book *Ecotopia* by Ernest Callenbach, man is able to modify technology into a perfect state of recycling and frugality. Sustainability is the new updated version of central economic planning.[39] The future society is perfectly balanced, like nature herself.

For many adherents, this gives mankind too much credit; it is better to return to the time when man had no technology. The state of the hunter-gatherer is idealized by this movement because the hunter-gatherer viewed himself as but one part of the overall scheme of nature. Many fanatics will say this is only an abstract ideal and to expect this to happen today is impossible—there are too many people. The hunter-gatherer population was only 5 million strong 15,000 years ago. But given the conduct of the Modern

---

[39] In the extreme one can imagine a variation on the American FDA. Such an agency of the government would require all new products to be approved first by this new agency to ensure sustainability. Innovation is a threat to the established order and needs to be crushed.

Dictatorship, Utopian Visions have a life of their own. No one would have thought in 1933, ten years later people would be contemplating genocide of the Jews. The Communists in the 20th century murdered upwards of 100 million people in their quest for utopia. The Khomeinists have made it clear their desire to use weapons of mass destruction. Pol Pot was able to exterminate thirty percent of his own countrymen as he cleansed society of western influences. Talk of the need for huge reductions in the earth's human population should be therefore viewed in this light as very troubling.

5.2

The Party is the new priesthood of the Modern Dictatorship. It guides the society in its total transformation.

The Party is the keeper of the orthodoxy of the Utopian Vision and replaces the role played by the priesthood in pre-industrial societies. Whereas religions of the past had both public and private aspects, the Utopian Vision can be viewed as a civic religion. Like the ancient past, the Party controls the interpretation of the modern sacred books. *Mein Kampf* was the Nazi sacred book. The writings of Marx were the same for the Russians. Any writings of the dictator take on special significance, as did Mao's *Little Red Book* or Lenin's *Imperialism, the Highest Stage of Capitalism*. The Party also rigidly controls censorship and the interpretation of history. The Party's quest is to control every aspect of society so it can be remade to their desires.

The intense human desire to see all secular and spiritual authority concentrated in one man such as the god-king, resurfaces in the Modern Dictatorship as the cult-of-the-personality. In it, the dictator takes on superhuman characteristics. To the outsider, some of the propaganda sounds ridiculous. Hitler on his birthday was described as a combination of Goethe, Kant, Hegel, Fichte, Frederick the Great, and Bismarck. At rallies in almost any of the Modern Dictatorships huge pictures of the dictator are on display. Hereditary Dictatorships forced ministers of the king to take the blame for mistakes of the king, and Modern Dictatorships do the same for any error of the dictator.

Mao did everything he could to reinforce the personality cult around him. His *Little Red Book* was everywhere. In "experience exchanges," young people would be transported by the military to travel to different parts of the country to meet other Red Guard members. The big draw to these events was always the possibility they might meet Chairman Mao. There was a rock-star atmosphere complete with tearful, fainting teenage girls and people trampled to death by the enthusiastic crowds.

Control of all sources of values is important, and the German example is instructive. Since ninety percent of Germans belonged to a church, the churches became a focus of the Nazi efforts of coordination or *Gleichschaltung*. *Gleichschaltung* was the Nazi term for the state's complete control over society. The Nazis were not satisfied with obedience; they wanted their message built into Church teachings if possible. For the Protestants, who made up about sixty-five percent of the population, their activities were coordinated under one central bishop. In 1933, Ludwig Muller was appointed Reich Bishop to facilitate Nazification. Not all went along with the new regime. Martin Niemoller, a decorated navy captain from World War I, was arrested in 1937 for his anti-Nazi sermons and eventually was sent to a concentration camp. Another member of the Confessional Church, Dietrich Bonhoeffer, was arrested in 1943 and hanged a month before the end of the war for his anti-Nazi activities. For the remaining third who were Catholic, Hitler got the Church to sign a concordat in 1933. He would leave worship alone if they stayed out of politics. In return for Hitler's promises, the Catholic bishops took an oath of loyalty to the state, and the Church closed down the Centre Party, a political party they supported.

The unions, more aligned with the Communists, were immediately hostile to the Nazi program of *Gleichschaltung*. Because of this, union halls were forcibly occupied and noncompliant leaders arrested. All workers were forced to join the German Work Front (DAF), which was subservient to the Nazi Party. For major businesses and business leaders the Nazi Party was more cautious as they did not want to do anything to disrupt their rearmament program. Additionally, the Nazis did not have a rigid economic ideology like the Communists and could be more flexible depending upon the circumstances. Only businesses associated with Jews were attacked and sometimes taken over for personal gain.

When it came to the army, the Nazis were particularly careful. Since they had come to power via elections and not armed conflict, they had no power base of their own, and their street thugs were no match for a modern military. Their efforts to gain control had to be gradual, and they never completely controlled the military the way the Communists controlled theirs. In 1939 the Gestapo, the German secret police, fabricated a charge of homosexuality against General von Fritsch who was then army supreme commander. Hitler used this incident as an excuse to reorganize the army and make himself head of the armed forces.

The military indoctrination of the youth provides a different insight into how pervasive the Party's reach can be in the Modern Dictatorship. Since all good revolutionaries must be prepared for the class struggle, Soviet children spent time in class studying the military, taking part in drills, learning to fire weapons, and throw grenades. This was something not relegated to the Stalinist past. In 1984 a Latvian High School student was killed by a gunshot wound in mandatory drills. In 1985 an instructor died when his hand grenade exploded in front of twenty-six students during class. Starting early, elementary schools had military games, and students could go to regional and national levels of competition. While under intense budgetary pressure, in 1987 the government continued allocating funds to build new firing ranges at high schools since only fifty percent of high schools had modern firing ranges. In addition to regular schooling, the Soviet summer camps had training in small unit tactics, reconnaissance, and interrogation with thirty million children attending these camps each summer. This obsession continued right up to the fall of the Soviet Union.

When individuals required it, the Party forced them into intensive programs of indoctrination. In China a system of reeducation camps was created to supplement the *laogai* concentration camp system. The amount of time spent in the camps varied but could take up to a year. The reeducation was often conducted in a remote location where there was little chance for escape. The inmates would be divided into small groups under the guidance of an indoctrinator, and they would be assigned physically demanding tasks to weaken their will to resist. Breaking up into small groups, they would criticize each other's lives. Austerity measures would include Spartan-like living conditions and poor food quality.

As the individual made progress the quality of the living conditions improved, but the physical rigor was a constant. The small groups would continue, but classes would be added. The sacred texts of the dictatorship would be studied: Marx, Lenin, Stalin, and Mao. Propaganda would be everywhere. The past was a dark time before the advent of the Party, but now the future for the people was bright, and the people needed your help. Many would have an almost religious experience finally seeing the error of their ways and filled with a new purpose in their life. Like something out of the book *1984*, they finally learned to love Big Brother.

Pol Pot (1925 – 1998), the dictator of Cambodia, provides an example of how far the Party will go to dominate every aspect of society. The country was essentially turned into one giant concentration camp in an effort to wipe out western influences. The Four Year Plan went into effect in September 1977. The cities were mostly evacuated and left looking like ghost towns. The plan called for a "storming offensive" of the people.[40] There was massive forced collectivization with most of the population working in the rice fields twelve hours a day, 365 days a year. With little food, many dropped dead from physical exhaustion. Survivors described themselves as skin and bones.

For enemies of the state, the counterrevolutionaries, a regimen of torture, confession, and execution was their fate. Tuol Sleng, the interrogation center where thousands of innocent people were killed, is famous for pictures of the large piles of skulls of its victims. One was guilty until proven innocent when implicated by the forced confessions of three other people, and in the end approximately 2 million people were murdered.

Pol Pot's communist version of the Modern Dictatorship holds the record for killing the largest percentage of its total population—nearly one third. The Cambodian killing fields were the new Black Death of modern times.

---

[40] Party propaganda actually told people they would eventually enjoy dessert on a daily basis by 1980 if they kept up their revolutionary zeal. Hearing this one does not know if one should laugh or cry.

5.3

The human weakness of mass hysteria is an important part of any Modern Dictatorship via its Utopian Vision.

The role of mass hysteria is critically important in any utopian movement, and something every dictator exploits. The human mob tendency toward hysteria runs deep and should be seen as an inherent human weakness. The witch hysteria in Europe is an ideal example. Witchcraft was something always banned in Europe. Charlemagne had on several occasions declared all necromancers, astrologers, and witches be driven from his kingdom, but it was not until Pope Innocent VIII issued a Papal Bull in 1488 that the witch mania began. Both women and livestock were having more miscarriages and losing their young. Vast amounts of crops were lost to 'natural' calamities caused by spells with entire cornfields being laid flat. Mostly women but also sometimes men were accused of causing havoc across Europe.

The challenge posed by this perceived evil was met by men and women who claimed an expertise in helping find these witches and bringing them to justice. Sprenger of Germany was such an individual. He wrote, *Malleus Maleficarum*, which contained extensive information about witches. It detailed instructions for Inquisitors on how to determine if someone was a witch, and the enterprising Sprenger soon was burning 500 women a year in Germany. Others followed his lead. Cumanus in Italy burned forty-one so called witches in one province alone. Bartolomeo de Spina wrote in the district of Como, Italy, for several years over a hundred witches were burned each year. The Italian Inquisitor, Remigius, convicted and burned 900 witches over a fifteen-year period.

Torture on the rack by the Inquisitors ensured the desired answers were obtained. In Poitiers (1564) three men and one woman confessed on the rack to killing sheep in their pens. In 1571, the personal physician to the King of France confessed to a vast array of both miraculous cures and despicable deeds. He named 1,200 others in a vast conspiracy, many of whom were also arrested and burned. At Dole, a man was accused of being a *loup-garou* or man-wolf. Fifty witnesses testified against him and he confessed everything on the rack. Sometimes the witch would be asked if she had any children by a devil. No woman with children would admit to such a crime despite the most severe torture, as any children would have been burned at the stake with their mothers.

Many times the testimony in favor of the accused was ignored. When a group of witches were accused of meeting a devil at night, the husbands protested saying their wives were next to them in their beds. The archbishop informed them this was an illusion from the devil and burned the women anyway.

Only on rare occasions were people acquitted. In Paris (1589) an appeal from fourteen people forced the establishment of a royal commission to investigate the accusations made against them. The women were stripped naked and prodded with needles to see if they felt pain and drew blood. The report stated they were not witches but instead either stupid or insane and while several wanted death, what they needed was medicine and not punishment.

Once the Reformation got underway the Protestants were no better than the Catholics. Both Luther and Calvin believed in witches while Protestant England passed laws against witchcraft in 1551, 1554, and 1562. The hysteria continued into the early part of the 17th century. In many cases, angry mobs would take care of the problem without the bother of a trial.

The town of Warbois, England provides a remarkable look into how an accusation grows into hysteria. A girl, Mistress Joan Throgmorton, had passed by an old lady's house many times. Once, when the old woman was looking back at the girl, the girl was hit with a pain jolting her entire body, and she told her parents immediately. Soon other children would go into fits whenever they passed by the old lady's house. The story grew in the telling, and soon there were seven spirits involved with names the children all knew. Eventually, Joan Throgmorton's family along with friends confronted the woman and her family. They used pins to see if they could draw blood, and she cursed them. For over a year they tormented the alleged witch until a family friend died, and then the accusers were convinced the curse done the year before had worked its magic. Soon a large crowd confronted the old lady's family, and they were arrested. Her husband and daughter refused to concede anything under torture, but the old lady could not stand the rack and confessed. All three were hanged and their bodies burned on 7 April 1593.

Over time the hysteria subsided. By the year 1736 the death sentences for witchcraft in England and Scotland were replaced with prison or the pillory. In continental Europe the same general trend was observed. German princes would reduce death sentences to prison terms using the argument only the crime of witchcraft itself had been proved and not other crimes committed using spells. Professors and intellectuals attacked the belief in witches. The whole scare was soon gone.

In the area of economics, hysterias can be driven by the desire to get rich quickly. The tulip was introduced to Europe in the 16th century from Turkey. The bulb was highly prized, and the wealthy would order it directly from Constantinople. Gradually its value passed any reasonable expectation as it became a symbol of status, and in 1634 they became a craze mainly in Holland. Tulipomania had arrived! By 1635 it was not uncommon for people to spend incredible sums on tulips—one man spending 100,000 florins for forty bulbs. Certain varieties were particularly expensive. In Amsterdam 4,600 florins would buy two horses and a new carriage with a harness while at the same time one could also expect to pay 4,400 for an Admiral Van der Eyck bulb, and the Semper Augustus would go for a price of 5,500 florins.

Foreigners unaware of the madness could find themselves quickly in a financial or legal disaster. A sailor once mistook a tulip bulb for an onion and ate it for dinner. He would spend several months in jail trying to sort it out with the judge. In a similar case, an English amateur botanist dissected a bulb and ended up in debtor's prison. The tulip craze produced an army of tulip speculators. When sanity finally prevailed in 1636, the prices collapsed. Dutch judges declared tulip contracts were null and void since they fell under the category of gambling.

5.4

To maintain power, the Modern Dictatorship and its Utopian Vision make full use of scapegoats and the emotion of hate.

The role of the scapegoat and an internal enemy keeps the nation close to a wartime footing and justifies almost any police action. Combining this with the powerful emotion of hate and the dictator can make people obey any order. The Jews have been scapegoats throughout history, and the Nazis took it to unbelievable levels never seen by any dictatorship before. Typical anti-Semitism combines racism against a minority with envy of the rich. The international Jewish conspiracy of bankers is the perfect storm of these two powerful negative emotions.

In September 1939 fewer than 200,000 Jews were living in Germany— about half of the original number of 1933. The forced emigration of Jews was the job of the SS under the direction of Heinrich Himmler. Prior to *Kristallnacht*, Night of the Broken Glass, Jews were not summarily rounded up. A policy of gradually eliminating them from all public positions forced many to wisely choose to voluntarily leave after paying an exit tax. This all changed on 9 November 1938 when the Brown Shirts attacked Jewish stores, homes, and synagogues. It was called the Night of the Broken Glass because of the broken glass left upon the street from the smashed windows of Jewish stores. Though obviously in preparation for some time, the immediate excuse given was the assassination of a minor German diplomat in Paris. The assassin, Herschel Grynszpan was a seventeen year-old Jewish boy.

The conquest of the eastern countries of Europe presented a completely different problem as each country had a large Jewish population—nearly 3 million in Poland alone. Most of these people were poor and were in no position to pay the leaving tax. The SS would clear areas of living space, *Lebensraum*, in Poland, confiscating land. A non-Jewish Polish family was left with a small suitcase, a blanket, a little food, and some cash, but the Jews, if not shot on the spot, were forced into ghettoes or taken to Germany to become slave labor. As the German armies advanced into Russia, they were followed by the Special Action Group, *Einsatzgruppen*, a specially selected group of SS members charged with the task of exterminating all Jews. They would round up the Jews in each village, take them to the outskirts in trucks, and shoot them. Despite being staffed with specially selected Nazi fanatics, the units had a high psychological dropout rate.

The infamous Final Solution, was a systematic extermination of people using industrial principles. These were the true death camps, not the ordinary concentration camps regulating the death rate to make room for more enemies of the state. These new installations were designed to murder people as quickly and efficiently as possible. Men, women, and children were brought in trains to an industrial plant like any other commodity, and various deceptions were used to get enough cooperation to keep the process moving smoothly. The victims were literally stripped of all belongings, forced into gas chambers made to look like showers for louse decontamination, and the bodies were incinerated.

The most infamous death factory was Auschwitz. Located in Nazi-occupied Poland, it had four large gas chambers for the total eradication of all Jews in Europe, and these large chambers holding 2,000 victims located near a crematorium made it the perfect killing machine. Its capability was far beyond the other extermination camps of Treblinka, Belsec, Sibibor, and Chelmno, all located in Poland.

When Auschwitz was under construction, the future commandant of the camp, Rudolf Hoess, toured Treblinka to improve upon the killing methods used there. As a member of the Death's Head SS it was his responsibility to ensure maximum efficiency. At Treblinka a chamber could only kill about 200. Treblinka had been used to murder the Jews from the Warsaw ghetto with carbon monoxide gas, but Hoess devised a new poison, Zyklon B, as a more effective method. Russian prisoners of war were used to test the new factories of death. Once in operation, the Death's Head SS knew the new gas had done its work when the screaming stopped. The doors would be opened, and the bodies stripped of all valuables, including gold teeth. The valuables would be deposited in a secret SS bank account in Berlin.

Auschwitz near the end of the war could murder 6,000 people in one day. Nearly six million Jews as well as Gypsies, Jehovah Witnesses, homosexuals, and Communists were murdered in this manner. It is because of this crime the Nazis are considered the most evil of all the Modern Dictatorships. It is true they did not kill as many people as the Communists, but this can be attributed to the short duration of their reign of terror. The regime had a palpable love of death and sadism.

The Russians had their own scapegoats and used their desire to eradicate successful peasants, *Kulaks*, as a justification for collectivization of farming. The war against the *Kulaks* began on 27 December 1929 when Stalin called for the elimination of *Kulaks* as a class. Each district's activities were coordinated by the head of the local Party, the president of the local Soviet, and the local chief of the GPU. Local *dekulakization* brigades would carry out the actions.

These enemies of the state were divided into three categories. A quota of 60,000 *Kulaks* for the first category was established by the Soviet Political Police, the *Cheka*. These *Kulaks* were ones who had taken part in counter-revolutionary activities, and they would be transferred to the GPU who controlled the concentration and work camps. If they showed any sign of resistance, they would be executed. Their family members were deported to the interior of the country, often Siberia, and all their property became the property of the state. The second group was called the arch-exploiters of the people, and they would merely be deported. The third group, those loyal to the revolution, would be forced to relocate from the district they currently resided to a different district.

The scapegoats of the Cultural Revolution in China were the intellectuals and artists. The adjective "stinking" was always attached to the word intellectual. The universities in particular suffered as study was branded as bourgeois. The more you learned the more stupid you became, and as proof the Red Guards would test a professor with some obscure question, such as how many types of grains are there and how do you differentiate. Answers only a peasant would know. Admission to the universities was increasingly based on ideological purity and nothing else. Resistant professors could have their life's work destroyed.

The Taliban in Afghanistan are a Khomeinist group. For this Utopian Vision, women are hated and made the scapegoats. Maulvi Qalamuddin was the head of the Taliban's religious police and as head of the Department of the Promotion of Virtue and the Prevention of Vice, it was his job to issue edicts on virtually everything regarding daily living and to enforce those edicts. No woman was allowed into his building. The religion police, with their Kalashnikov rifles at their side, would use whips and long sticks to enforce the edicts with street justice. Girls and women were not to go to school, the wearing of the *burkha* was mandatory, and they were banned from all sports. In the religious schools called *madrassas*, boys were taught oppressing women was a symbol of manhood and evidence of a man's commitment to *jihad*.

Giving freedom to women would result in adultery, which would be followed by the collapse of society and Islam, and once Islam was gone there was nothing to stop the dreaded infidel from ruling.

6

Like the Hereditary Dictatorship, the Modern Dictatorship attempts to dominate intellectual life. Propaganda and the Utopian Vision are effective in winning over individuals in Free Societies.

Propaganda plays a central role in the Modern Dictatorship like it did in the Hereditary Dictatorships of the past. Leni Riefenstahl's documentary film of the 1934 Nuremberg Nazi Party gathering, *Triumph of the Will*, is regarded by many as one of the most masterful examples of propaganda ever created. Her opening scene is most telling. Wagnerian music plays as a plane comes down out of the clouds to land while the plane's shadow clearly makes a Christian cross on the ground. Hitler appears at the plane door while the background lighting gives him a halo. As he travels into town, vast crowds are shown enthusiastically cheering—the messiah of Germany has arrived. Hitler takes the massive podium in the rally symbolizing the concentration of all secular and spiritual authority in one man. A spectacle satisfying a deep-seated human need and identical to an ancient priest-king in his full regalia mounting a step-pyramid 5,000 years ago.

Good propaganda requires several elements including a good conspiracy. When a conspiratorial worldview is established, new facts either fit into the framework or are dismissed as rare exceptions or fabrications. Once a person believes a conspiracy it is difficult to overthrow. Conspiracies are also useful vehicles to generate hate, as the believer feels cheated and betrayed. There is always something profoundly unfair about being tricked by cowards who can manipulate you from the shadows while fools go about their business blindly ignorant. A conspiracy also adds an important feature needed by the Utopian Vision—its certainty. If the great events of the day are controlled by a conspiracy then, once the conspirators are dead, great events can then be controlled by the Party. In Russia the plots varied from Trotskyites, the secret

225

rule of the 300 richest families to plots by British or American secret services. The Nazis always used the international Jewish conspiracy.

Good propaganda must be consistent and often repeated. Hitler said when you lie you must make it a big lie and repeat it over and over again. It is within this environment the dictator will appear to make predictions when in fact he is telegraphing his next move as he is in the unique position of being able to make his prediction come true by his actions. In a speech to the Reichstag in January 1939, Hitler predicted war might happen in Europe due to the international Jewish financiers. Before the Central Committee in 1930, Stalin predicted right-wing elements and deviant socialists were a dying class. In both cases their predictions came true thanks to their own actions.

More than any efforts at general persuasion, the goal of propaganda is to gather new followers. This is typically facilitated by a front organization grouping together a diverse collection of people for a common cause, and then these fellow travelers can be evaluated for eventual membership in the Party. It is important for the dictator to keep sympathizers distinct from worthy true believers as this gives sympathizers something to strive for and gives the dictator a cadre of worthy believers he can count on. Hitler was conscious of this, and while he made every effort to vastly increase the sympathizers, he also kept tight control on the number of Party members.

Propaganda is most effective if foreigners or other neutral parties repeat the story as if it was their own and the Soviet show trials taking place in August 1936, January 1937, and March 1938 were powerful propaganda. In these trials, Lenin's old companions were eliminated, and anyone who was a new threat to Stalin was also added to the collection. It was theater, and every effort was made to make the trials appear fair. In all, fifty-four people were put on trial, convicted, and most were executed. The most dramatic events in the trial were the seemingly honest confessions in open court—although it is now known torture and threats were used to force those confessions. Many foreign observers at the time reported they were honest confessions without coercion.

The ability of ordinary people to be fooled by the dictator's propaganda is an important way he can subvert Free Societies. The recent 'lone wolf' terrorist persuaded to act by a *jihad* website is an example. The parade of journalists returning from Modern Dictatorships singing their praises is now an unfortunately long list. The Swedish journalist Jan Myrdal and Scottish academic Malcolm Caldwell were both strong supporters of Pol Pot after visiting the country. Another good example is the cover up of the Ukrainian famine perpetrated by a correspondent for the *New York Times* in Moscow, Walter Duranty. Writers and artists, too, sing dictator's praises. The American poet Ezra Pound was an ardent supporter of Mussolini and also praised Hitler. A long list of American Hollywood stars has paid the brutal Castro a visit in Cuba from solid actors like Robert Redford, Robert Duvall, and Jack Nicholson, to producers like Oliver Stone.

7

There are a variety of dictatorships in the modern era as in the past, and they are all militarily aggressive. The Free Societies should always be vigilant.

As less violent forms of the Hereditary Dictatorship emerged from time to time, one can expect more 'tolerable' forms of the Modern Dictatorship will also develop. It is common for historians to lavish praise on certain dictators for being a patron of the arts, or science, or for some other reason being particularly enlightened. Such 'good' dictators have created important public works such as the Great Canal in China and the Coliseum in Rome. The false distinction of the despot versus a 'good' ruler is part of this thinking. A 'good' dictatorship may be a bigger threat than a despot if the Free Societies are lulled into a sense of complacency.

Otto von Bismarck was born to the Junker aristocracy in Prussia. His mother wanted him to pursue a civil service career like her father and made sure he attended some of the best schools. Undisciplined in both his personal and academic endeavors, he managed to pass the civil service exam at age twenty. However, he was well read in those subjects that interested him—the romantics like Goethe and recent German history.

While working at his civil service job, he took off with a young English woman for three months to tour Germany but returned to fulfill his military obligation. Then, at age twenty-four, his military training complete, he resigned his civil service appointment. For the next eight years he retired to a family-owned Pomeranian estate and it was there he had a religious conversion to a pietistic version of Lutheranism, married a woman similarly disposed, and settled down to married life.

In 1847, King Frederick Wilhelm IV summoned the meeting of the Estates of his kingdom for a united *Diet* in Berlin to not only avoid creating a true parliament but also to raise revenue for a new railroad to the eastern parts of Prussia. Bismarck was appointed to attend when the current occupant of the appointment resigned for ill health. He became the spokesman for the Prussian state, the Hohenzollern dynasty, and an outspoken critic of the liberals. He stated privately his Lutheran faith gave him a newfound strength, and later in life he would say he felt he was doing God's work building the German Reich.

During the revolutions sweeping Europe in 1848, Bismarck organized against the tide by supporting the king. When a new parliament was formed despite his best efforts, he was elected to a seat. In 1852, he was sent by the king as his representative to the *Diet* of the German Conference in Frankfurt. Becoming the leader of the pro-Prussian group, he resisted attempts by Austria to dominate German affairs, managing to exclude Austria from the German customs union, the *Zollveren*.

Bismarck next became Ambassador to France. His leadership skills were needed when a military reform bill had been stalled in Parliament for two years, and the new Prince-elect Wilhelm asked him to return to Germany to guide the bill's passage. Bismarck put off the request for months captivated by the twenty-two year-old wife of Russia's ambassador to Belgium. When he finally left her he would never resume the liaison but in typical Bismarck fashion would wear a small gift from her on his watch chain for the rest of his life.

When Prince Wilhelm and Bismarck met on 22 September 1862 it was the beginning of a long successful partnership, and the next day Bismarck became Prime Minister of Prussia. In his first speech to the parliament he made the famous statement characterizing his career saying the pressing issues of the day were not settled by debates but by "iron and blood." For the next thirty years he would dominate the European landscape as the archetype practitioner of Realpolitik, where practical considerations override moral or ideological judgments.

Bismarck's first crisis to overcome was the refusal of the liberals to support a military reform bill, and he did this by simply proclaiming a gap existed in the new Prussian constitution of 1848. The new constitutional interpretation, the *Luckentheorie,* allowed the government to keep collecting taxes and spending money when no legislation said otherwise. In this way the military modernization the King and Bismarck wanted could take place.

Those first five years as Prime Minister were Bismarck's learning years when he realized how important a foreign policy success could be to domestic power. He also became sensitive to the trends in his time, deciding not to fight them. Nationalism was such a trend and became the primary force behind liberal demands for parliamentary rights to represent the nation. Bismarck would channel nationalism into a force for King and Country. The German unification under a Prussian solution would provide the means.

Because of Bismarck's military reform efforts, Prussia had the most advanced army in Europe. The German wars of unification first began with the Prusso-Danish war of 1864. After the Prussian victory over the Danish, a joint administration was proposed, much to Austria's dislike. As the tensions with Austria grew, Bismarck took steps to isolate them diplomatically with both Russia and France agreeing this was a purely German affair. He then arranged an alliance with Italy before attacking Austria in 1866 and dispatching them in six weeks. Bismarck exacted mild terms from the Austrians so their motivation for revenge was small, and he lived up to all obligations with the Italians by transferring Venetia to the Kingdom of Italy despite the lackluster support the Italians provided.

Bismarck used his recent foreign policy successes to secure his position at home. In 1867, he introduced a bill to retroactively approve the war expenditures. The liberals had always opposed this spending but now could not help but vote for these unconstitutional measures because they were both successful and popular. Prussia was now head of the newly created North German Confederation, and Bismarck continued his drive to unite all of Germany.

Three German states, Baden, Württemberg, and Bavaria, remained independent and under the protection of the Catholic Napoleon III of France. Bismarck looked for any opportunity to isolate France. When in 1870 the Hohenzollern dynasty had a candidate to the Spanish throne, the French protested. King Wilhelm was preparing a response with Prussia backing down, but Bismarck modified the reply, known as the Ems Dispatch. The Dispatch cleverly insulted the French, and they responded with a declaration of war, thereby losing both British and Russian support. Bismarck had isolated his enemy again, and when the Prussian army crushed the French at the Battle of Sedan and the Franco-Prussian War (1870) was over, King Wilhelm ruled a united Germany.

Over the next twenty years until his resignation as German Chancellor in 1890, Bismarck attempted internal reforms moving the different states toward a consolidated Germany. Under the constitution, Prussia dominated the new upper chamber making any constitutional change impossible while at the same time, a lower chamber, the *Reichstag*, could only debate bills submitted by the Chancellor. The *Reichstag* also had no role in government oversight and could not compel ministers to testify.

Bismarck had a strong hand to play and went after two centers of power in the new Germany—the Catholic Church in the south and the Socialist Party. He allied himself with the liberals to outlaw religious orders, eliminate Catholic influence in German education, and limit the authority of bishops. Bismarck called this his *Kulturkampf*—his culture war. When liberal strength began to grow, particularly in the Socialist Party, he switched alliances. With help from the conservatives and the Church, he proposed a new set of legislative initiatives. The Socialist Party was banned, as were their publications, and trade unions were outlawed. At the same time he proposed the best social welfare program in all of Europe, including an insurance system for sickness, accidents, old age, and disability with contributions from the company, government, and the worker. Bismarck had out maneuvered his internal opposition as effectively as he had his external enemies.

Bismarck stands out as a leader who was able to guide the Hereditary Dictatorship into the modern era. Because of his policies the Hohenzollern dynasty was unique—an industrialized society under a king—unlike the other decaying dynasties of Europe. Although there was strong nationalism, there was no Utopian Vision to remake society. The society was instead conservative and only selectively embraced change. Bismarck proved other forms of dictatorship could survive the transition caused by industrialization.

8

The two innovations of the Terror and the Utopian Vision have transformed the Modern Dictatorship into a killing machine. In its ultimate abstraction, the Utopian Vision demands alteration of mankind to attain the perfection of man.

The Modern Dictatorship is the application of science and industrialization to the ancient human tendency toward dictatorship. Using modern methods, the dictator can completely remake society to his desires with a state totally devoted to the dictator and centering on a Utopian Vision. Once the dictator can create hysteria around the Vision, he can motivate people to do anything. Four types of Modern Dictatorships have emerged since the dawning of the Industrial and Scientific Revolutions—Extreme Rationalism, Fascism, Communism, and Khomeinism.[41] In each case, an ideal pure society is the ultimate goal with the entire world to be eventually encompassed by the Utopia. No amount of violence is too extreme in furthering this goal. Nazism, the most evil expression of the Modern Dictatorship, went so far as to build industrial facilities for the sole purpose of murdering people as quickly and efficiently as possible.

All the old props of the Hereditary Dictatorship find a new expression in the Modern Dictatorship. The Party becomes the new priesthood while the Utopian Vision is the new state religion. The cult-of-the-personality replaces the ancient god-king, and the writings of the dictator become the new sacred texts. While the pre-industrial society was shaped like a pyramid,

---

[41] It has been demonstrated how Fascism and Communism, Maoism and Nazism, Khomeinism and Marxism are all basically the same thing. Political discourse should not have terms blurring this insight like the traditional usage of left and right. It is instead a spectrum from dictatorship to anarchy varying the amount of government power.

the Modern Dictatorship is shaped like an inverted thumbtack—the dictator is at the point, and everyone else is at the bottom.

As before, political power rests with the military, so nothing about the monopoly of violence in human government has changed. However, the Modern Dictatorship adds the secret police and the Terror. By creating vast systems of prisons, camps, and torture facilities to establish ideological purity, this dictatorship ensures the Party is always in control, especially of the military. The Gulag Archipelago of the former Soviet Union was the most famous of these systems. Several waves of Red Terror swept through the dictatorships of Lenin and Stalin. The Nazi's had their Gestapo and *Kristallnacht*. Mao had his Red Guard and the Cultural Revolution. Pol Pot turned an entire nation into one big concentration camp, while the Khomeinists have their Revolutionary Guard.

The warlike nature of dictatorships is magnified many times over by the Modern Dictatorship. Fascism was notoriously aggressive. The Japanese conquered Korea, Manchuria, and were in the process of conquering China when they attacked the United States. Germany overran Austria, Czechoslovakia, Poland, Belgium, the Netherlands, Denmark, Norway, and France before attacking Russia. Hitler declared war on the United States for no valid strategic reason. The Communists, though militarily weaker, were expansive as well, spreading to Eastern Europe, the Baltic countries and China. After China, Communism spread to Southeast Asia, Latin America, and Africa.

The Modern Dictatorship's control over information and its propaganda make Free Societies vulnerable. The dictatorship would not exist if its Utopian Vision was not an effective one. The Vision has already attracted numerous recruits, and it will attract some members of any Free Society as it provides an answer to all of society's problems and furnishes them with a higher purpose greater than themselves. The Vision creates hysteria and taps into hate—a powerful human emotion.

Despite the horror of the Modern Dictatorships, the Free Societies should not be complacent in the face of more conventional dictatorships, and they should not automatically assume dictatorships follow counter-productive economic policies. Bismarck's Germany was a technological and economic leader in Europe. A more benign form of dictatorship can conquer a Free Society as well as any.

The Utopian Vision postulates a new man and this remains the most important long-term danger from the Modern Dictatorship. Human nature has proved to be the final barrier dictators of the past could not overcome. It is likely, at some future date, a Totalitarian regime will biologically alter the human being to realize its utopian fantasy and the perfection of man. The monopoly of violence will then extend to the essence making a human being human. But whatever the next form the Modern Dictatorship takes, a new form will arrive some day. The Free Society, so unlikely to have been created at all, will never be free of this threat. There is no end to history.

Epilogue

Mankind's government is a struggle for power while the freedom we love and cherish is a fluke of history. Except for Athens, Rome, and a few hints elsewhere, the pre-industrial world only provides examples of dictatorship. The characteristics of this dictatorship, the Hereditary Dictatorship, have been documented here in some detail. The one who is victorious in this struggle, the dictator, creates a monopoly of violence. Using this primary monopoly, he creates secondary monopolies over the body, mind, and soul of the kingdom. Should the dictator be overthrown, men so love security over freedom a new dictator replaces the old.

Only a flawed civilization allows a weaker human tendency to emerge: the desire for freedom. Europe was mired in a permanent warring states condition with no single unifying dynasty to crush dissent and enforce orthodoxy. Each of the secondary monopolies was weakened by a set of special circumstances the dictators could not stop due to the fractured political landscape of Europe. But this was still not enough. An accident of geography, as well as timing, was needed. The Free Society in Britain and America, both isolated from the European continent, came at the dawn of the Industrial Revolution, which was undermining the Hereditary Dictatorships of Europe. This was the final blow to the Hereditary Dictatorships. Without it, Britain and America would have gone the way of Athens and Rome.

Many mistakenly believe it only took the triumph of reason to smash ignorance and superstition ushering in a new age. This would be a reasonable position if the year was 1788, but knowledge about the results of 'pure reason' during the French Revolution should dispel any such notions. Science is neutral in the struggle between good and evil. Instead, the French Revolution stands as a warning to those who wish to use the monopoly of violence for good thinking they can remake society.

The real story is the story of freedom: freedom to worship, to question, to discover, to innovate. It is the freedom of people to govern one's country and the freedom of the individual to govern one's life. Science and industrialization, each a manifestation of freedom, are only part of the story. While a clever dictator can harness science and industrialization for his own purposes, he cannot unleash freedom because that would destroy him. It is also why the story did not end with Europe. Europe simply had too much historical baggage to fully implement parts of the Enlightenment devoted to liberty.

America is so exceptionally important because while virtually all nations are founded around a people or ethnicity, America is a nation founded on ideas. Its lucky founding placed it in the most excellent of locations with a special set of conditions allowing the practice of those ideas to grow to fruition. Only the scourge of slavery marred this founding and almost killed the experiment. Fortunately, the experiment survived. America grew into the most powerful nation on earth; demonstrating how powerful freedom can be in unleashing human potential. America proves not only can freedom survive—it can thrive.

The Age of European Domination (c. 1450 – 1945) is over. The human race is in the early stages of the Scientific and Industrial Age. Will this be an age of freedom, democracy, and human rights? The realist would say the 5,000-year history of dictatorship, and the recent bloody dictatorships of the 20th century, argue for a clear no. At the human race's highest point of development, instead of producing a golden age, the 20th century spawned Hitler, Stalin, and Mao. The Free Society could, within a century or two, disappear like ancient Athens overtaken by the Modern Dictatorship.

Today, humanity stands at a perilous crossroads. The Free World as we know it is a new and potentially transient phenomenon coming into existence only since 1945. In the recent past, democracy was limited to a few Western countries. As worldwide democracy is less than 100 years old, over-confidence in its longevity is misplaced. The American President, Ronald

Reagan, stated freedom was like a chain linking each generation, and would be lost when any single generation failed to make the necessary sacrifices.

Never were the stakes higher. The Modern Dictatorships of the 20th century are the first of many yet to come. Because the full power of the Scientific and Industrial Revolutions are now at the service of the dictator, the ubiquitous and unbounded monopoly of violence can now be fully realized, resulting in disastrous consequences for humanity.

Finally, a few comments are in order about the current threats to the Free Society. Four actual and two hypothetical Utopian Visions have been identified in the previous discussion. Aspects of four out of the six are active in the Free Societies today: Communism, extreme Rationalism, Ecotopianism, and Khomeinism. Communism in its more pure form has lost some of its appeal, but the fundamental paradigm of oppressor versus oppressed has metastasized into many areas. Many believe using the power of government to help the have-nots at the expense of the haves will create social justice. They see the world as rich versus poor, white versus black, men versus women, Western Civilization versus the Third World, etc. It only takes the right leader using the proper crisis for these beliefs to be easily exploited.

Extreme Rationalism is also evident particularly in the West. People who pray are viewed in many quarters with suspicion. Public displays of religion are met with opposition. Anything claiming to be scientific is held to be beyond debate an attitude contrary to the openness of the scientific method. Likewise, legitimate concerns about the environment have morphed into hysterical declarations of impending ecological catastrophe. It does not matter these declarations have universally turned out to be wrong. The world did not enter into an Ice Age as predicted in the 1970s, nor did the world face mass starvation due to the "population bomb." Rhetoric about an impending extinction of the human race or how there are too many humans is dangerous. This is exactly the kind of talk a 'Green Hitler' needs to grab power.

The most aggressive of the four currently is the Utopian Vision of Khomeinism. It has taken root in an area of the world economically weak and unlikely to produce a Nazi Germany or Soviet Union anytime in the near future. However, because of their economic weakness, they resort to terrorism. Only nations with large Islamic populations like Indonesia, Nigeria, or Pakistan potentially could rise to major power status. In the Arab world, Egypt with its large population could form the basis of a Khomeinist regional power. Certainly it, unified with the oil wealth of Arabia or the Persian Gulf, would be a major source of trouble for the Free Societies. In the same way Turkey with its large population could pose a similar threat should it succumb to Khomeinism, as does Iran.

Iran today is the only major nation ruled by a Khomeinist dictatorship. They are devoted to expanding their ideology and are actively pursuing ballistic missile delivery systems with nuclear weapons technology. They have repeatedly called for the destruction of a neighboring Jewish state, Israel. These threats should not be lightly dismissed since hatred of the scapegoat in an atmosphere of hysteria is part of any Utopian Vision. The Free Societies should deal firmly with this expansionist dictatorship or disaster awaits. A regional nuclear arms race is almost inevitable.

A Modern Dictatorship stretching from Tunisia to Mecca with its capital in Cairo would also fulfill the Caliphate the Khomeinist Bin Laden desired. Since none of these countries have a modern armament industry and would be required to buy the military equipment they would need to wage war, such a power would require an outside ally with China or Russia being likely suppliers (although one cannot dismiss a European country trying to make a fast buck). They would also be highly attracted to nuclear weapons since this is a fast way to claim major power status and a 'great equalizer' in potential conflicts with real industrial powers, which explains the motivation behind Iran's nuclear weapons program. The current War on Terror can be viewed as the start of a new Cold War against Khomeinism.

In addition to the current crisis in the Islamic world and the continuing appeal of Communism in Latin America and Africa, the world must deal with the Bismarckization of China. It is a real possibility China will be the Germany of the 21st century. The Chinese are a proud, industrious, inventive people with a sense history has treated them unfairly. Currently they are experiencing rapid economic growth and are developing a modern military. They have a large population, a large country with plentiful resources, and territorial ambitions from Siberia to Taiwan—all ruled by a dictatorship. As the previous analysis confirmed—dictatorships are expansive by nature.

It has been a common mistake to think because different countries are economically interconnected a war will not come. Prior to Napoleon, a person could travel about Europe and no matter what country they visited they would have had the sense it was all one place. The elites read the great works from each other's country and listened to the musical masterpieces from each other's gifted composers. They shared their scientific discoveries. The same feeling existed prior to the Great Western Civil War when it was believed Great Britain, France, and Germany were too intertwined economically to fight. Norman Angell made this argument when he published *The Great Illusion* in 1910. In his view, the disruptions to international credit made a war impossible. That the Chinese and Americans are too intertwined to fight is a similar argument being made today—the world is one giant economy making a general war impossible. As before, this belief is equally wrong today: as already stated, there is much more to fear from men who love power than those who love profits.

The Free Societies would be wise to adopt a freedom and human rights based approach to foreign policy. For instance, they should be less inclined to trade with China and should instead insist upon democratic reforms, an end to human rights abuses, and freedom for Tibet. But in order for this strategy to become effective, the Free Societies must liberate themselves from any dependency upon these dictatorships. First, the Free Societies must become energy independent from the Middle East because they cannot actively oppose Khomeinism if they depend upon those dictatorships for their economic health. One might also add, the Hereditary Dictatorships in the region are a thing of the past as they will fall, and a Modern Dictatorship will replace them. Depending upon them for oil is a foolish short-term expediency.

Second, the Free Societies cannot depend upon China for their financial health. They must free themselves by putting their fiscal houses in order and modify their stance from simple free trade to free trade with free countries. A freedom and human rights based foreign policy is almost a necessity since it is likely Khomeinism and the Chinese Dictatorship will find common cause against the Free Societies. A unified insistence upon equal rights for women and religious tolerance would strike at both dictatorships.

The human race has a clear choice. At this juncture in history, it is vitally important freedom, democracy, and human rights be made a priority across the globe. Given humanity's sad history, we likely will never have such a golden opportunity again.

Acknowledgments

When I first began this project I attended a book fair at a local university to see what I could learn about writing a book. In each seminar, speaker after speaker told of a process taking years and gradually becoming a dominating presence in their lives. They also spoke of the joy, as their dreams became a reality. I confess I have experienced both. More than once I came either to a roadblock to further progress or to a simple fatigue wishing the project was over. But I also experienced the joy. There is simply no comparable feeling to be immersed in a pile of great books as your ideas, only vaguely defined at first, come alive with each additional insight.

I am therefore grateful and want to express my thanks first to my immediate family for all their encouragement, support, and helpful suggestions. They, more than anyone, were on this five-year journey with me, both the ups and downs. I want to especially thank my wife who along with many good suggestions was my most important cheerleader in this long process. I likewise want to express my thanks to other family members and friends who took the time to read my early manuscript. Your helpful ideas made the book better. Lastly I wish to acknowledge my debt to my editor Mary Martha Miles and my publicist Lynn Wiese Sneyd of LWS Literary Services. Their expert guidance and professionalism helped turn my dream into a reality.

Note on Sources

Almost all numbered sub-sections are simple summaries of two or three sources found in the bibliography. A few sub-sections are summaries from a single source. For example, sub-section 5.3 in chapter six, is a summary of information found in *Extraordinary Popular Delusions* by Mackay, a wonderful book I strongly recommend. Sub-section 5 chapter five is another example taken substantially from Norman Freidman's *The Fifty Year War Conflict and Strategy in the Cold War* another informative book. For nearly all sub-sections, particularly if I used multiple sources, I would double-check against Wikipedia for consistency in names, places, and dates. I apologize for the lack of footnotes but thought it pointless since almost every sentence would require a footnote, and the sources for each sub-section are self-explanatory. Furthermore, a significant portion of the sources I cite declined to use footnotes in their own work. In retrospect, I could have written much of my work using only Wikipedia. The facts I cite are not controversial or in doubt, it is only the interpretation of these historical events that are original and unique.

There are, however, a few sources providing key ideas found throughout the book, I wish to highlight. Patricia Crone's *Pre-Industrial Societies* was an eye opener. Her concise and lucid description of these early societies helped me organize my thoughts. It helped me see the pattern present in many of the other sources. Likewise, Finer's *The History of Government* (in three volumes) was important for the same reason. He is also the source for the comments in sub-section 2 chapter three about ancient Israel, and for much of the information in sub-section 3 chapter three. It is truly a loss he never finished the chapter about Totalitarianism in volume III. Paul Johnson's *A History of the American People* was used throughout chapter four particularly in the discussion on the American Supreme Court. Finally, I wish to credit Machiavelli's *The Prince*, the first serious book I read many years ago. Although I reference the original copy I read in 1969 in the bibliography, I recommend *The Prince and Other Writings* translated by Wayne Rebhorn for those interested in Machiavelli's thoughts. Machiavelli was a realist and it was in this spirit I wrote the book. It is only by seeing the world, as it truly is, that we can make it better.

Bibliography

Andrew, Rod, Jr. <u>Long Gray Lines</u>. Chapel Hill, North Carolina: The University of North Carolina Press, 2001.

Archaeology Magazine. <u>Secrets of the Maya</u>. New York: Hatherleigh Press in affiliation with W. W. Norton & Co. Inc., 2003.

Arendt, Hannah. <u>The Origins of Totalitarianism</u>. New York: Harcourt, Brace & World, 1966.

Baehr, Peter. <u>Hannah Arendt, Totalitarianism, and the Social Sciences</u>. Stanford, California: Stanford University Press, 2010.

Baigent, Michael and Richard Leigh. <u>The Inquisition</u>. London: Penguin Books, 1999.

Balot, Byan K. <u>Greek Political Thought</u>. Malden, Massachusetts: Blackwell Publishing, 2006.

Barber, Noel. <u>The Lords of the Golden Horn</u>. London: Macmillan, 1973.

Barnard, Toby. <u>The English Republic 1649 – 1660</u>. London: Longman, 1997.

Bauer, K. Jack. <u>The Mexican War 1846 – 1848</u>. Lincoln, Nebraska: University of Nebraska Press, 1992.

Bauer, Lt. Colonel E. <u>The History of World War II</u>. London: Orbis Publishing, 1979.

Bauer, Susan Wise. The History of the Ancient World. New York: W. W. Norton & Co. Inc., 2007.

Beddard, Robert, ed. The Revolutions of 1688. Oxford: Clarenoon Press, 1991.

Bell, David A. The First Total War. New York: Houghton Mifflin Co., 2007.

Benjamin, Sandra. Sicily Three Thousand Years of Human History. Hanover, New Hampshire: Steerforth Press, 2006.

Blanning, T. C. W. The French Revolutionary Wars 1787 – 1802. New York: Arnold, 1996.

Blumenthal, Uta-Renate. The Investiture Controversy. Philadelphia: University of Pennsylvania Press, 1988.

Bolton, Herber E., and Thomas M. Marshall. The Colonization of North America. New York: The MacMillian Company, 1949.

Boreisza, Jerzy W., and Klaus Ziemer ed. Totalitarian and Authoritarian Regimes in Europe. Warsaw, Poland: Berghahn Books, 2006.

Brook, Timothy. The Troubled Empire. Cambridge, Massachusetts: Belknap Press, , 2010.

Brown, Travis. Historical First Patents. Metuchen, New Jersey: The Scarecrow Press, Inc., 1994.

Buckley, Terry. Aspects of Greek History 750-323 BC. New York: Routledge, 2010.

Carlton, Eric. The Faces of Despotism. Brookfield, Vermont: Ashgate, 1995.

Carson, Clayborne, ed. The Autobiography of Martin Luther King, Jr. New York: Warner Books, 1998.

Carsten, F. L. The Rise of Fascism. Berkeley, California: University of California Press, 1982.

Chandler, David P. A History of Cambodia. Boulder, Colorado: Westview Press, 1992.

Churchill, Winston S. The Gathering Storm. Boston: Houghton Mifflin Company, 1948.

Clark, Martin. Mussolini. Harlow, United Kingdom: Pearson Longman, 2005.

Cooper, William J., Jr., and Thomas E. Terrill. The American South. New York: McGraw Hill, 1996.

Courtois, Stephane, et al. The Black Book of Communism. Cambridge, Massachusetts: Harvard University Press, 1999.

Crone, Patricia. Pre-Industrial Societies. Cambridge, Massachusetts: Basil Blackwell Inc., 1989.

Cronin, Vincent. The Florentine Renaissance. London: Pimlico, 1996.

D'Altroy, Terence N. The Incas. Malden, Massachusetts: Blackwell Publishers, 2002.

Dahl, Hans F. Quisling A Study in Treachery. New York: Cambridge University Press, 1999.

Daniel, Elton L. The History of Iran. Westport, Connecticut: Greenwood Press, 2001.

DeLuca, Anthony R. Personality, Power and Politics. Cambridge, Massachusetts: Schenkman Publishings, 1983.

Diamond, Jared. Guns, Germs, and Steel. New York: W. W. Norton & Co. Inc., 1999.

Dorey, T. A. and D. R. Dudley. Rome against Carthage. Garden City, New York: Doubleday & Co., Inc., 1972.

Drew, Katherine Fischer. Magna Carta. Westport, Connecticut: Greenwood Press, 2004.

Dunn, Richard S. The Age of Religious Wars 1559 – 1715. New York: W. W. Norton & Co., 1979.

Dynneson, Thomas L. City-State Civism in Ancient Athens. New York: Peter Lang, 2008.

Eatwell, Roger. Fascism A History. London: Chatto & Windus, 1995.

Edelstein, Dan. The Terror of Natural Right. Chicago: The University of Chicago Press, 2009.

Ellis, John. World War II A Statistical Survey. New York: Fact On File, 1993.

Estep, William R. Renaissance and Reformation. Grand Rapids, Michigan: William B. Eerdmans Publishing, 1986.

Evans, David Air Marshal. War: A Matter of Principles. Ipswich, Suffolk, United Kingdom: Ipswich Book Company, 1997.

Fadiman, Clifton, and Jean White ed. Ecocide. Santa Barbara, California: Center for the Study of Democratic Institutions, 1971.

Falola, Toyin. Key Events in African History. Westport, Connecticut: Greenwood Press, 2002.

Finer, S. E. The History of Government Vol I Ancient Monarchies and Empires. New York: Oxford University Press, 2003.

—-. The History of Government Vol II The Intermediate Ages. New York: Oxford University Press, 2006.

—-. The History of Government Vol III Empires, Monarchies, and The Modern State. New York: Oxford University Press, 2005.

Fletcher, Richard. Moorish Spain. Berkeley, California: University of California Press, 1992.

Folsach, Kjeld von, Torben Lundbaek, and Peder Mortensen eds. Sultan, Shah, and Great Mughal. Copenhagen, Denmark: The National Museum, 1996.

Frazier, Donald S., ed. The United States and Mexico at War. New York: Simon & Schuster, 1998.

Freidman, Norman. The Fifty Year War Conflict and Strategy in the Cold War. Annapolis, Maryland: Naval Institute Press, 2000.

Frey, Linda S., and Marsha L. Frey. The French Revolution. Westport, Connecticut: Greenwood Press, 2004.

Fritze, Ronald H. New Worlds The Great Voyages of Discovery 1400 – 1600. Phoenix Mill, United Kingdom: Sutton Publishing, 2002.

Gabba, Emilo, trans by P. J. Coff. The Republican Rome, The Army, and the Allies. Oxford: Basil Blackwell, 1976.

Gabriel, Richard A. Scipio Africanus. Washington D.C.: Potomac Books, Inc., 2008.

Garraty, John A. and Peter Gay ed. The Columbia History of the World. New York: Harper & Row, 1972.

Gates, David. The Napoleonic Wars 1803 – 1815. New York: Arnold, 1997.

Gay, Peter. Age of Enlightenment. New York: Life-Times Books, 1976.

Giardina, Andrea ed. The Romans. Chicago: University of Chicago Press, 1993.

Glahe, Fred R. ed. Adam Smith and the Wealth of Nations. Boulder, Colorado: Colorado Associated University Press, 1978.

Gordon, John S. An Empire of Wealth. New York: Harper Collins, 2004.

Grant, Michael. The Antonines. London: Routledge, 1994.

Grant, Susan-Mary. The War for a Nation, New York: Routledge, 2006.

Haine, W. Scott. The History of France. Westport, Connecticut: Greenwood Press, 2000.

Hammond, N. G. L. The Classical Age of Greece. London: Phoenix of Orion Books Ltd., 1999.

Hannam, James. The Genesis of Science, Washington D. C.: Regency Publishing, Inc., 2011.

Hardon, John A. <u>Modern Catholic Dictionary</u>. Bardstown, Kentucky: Eternal Life Publishers, 1999.

Harries, Karsten, and Christoph Jamme ed. <u>Martin Heidegger Politics, Art, and Technology</u>. New York: Holmes & Meier, 1994.

Heidler, David S., and Jeanne T. Heidler. <u>The Mexican War</u>. Westport, Connecticut: Greenwood Press, 2006.

Heilbroner, Robert L., and Laurence J. Malone. <u>The Essential Adam Smith</u>. New York: W. W. Norton & Company, 1986.

Higgs, Robert. <u>The Transformation of the American Economy 1865 – 1914</u>. New York: John Wiley & Sons, Inc., 1971.

Hof, Ulrich Im. <u>The Enlightenment</u>. Cambridge, Massachusetts: Blackwell, 1994.

Hoffer, Eric. <u>The True Believer</u>. New York: Harper Perennial, 1989.

Holmes, George. <u>The Florentine Enlightenment 1400 – 1450</u>. New York: Clarendon Press, 1992.

Holt, P. M., Ann K. S. Lambton and Bernard Lewis eds. <u>The Cambridge History of Islam Vol I</u>. New York: Cambridge University Press, American Branch, 1970.

Hsu, Immanuel C. Y. <u>The Rise of Modern China</u>. New York: Oxford University Press, 1995.

Huxley, Aldous. <u>Brave New World</u>. New York: HarperCollins, 2006.

Imber, Colin. <u>The Ottoman Empire 1300 – 1481</u>. Istanbul: The Isis Press, 1990.

Johnson, Paul. <u>A History of the American People</u>. New York: Harper Perennial, 1999.

Jones, Eric. <u>The European Miracle</u>. New York: Cambridge University Press, 2003.

ography*

Jones, Nicholas F. <u>Politics and Society in Ancient Greece</u>. Westport, Connecticut: Praeger Publishers, 2008.

Keay, John. <u>India A History</u>. New York: Grove Press, 2000.

Keddie, Nikki R., and Eric Hooglund eds. <u>The Iranian Revolution & the Islamic Republic</u>. Syracuse, New York: Syracuse University Press, 1986.

Keene, Jennifer D. <u>The United States and the First World War</u>. London: Longman, 2000.

Kekewich, Lucille, ed. <u>The Renaissance in Europe: A Cultural Enquiry</u>. New Haven, Connecticut: Yale University Press, 2000.

Kingseed, Cole C. <u>The American Civil War</u>. Westport, Connecticut: Greenwood Press, 2004.

Kirkwood, Burton. <u>The History of Mexico</u>. Westport, Connecticut: Greenwood Press, 2000.

Klein, Maury. <u>The Genesis of Industrial America 1870 – 1920</u>. New York: Cambridge University Press, 2007.

Konstam, Angus. <u>Historical Atlas of the Crusades</u>. New York: Thalamus Publications, 2002.

Kramer, Samuel Noah. <u>The Sumerians</u>. Chicago: The University of Chicago Press, 1963.

Kuykendall, Ralph S., and A. Grove Day. <u>Hawaii: A History</u>. New York: Prentice-Hall, Inc., 1948.

Leder, Lawrence H. <u>America 1603 – 1789 Prelude to a Nation</u>. Minneapolis, Minnesota: Burgess Publishing Company, 1978.

Lee, Stephen J. <u>European Dictatorships, 1918 – 1945</u>. London: Routledge, 1987.

Leick, Gwendolyn. <u>Mesopotamia</u>. New York: Allen Lane The Penguin Press, 2001.

Liddick, Donald R. <u>Eco-Terrorism</u>. Westport, Connecticut: Praeger, 2006.

Lin, Nan. Struggle for Tiananmen. Westport, Connecticut: Praeger, 1992.

Lineham, Peter. Spain, 1157 – 1300 A Partible Inheritance. Malden, Massachusetts: Blackwell Publishing, 2008.

Locke, John, and Peter Laslett ed. Two Treatises of Government. New York: Cambridge University Press, 1988.

—-, and Tim Crawford ed. Two Treatises of Government and a Letter Concerning Toleration. Mineola, New York: Dover Publications, Inc., 2002.

Luard, Evan. The Balance of Power The System of International Relations, 1648 – 1815. London: Macmillan, 1992.

Machiavelli, Niccolo. The Prince. New York: The American Library, Inc., 1952.

Mackay, Charles. Extraordinary Popular Delusions. New York: Prometheus Books, 2001.

MacLeod, Christine. Inventing the Industrial Revolution. New York: Cambridge University Press, 1988.

Manes, Christopher. Green Rage. Boston: Little, Brown and Company, 1990.

Manuel, Frank E. ed. The Enlightenment. Englewood Cliffs, New Jersey: Prentice-Hall, Inc., 1965.

Mason, David. Verdun. Gloucestershire, United Kingdom: The Windrush Press, 2000.

Matyszak, Philip. Chronicle of the Roman Republic. London: Thames & Hudson, 2003.

McCarthy, Justin. The Ottoman Turks. New York: Longman, 1997.

McGrath, S. J. Heidegger a (very) critical introduction. Grand Rapids, Michigan: William B Eerdmans Publishing Co., 2008.

McKivigan, John R. The War Against Proslavery Religion. Ithaca, New York: Cornell University Press, 1984.

Miller, John. The Glorious Revolution. London: Longman, 1997.

Mombauer, Annika. The Origins of the First World War. London: Longman, 2002.

Montaigne, Michel de, Donald M. Frames, ed. The Complete Works of Montaigne. Stanford, California: Stanford University Press, 1957.

Montgomery, Bernard, Field-Marshal Viscount. A History of Warfare. London: Jane's, 1962.

Morrill, John. Revolt in the Provinces. London: Longman, 1999.

Morris, Ian. Why The West Rules – For Now. New York: Farrar, Straus and Giroux, 2010.

Morton, Joseph C. The American Revolution. Westport, Connecticut: Greenwood Press, 2003.

Nicolson, Harold. Kings, Courts, and Monarchy. New York: Simon and Schuster, 1962.

Oakely, Francis. Kingship. Malden, Massachusetts: Blackwell, 2006.

Oliver, Roland, and J. D. Page. A Short History of Africa. New York: New York University Press, 1963.

Orwell, George. 1984. New York: Plume, 1983.

Overy, Richard. Why The Allies Won. London: Jonathan Cape, 1995.

Panah, Maryam. The Islamic Republic and the World. London: Pluto Press, 2007.

Parry, Albert. Terrorism. New York: The Vanguard Press, Inc., 1976.

Perez, Louis, G. The History of Japan. Westport, Connecticut: Greenwood Press, 1998.

Pomeranz, Kenneth. The Great Divergence. Princeton, New Jersey: Princeton University Press, 2000.

Pope, Stephen. <u>Dictionary of the Napoleonic Wars</u>. New York: Facts On File, Inc., 1999.

Popper, Karl R. <u>The Open Society and Its Enemies The Spell of Plato</u>. Princeton, New Jersey: Princeton Paperback Printing, 1971.

Post, Ken. <u>Communists and National Socialist</u>. London: Macmillian, 1997.

Powell, Jim. <u>Great Emancipations</u>. New York: Palgrave Macmillan, 2008.

Puddington, Arch. <u>Failed Utopias</u>. San Francisco, California: Institute for Contemporary Studies, 1988.

Raaflaub, Kurt A. and Mark Toher eds. <u>Between Republic and Empire</u>. Berkeley, California: University of California Press, 1990.

Raphael, D. D., Donald Winch and Robert Skidelshy. <u>Three Great Economists</u>. New York: Oxford University Press, 1997.

Rashid, Ahmed. <u>Taliban</u>. New York: I. B. Tauris Publishers, 2000.

Raudzens, George. <u>Empires Europe and Globalization 1492 – 1788</u>. Phoenix Mill, United Kingdom: Sutton Publishing, 1999.

Reed, Christopher A. <u>Gutenberg in Shanghai</u>. Toronto, Canada: UBCPress, 2004.

Reilly, Bernard F. <u>The Contest of Christian and Muslim Spain 1031 – 1157</u>. Cambridge, Massachusetts: Blackwell, 1992.

Reinhold, Meyer. <u>The Golden Age of Augustus</u>. Sarasota, Florida: Samuel Stevens & Co., 1978.

Reynolds, Bruce E., ed. <u>Japan in the Fascist Era</u>. New York: Palgrave Macmillian, 2004.

Richard, Jean. <u>The Crusades 1071 – 1291</u>. Cambridge, United Kingdom: Cambridge University Press, 1999.

Risjord, Norman K. <u>Jefferson's America 1760 – 1815</u>. New York: Rowman & Littlefield Publishers, 2002.

Robb, Peter. <u>A History of India</u>. New York: Palgrave, 2002.

Robinson, Eric W. ed. <u>Ancient Greek Democracy</u>. Malden, Massachusetts: Blackwell Publishing, 2004.

—-. <u>The First Democracies: early popular government outside Athens</u>. Stuttgart, Germany: Steiner, 1997.

Rothenberg, Gunther E. <u>The Napoleonic Wars</u>. London: Cassell, 1999.

Roussea, Jean-Jacques. <u>The Social Contract</u>. New York: Barnes & Noble, Inc., 2005.

Rousso, Henry ed. <u>Stalinism and Nazism</u>. Lincoln, Nebraska: University of Nebraska Press, 2004.

Rudgley, Richard. <u>Barbarians Secrets of the Dark Ages</u>. London: Channel 4 Books, 2002.

Schulz, Regine, and Matthias Seidel. <u>Egypt The World of the Pharaohs</u>. Cologne, Germany: Konemann Verlagsgesellschaft mbH, 1998 English Edition.

Schwoerer, Lois G. <u>The Declaration of Rights, 1689</u>. London: Johns Hopkins University Press, 1981.

Shirer, William L. <u>The Rise and Fall of the Third Reich</u>. New York: Simon and Schuster, 1960.

Smith, Denis Mack. <u>A History of Sicily Medieval Sicily 800 – 1713</u>. New York: Dorset Press, 1968.

Smith, Hugh. <u>On Clausewitz</u>. New York: Palgrave, 2005.

Smith, Roy C. <u>Adam Smith and the Origins of American Enterprise</u>. New York: St. Martin's Press, 2002.

Sofri, Gianni. <u>Gandhi and India</u>. Gloucestershire, United Kingdom: The Windrush Press, 2000.

Southern, Pat. <u>Augustus</u>. London: Routledge, 1998.

Stalecup, Brenda ed. <u>Ancient Egyptian Civilization</u>. San Diego, California: Greenhaven Press Inc., 2001.

Staveley, E. S. <u>The Greek and Roman Voting and Elections</u>. Ithaca, New York: Cornell University Press, 1972.

Steinberg, S. H. <u>Five Hundred Years of Printing</u>. New Castle, Delaware: The British Library & Oak Knoll Press, 1996.

Stevenson, David. <u>1914 – 1918 The History of the First World War</u>. London: Allen Lane, 2004.

Swain, Hilary, and Mark E. Davies. <u>Aspects of Roman History, 82 BC – AD 14</u>. New York: Routledge, 2010.

Swanson, Mark. <u>Atlas of the Civil War</u>. Athens, Georgia: University of Georgia Press, 2004.

Taber, Robert. <u>War of the Flea</u>. Washington D.C.: Brassey's, Inc., 2002.

Tierney, Brian. <u>The Crisis of Church and State 1050 – 1300</u>. London: University of Toronto Press, 1989.

Tocqueville, Alexis De, edited Richard D. Heffner. <u>Democracy in America</u>. New York: Mentor, 1984.

Totman, Conrad. <u>A History of Japan</u>. Malden, Massachusetts: Blackwell Publishing, 2005.

Vivante, Bella. <u>Events That Changed Ancient Greece</u>. Westport, Connecticut: Greenwood Press, 2002.

Wade, Rex A. <u>The Bolshevik Revolution and Russian Civil War</u>. Westport, Connecticut: Greenwood Press, 2001.

Wallace, Peter G. <u>The Long European Reformation</u>. New York: Palgrave Macmillan, 2004.

Wallace-Hadrill, J. M. <u>The Barbarian West 400 – 1000</u>. Oxford, United Kingdom: Basil Blackwell, 1996.

Washington, James M. <u>A Testament of Hope</u>. San Francisco: Harper & Row, 1986.

Weinstein, Leo ed. <u>The Age of Reason</u>. New York: George Braziller, 1965.

Wiesner-Hanks, Merry. <u>Early Modern Europe 1450 – 1789</u>. New York: Cambridge University Press, 2006.

Wikipedia.org

Wilson, Keith ed. <u>Decisions for War</u>. 1914, University College, London: UCL Press, 1995.

Wood, Gordon S. <u>The Idea of America</u>. New York: Penguin Press, 2011.

Woodruff, William. <u>The Struggle for World Power 1500 – 1980</u>. New York: St. Martin's Press, 1981.

Wright, David Curtis. <u>The History of China</u>. Westport, Connecticut: Greenwood Press, 2001.

Wright, Louis, B. <u>The Cultural Life of the American Colonies</u>. New York: Harper and Row, 1962.

CPSIA information can be obtained
at www.ICGtesting.com
Printed in the USA
BVHW070722060219
539569BV00001B/55/P